Bill Shields was the former risk manager for the Modern Continental Construction Company during the 1970s and 80s. He then went on to start 'Shields & Associates Insurance Agency' with his wife, Maria. Bill and Maria have been happily married for fifty years. Together, they have three children and six grandchildren. Bill was also the author of the best-selling memoir, *The Farewell Christmas*, which was a tribute to his brother, Jackie, who was a U.S. Naval Aviator who flew with the 'Blue Angels' and was killed in a tragic plane crash when Bill was ten years old. Bill and his wife, Maria, live in Middleton, Massachusetts. Bill enjoys frequently traveling to far-off places with his wife and spending time with his family. He especially enjoys being involved with his grandchildren.

Ken Anderson was one of the founders of Modern Continental Construction Company. Ken spent the crux of his life dedicated to the endeavors and successful achievements associated with the company. Ken married his sweetheart, Roseanne, in 1981. Together, they have two children and four grandchildren. Ken has been involved with numerous philanthropic undertakings over the years. However, the charity that has been near and dear to his heart has been The Brigham & Women's Hospital in Boston, Massachusetts, which has helped him through some trying times. Ken enjoys the competitive card games that he and Roseanne get involved with almost daily. He also loves being part of his grandchildren's lives and supports their numerous activities.

The writing of this book has been a labor of love for both Ken Anderson and Bill Shields. They would like to dedicate the book to Les Marino and his family and, of course, to their better halves; Roseanne Anderson and Maria Shields.

Bill Shields and Kenny Anderson

NEVER TAKE NO
FOR AN ANSWER

AUSTIN MACAULEY PUBLISHERS™

LONDON ● CAMBRIDGE ● NEW YORK ● SHARJAH

Ordering Information
Quantity sales: Special discounts are available on quantity purchases by corporations, associations, and others. For details, contact the publisher at the address below.

Publisher's Cataloging-in-Publication data
Shields, Bill and Anderson, Kenny
Never Take No for an Answer

ISBN 9798891554641 (Paperback)
ISBN9798891554658 (Hardback)
ISBN 9798891554665 (ePub e-book)

Library of Congress Control Number: 2024906460

www.austinmacauley.com/us

First Published 2024
Austin Macauley Publishers LLC
40 Wall Street, 33rd Floor, Suite 3302
New York, NY 10005
USA

mail-usa@austinmacauley.com
+1 (646) 5125767

The writing of this book would not have been feasible without the help, support, and direction that have been provided by many. It is with great appreciation that we acknowledge those who provided input and assistance in making this project possible.

Thank you to Tony Gika; he took the time to review the writing and provided valuable feedback. You are a good friend who is an intelligent and sincere individual.

R.J. Vincente, our good friend from Pine Ridge Technologies, Inc., was one of the first to take a look at the early ramblings that were put on paper. His encouragement and contributions are greatly appreciated.

Joesph M. Brito, Jr., a former competitor and rival of Modern Continental and the driving force behind one of Rhode Island's and New England's premier utility contractors, C.B. Utility Company and C. Brito Construction, read the rough manuscript and provided comments and insights that were very valuable. We are thankful for Joe's advice and guidance.

We would like to acknowledge the help and assistance provided by our illustrious technical support people, 'Geek Support'—Roman, David, and Chris—for their valuable and extremely beneficial assistance with all the technical computer issues that tend to befuddle a couple of old dogs!

During our 'Dunkin Donuts' sessions, Kenny and I would sometimes need clarification or confirmation regarding a particular time frame or a specific occurrence; therefore, Kenny would pull out his phone and call John Pastore or John MacNamara for clarification. They were both always there and were extremely helpful.

A sincere thank you to the very competent and capable staff at Austin Macauley Publishing Company for their expertise and assistance in making this book possible.

Thank you very much to the two spouses, Maria Shields and Roseanne Anderson. You were both very supportive and understanding when Kenny and Bill would go off and drink coffee and spend time reminiscing when we should have been helping with grandkids!

The last acknowledgement and thank you would be to the Marino family for supporting us with the story of such an intelligent, vibrant, and unique individual. Les Marino was one in a million and will forever be remembered as a great and benevolent visionary, a wonderful husband, father, grandfather, brother, and friend. Rest in peace, Les!

Table of Contents

Introduction
Modern Continental Construction Company, Inc.

"The Valiant Years"

This is the tale of how two strangers met, through an act of goodwill, would eventually put their expertise and experience together to form and build what would become one of the world's largest construction conglomerates.

Lelio "Les" Marino and Kenneth "Kenny" Anderson formed an everlasting friendship that would allow them to create a diversified company that at one point was performing over $1.1 billion dollars' worth of work a year and employed more than 5,000 people.

The story begins with a "humble" act of kindness that brought the two individuals together and would conceive a brotherhood and a bond between these two men that would last throughout their time together.

Two guys, that came from totally different backgrounds and cultures but they had a mutual shared characteristic of a powerful work ethic, diligence, commitment and a love for accomplishment, their undying love, loyalty and belief in America would allow them to create and ultimately live the "American dream".

Starting with a pick-up truck, a wheelbarrow and "some pick and shovel" hand tools, these industrious guys worked until "they earned a day's pay" and completed their first construction job, building sidewalks in the City of Peabody, Massachusetts in 1967.

The road to success wasn't easy and it did not happen overnight. However, the mind set of "perseverance, hard work, and sacrifice" kept these two guys going. They both had a common dream; become the biggest contractor in the world. A lofty goal for two guys that started from nothing and did not have the background or experience necessary to go up against the "big boys".

You might say this story begins as a "David vs Goliath" type of situation. So many of these types of scenarios always have a good beginning but seldom do they have the staying power and the fortitude to make it past the beginning. These guys sure did!

This company grew from their simple "sidewalk job" in Peabody, Massachusetts to participate in some of the biggest construction projects throughout the world. Numerous people in the United States of America and in many far-off lands as well, can thank these two guys for the roads, bridges and tunnels that they travel in and on, the runways that their airplanes land on, the buildings and houses that they live and work in, the water that they drink and the sewer pipes that bring the soiled water to the treatment plants that they have built and oh yeah, let's not forget the sidewalks that they walk on!

Chapter One
In the Beginning

1959–1962

Anything worth achieving is worth the effort—**Les Marino**

Quincy, Massachusetts
A parking area adjacent to the Furnace Brook Parkway
Monday, 3 August 1959
7:25 a.m.

It was another hot summer day; the 'dog days' of summer; there had been quite a few in this summer of 1959. The gray 1954, Plymouth Station wagon pulled up to the parking area where the three guys were waiting. The driver parked the car and got out and went over to the waiting men to introduce himself, he cleared his throat and then said, "Hi, I'm Lelio Marino, I'm the new crew chief for the survey party." The three guys just stood there and sized up the new guy for a moment, his English was broken and it was not easy to understand him with his heavy Italian accent. He was small in height, maybe 5 foot 8 inches tall, his hair was thinning, he had a good build, and big arms, and very muscular. Not much was said. The first guy to stick his hand out to welcome him was Paul Tibbets the rodman; Kenny Anderson the transit man then put his hand out as well and said, "Hi, I'm Kenny." Then the final man to greet the new guy was the junior rod man Morris Casey; he gave a weak handshake but did not say anything to Lelio.

****

Lelio (Les) Marino was born in Chieti Italy on 6 May 1935. Cheiti is part of the Abruzzo section of Italy not far from the Adriatic coast. He attended the University of Cheiti and received a degree in civil engineering. His father owned and operated a small construction company in the Cheiti region. Post-World War Two reconstruction had taken place in Italy which kept the small company busy at that time. Les's older brother, by two years, Luciano, who also had an engineering background, had become quite involved with the family construction operations.

Upon graduating from college in 1956, Les met and subsequently fell in love and ultimately married, his wife, Anna Maria. She was brought up and had been living in the Cheiti area, although she was actually an American by birth. After graduating college and soon after being married, Les began getting more involved in the family construction company. As a graduate civil engineer, he was very astute at surveying and civil engineering. However, in the short time that he worked for the family business, he was under the tutelage and guidance of his older brother Luciano. Their working together seemed to create a bit of 'discordance' which became quite evident between the two brothers. Sibling rivalry exists in all cultures and countries. The old saying *too many cooks spoil the broth,* was somewhat evident in the operation of the family construction company as Les was having some 'difficulties' dealing with his older brother.

Discouraged, bewildered, and disappointed at the end of his days' work, he would commiserate with his new bride Anna Maria when he got home at night. Noticing that there must be a certain amount of frustration with his duties at work, as he would be quiet and somewhat contrite, Anna Maria, having been born and having lived in the United States for a period of time when she was young mentioned to Les that the United States of America, after World War Two was building a whole new road system throughout the country and that maybe, he might consider moving to America to ply his trade of civil engineering and surveying. Anna Maria let Les know that she had family connections over there and that it was a wonderful country with many opportunities.

Les gave the suggestion of coming to America some deep thought and contemplation. Although it would be a difficult challenge, moving to a new country and dealing with both language and culture issues; he still liked the idea. It was also somewhat comforting and reassuring knowing that Anna Maria had family and relatives in the Boston area in the United States. Therefore, after much scrutiny, further contemplation, and deep thought, Les agreed with Anna Maria's idea. In the spring of 1957 with his hopes of getting more involved in the family construction business fading fast, Les and Anna Maria left Chieti Italy, and traveled to Cambridge, Massachusetts, and rented an apartment. The pursuit of the American Dream had thus begun for Les Marino!

Anna Maria was absolutely right, the United States of America, was a wonderful country with many opportunities for a young, hardworking guy. In the mid-1950s under the direction of the 34th president of the United States Dwight Eisenhower, through his foresight and vision, the United States was actively creating and building a detailed highway system to accommodate the country's rapid growth that had taken place after World War Two. With the soldiers returning from active duty, marrying, and starting families, the country was booming with road-building and developments.

Prior to making the move to America, Les Marino made inquiries regarding employment opportunities. He knew that he could not come to America without the assurance of a job and an income. He was pleased to learn that with his education, background, and training in civil engineering, he would be able to secure employment with 'Unites Engineering Company', a surveying and engineering company that was situated in the Boston area that provided survey parties to entities that performed land development, road-building, and construction activities.

Les started working as a 'transit' man for Unites Engineering Company. The transit man is the guy who operates the optical surveying instrument that is used to establish straight reference lines, read angles, and measure distance. The transit man holds an important position in the survey crew as he must be accurate, precise, and correct with the measurements that are taken. Les settled right into his new home and job. He had been working in a survey party as the transit man for a little over a year. His quick thinking and strong mathematical skills allowed him to succeed in the surveying and engineering fields. However, the difficulties that he had with the English language and the American working culture had him a little tentative about making a move to become a 'crew chief' which is the head of the survey party who is responsible for final calculations and the overall production of work that the survey party must complete. He wanted to move up to this position and had mentioned this to the managers of Unites Engineering Company, but he was just a bit tentative about actually making this move.

Much of the road work that was taking place in the Greater Boston area that was being built after World War Two, which was part of the massive country-wide road-building and development program, was under the direction of the Commonwealth of Massachusetts Department of Public Works.

Just about the time that Les had become comfortable with his duties as a transit man, Unites Engineering Company secured a contract to provide survey and engineering services for a new section of an existing roadway which was Route #3 that was going to be built in Braintree, Massachusetts. This contract was with The Commonwealth of Massachusetts Public Works Department and was Unite Engineering's first contract with the State of Massachusetts. As a result of this new contract, the management of Unites Engineering Company decided to take a chance with Les Marino and elevate him to 'crew chief'. This would require a shuffling of employees and the creation of a new survey party. Les was eager to prove that he was capable of running a survey crew and to show how productive and proficient he could be in this new position. With his promotion to party chief in place, Les was now anxious to meet his new crew and start working on the new road project.

****

It was customary that the four-man survey crew traveled in one vehicle to the job site. They would usually meet at a convenient designated meeting place; in this case, it was the parking area off Furnace Brook Parkway in Quincy. They would then travel in the crew chief's vehicle to the job site. The crew, having made introductions in the parking area off of Furnace Brook Parkway, all started moving toward Les's 1954 Plymouth station wagon so that they could head off to the job site. It was a short, quiet ride to the area where they would begin performing layout work relating to the new section of roadway that was to be built. All of the equipment was in the back of the station wagon, the transit and tripod legs, the stakes, sledge hammer, bull point, sickle, flagging, steel measuring tape, and the surveyor's 16-foot collapsible measuring rod.

Upon arriving at the work location in Braintree, the engineering drawings were spread out on the hood of the vehicle and the work began. Some brush had to be cut so that the transit could be set up, then work progressed on his very warm Monday morning.

As the work commenced, the guys in the crew were sizing up their new boss. He seemed to know what he was doing; he did understand the engineering and surveying aspect of the job as crew chief but then again, it was only this first morning. He had a lot to prove that would substantiate this promotion to survey party chief.

At a little before ten o'clock on this steamy Monday morning, the crew took a scheduled coffee break. They were all sitting around drinking their beverages and nibbling on their snacks when Les decided to check on when the noon-time lunch break should take place. Although he had worked in survey parties before, he was not quite sure how to work with this new crew and with this being the company's first 'state' job, things might possibly be different. Les said to the crew, "When do you guys want to take your lunch break?"

The guys kind of hesitated after Les's question was asked regarding the lunch break. They looked at each other and then after an awkward pause, Morris Casey kind of snickered and then offered a response, "In this country, when work is being done for the 'State', you start your lunch break at 11:30 a.m. and don't return to work until 1:00 p.m., and oh yeah, you also have to drive only five miles per hour back and forth from the restaurant." Les looked at Morris with a pained look on his face. You could see in Les's eyes that he questioned Morris's answer and that there was a certain amount of doubt regarding Morris's reply to his question. Les then looked at the other two guys, Paul Tibbets and Kenny Anderson to see if he could find out if there was any truth to Morris's edict.

There was dead silence and then Kenny Anderson thought for a moment about what was taking place, he was the youngest guy in the crew and had only worked with this group for a couple of hours. Having been brought up to be respectful to people older than him, he knew that it was really not his place to speak up. But then again, Kenny knew from experience that it wasn't right for someone to be taken advantage of. Therefore, with an explicit amount of certainty and a bit of disgust in his voice, Kenny Anderson looked at Morris as he replied to Les Marino's question and said, "Hey, Morris, you know that's not true, why are you trying to take advantage of this guy, you know better than that."

Kenny then said to Les, "We go for lunch at noon and come back at 12:30."

At this point, Paul Tibbets, who had also been a little disgusted at Morris's response to Les chimed in, "Yeah, Morris, why are you being such a jerk? It's his first day as crew chief, why are you messing with him."

The situation had been clarified; Les was a bit flushed and he had a look of abhorrence on his face as he stared intently at Morris and then he said, "Thank you," to Kenny Anderson. This simple act of kindness, a gesture of ethical and moral countenance was not a very big deal; someone trying to take advantage of a situation to make life easier for themselves was somewhat common in America. Having been around the business for a while working as a transit man, I'm sure that Les might have understood that Morris was just being an asshole. However, the kindness that was shown by Kenny Anderson when he came to his defense was more important to Les than the actual situation itself. You see, Italians never forget two things, who their enemies are and who helped them in a time of need. Kenny's kindness would never be forgotten by Les!

Les had been working in the survey business for a little over a year, the fact that he was married and had just had his first child, a little baby girl named Laura, who was born in 1958 not long after his arrival in America; this made him a busy family man which significantly curtailed his ability to establish friendships with guys that he worked with. This little 'dilemma', although a somewhat trivial matter, would prove to be the basis of what would show, beyond doubt, to be the start of a lifelong friendship.

****

The work progressed smoothly on the Route #3 Braintree project with little difficulty. Although Morris Casey would continue to be somewhat of an 'asshole', the crew got along well enough to perform in a manner that pleased both Les Marino and Unites Engineering Company. As Kenny Anderson was the transit man, he had a considerable amount of interaction with Les. They both seemed to possess the same qualities with regard to work; they were conscientious and diligent with a dedication to accuracy and punctuality along with a certain amount of perfection.

As the summer made its way toward fall, things seemed to become a little less tentative for Les, as a matter of fact, his friendship with Kenny Anderson, extended to include the rod man, Paul Tibbets. That little 'what time is lunch fiasco' kind of showed Les that both Kenny Anderson and Paul Tibbets had his back. Les felt that both Kenny Anderson and Paul Tibbets expressed a genuine quality that proved their friendship would be a lasting one. It was important to Les that he make an effort to understand and learn just how things went in the United States of America, a country that Les would become a staunch, loyal, and patriotic citizen of in the not-too-distant future. He had come to believe in America and took pride in all aspects of patriotism. After all, he lived in Massachusetts which is the cradle of liberty in this country, where it all began. The strong patriotic surroundings of Lexington and Concord did not go unnoticed by young Mr. Marino.

It was during this Route #3 project in Braintree, Massachusetts that a kind of 'Americanization' of Lelio Marino took place. It would become a memorable day for Les Marino, as on Monday, 21 September 1959 in a simple ceremony held at Cambridge District Court House on 3rd Street; Les was sworn in and became a citizen of the United States of America. With his wife Anna Maria standing beside him as she was his sponsor, Les proudly took the oath and became an American.

As his English language skills developed and improved, so did his confidence. The guys in the survey crew had been calling Les, by his given name of 'Lelio'. It's not been established who, or how, it exactly was changed, but through a process of, well let's call it 'transformation' Lelio was modified to become 'Les'.

On Friday, 9 October 1959 the day before the long Columbus Day weekend, the crew knocked off from work a little earlier than usual. Kenny Anderson had been dropped off at work that morning by his childhood buddy and good friend John Malm, a fellow Swede as Kenny's vehicle was being worked on in the auto repair shop. At the end of the day, Kenny asked Les if it would be possible for him to drop him off at his house in Randolph on his way back to Cambridge. Les said, "Sure, Ken, I can take you home after work." Les drove Kenny home from the job in Braintree. When they got to Randolph and were in front of Kenny's house, it had turned out to be a beautiful early autumn afternoon, the sun was shining through the fall leaves. Kenny noticed that his mother was sitting at a table in the back yard of the house with a pot of tea in front of her.

Kenny thought for a moment and then turned to Les and said, "Hey, Les, what do you say you stop by and say hello to my mother, I've mentioned you to her a few times so I'm sure that she'd love to meet you."

Les took a quick look at his wristwatch and understood that it was a little earlier than he was usually expected home so he said. "I'd like that; it would be nice to meet your mother."

Kenny and Les walked to the back of the house; Mrs. Anderson was surprised to see Les with Kenny as they approached the little table that she was sitting at. Upon their approach, she said, "Well, this is a pleasant surprise."

Kenny said, "Hi, Mom, this is Les Marino the survey party crew chief that I work with."

Mrs. Anderson said, "Well, it's so nice to finally meet you, Kenny talks about you all the time. I got home from work a little while ago and thought I'd sit out here in the backyard for a few minutes and take advantage of this beautiful autumn afternoon, please, sit down, Les. Kenny, can you be a dear and get two tea cups from the house for you and Les?" Kenny fetched the tea cups as they all sat at the little table in the backyard and drank tea. It was a picture-perfect setting; the fall colors were very vibrant; the autumn afternoon was superb, as they sat and sipped tea and chatted.

It was not very often that Les had the chance to just sit and relax for a few minutes and become engaged in idle conversation. As he sat and sipped tea, he had a moment to reflect upon his decision to leave Chieti Italy, and migrate to the United States. He was pleased with his choice. He had fallen in love with his newly adopted country. He was proud to be an American and quickly understood why its citizens were so loyal and supportive of their country. He found Kenny's mother to be a very humble and enjoyable lady who epitomized the true American mother who unconditionally loved her children and cared deeply about their health, welfare, and future.

As they finished with their tea, it was time for Les to head home to Cambridge to be with Anna Maria and his beautiful little baby girl Laura. As he got up from the table, he leaned over and gave Mrs. Anderson a slight kiss on her cheek and said, "Thank you very much for the tea and conversation." He then turned to Kenny and said, "Kenny, you are very fortunate to have such a beautiful and caring mother." Kenny and Mrs. Anderson said goodbye as Les left the back yard.

As Les walked away, Mrs. Anderson smiled and turned to Kenny and said, "He seems like a very nice young man, you would be wise to remain friends with him as I think that he will go a long way and be very successful." Kenny kind of nodded and just took in his mother's words of wisdom.

Kenneth Ludwig Anderson was born just before noontime on Wednesday, 18 February 1942 at the Brockton Hospital, in Brockton, Massachusetts. Kenny was the first child of Ludwig and Lulu 'Elizabeth' Anderson.

Kenny's dad was a house builder who performed the construction of single-family, wood-frame homes in the suburban Boston area in the Needham, Dedham, Braintree, and Randolph locations. Mr. Anderson was in business with his good friend and partner Paul Dahlberg. They both were Swedish immigrants who came to America with their respective families when they were just young children. They had been friends growing up in Randolph, Massachusetts, and at an early age they both got involved with carpentry and building projects.

Mr. Anderson was born Ludwig Emanuel Anderson in 1895, in the small village of Bagaregarden Sweden, which is a suburb of Gothenburg. His family migrated to the United States of America when he was just a child not long after the turn of the century. Kenny's mother's given name was Lulu Elizabeth Hanson. She liked to go by Elizabeth rather than 'Lulu' as she felt 'Lulu' was just a bit brash. Lulu Elizabeth Hanson was also of Swedish descent. She was born on 26 January 1903 in the Town of Easton, Massachusetts. Elizabeth and Ludwig fell in love and married in 1937 after their marriage, they lived in the house that was built by Ludwig Anderson in Randolph, Massachusetts.

In addition to their son Kenneth, another son Richard was born to Ludwig and Elizabeth Anderson, in January of 1944. In less than two years, Ludwig and Elizabeth had been blessed with two bouncing baby boys. The winter of 1944 was a very hectic time in the Randolph, Massachusetts home of the Anderson family.

It was not long after the birth of Richard in 1944 that Ludwig started to complain about having stomach issues. Needless to say, it was a frenzied time in his life with two small children and a bitter world war raging; it was no wonder that Ludwig's stomach was upset. Ludwig tried various upset stomach remedies with little comfort or relief from his constant stomach pain. A staunch tough Swede, Ludwig put off the telltale signs of stomach trouble and tried his best to work through the discomfort. By early March of 1944, his stomach issues became more severe, he finally realized that he was ill. The illness proved to be a form of stomach ulcers which unfortunately was later diagnosed as cancer. After a brief time from the diagnosis, Kenny's father, Ludwig Emanual Anderson passed away on 8 April 1944.

Life was not easy for the Anderson family after Ludwig passed away so suddenly. With two small children, one being a newborn infant, Elizabeth Anderson had to do her best to get through this unreal nightmare that had so quickly turned her world upside down. Being a woman of faith and understanding, she knew that she needed to work, yet still be close to her small children. It was not long before Elizabeth came up with an idea that incorporated both issues, work and child care. In late 1944 with World War Two raging in both the European and Pacific theaters of war, Elizabeth Anderson made a decision that would prove to be beneficial to all involved. In late 1944, Elizabeth Anderson was hired as a domestic worker at the Lutheran Children's House in Avon, Massachusetts.

She would work in the facility and still be able to attend to her small children. This position allowed Elizabeth to live at the Lutheran Children's House, as part of her employment conditions included accommodations for her and her two small children. Elizabeth then rented out the family's home in Randolph which became a small form of income for Elizabeth. The Anderson family lived at the Lutheran Children's House in Avon Massachusetts from late 1944 until early 1948.

Kenny Anderson and his little brother Richard survived their tumultuous childhood, thanks to a very strong mother who understood the importance of keeping her family together and the significant role that she, as a single parent, provided to her two young sons. Not long after New Year's Day in 1948, the Andersons moved back to the house that Ludwig built in Randolph, Massachusetts, and moved forward as a family.

Kenny and his little brother Dick helped out as much as they could, they both acquired paper routes along with shoveling snow in the winter and cutting lawns in the summer time. The Anderson boys learned quickly that in order for their family to survive, they needed to help their mother as much as possible. Growing up without a father was somewhat difficult for the Anderson boys. Fortunately, Elizabeth Anderson had a younger brother named Chester. Uncle Chester, who was a single man, was in the Merchant Marines. He would travel on merchant ships all over the world but when he was in port, he made it a point to spend time with his nephews. I guess Uncle Chester provided his two nephews with some guidance and a little bit of the rough and tumble side of things that might have been missing for the two boys.

Even though he spent most of his high school years working a full-time job, he did put the effort that he needed into his schoolwork. Kenny graduated from Randolph High School in the spring of 1959. Kenny excelled in math and seemed to have a mind for engineering. Upon graduating high school, a neighbor of the family, Mr. John Hannon, indicated to Kenny that he knew someone who was a manager at Unites Engineering Company and that he felt that they could probably use the services and mathematical mind of someone like Kenny. Mr. Hannon helped Kenny get an interview with the company. Not long after Kenny met with the people at Unites Engineering, he was hired as a junior rod man for one of their survey crews; this was in May of 1959.

Kenny proved to be a really quick learner. He developed a complete understanding of how surveying and engineering duties were performed. This type of understanding came rather quickly to this young and budding engineer. Kenny moved ahead rapidly and went from a junior rod man to a rod man to actually operating an intricate transit instrument which is the engineering apparatus that provides the measurements, angles, and distance necessary to calculate the locations and the intervals required in land surveying work. He learned quickly and at the tender young age of 18 years old, Kenny Anderson had become one of the youngest transit operators in the history of the land surveying industry. This was quite a feat!

****

With the survey work on the Route #3 Braintree, Massachusetts highway project rapidly coming to an end and the onset of winter approaching, the survey crew that was made up of Les Marino the survey party crew chief, Kenny Anderson the transit operator, Paul Tibbets the rod man and Morris Casey the junior rod man, they would all soon be on their way to starting another engineering project.

This new project for Unites Engineering Company would be performing layout and survey work at the intersection of the existing State Route #3 in Chelmsford, Massachusetts, and the construction of a new highway, U.S. Route #495. The new highway U.S. Route #495 that was being built was a connecting road, a calculated 'shortcut' that would basically cut off travel through the downtown Boston area if a motorist was traveling from Maine or New Hampshire south to Rhode Island. This new section of road U.S. Route #495 would begin at existing U.S. Route #95 in Amesbury, Massachusetts, and would reconnect with existing U.S. Route #95 in Mansfield, Massachusetts.

This connecting route would ultimately cut off a significant amount of mileage and time for a cross-country traveler as it would eliminate travel through Boston. The United States highway system was growing rapidly with new highways and roadways that connected to existing roads that had been built or were being built all over the country. The interstate numbering system that had been formed during this major highway initiative allowed for the absorption of Local Route #128, which is a road that circumvents the Greater Boston suburbs, into the nationwide highway system as it was incorporated and became part of the existing U.S. Route #95 roadway which begins in Maine and ends in Florida. There was road work taking place all over the country in the early 1960s. The existing Route #3 and new U.S. Route #495 interchange project began in the dead of winter in 1960.

Survey work is somewhat tedious as the many measurements and documentation of boundaries and landmarks must be calculated and recorded accordingly. Standing at a transit measuring instrument, holding a steel measurement tape, or hammering a wooden stake used as a boundary marker into the frozen ground can be interminable on a freezing cold winter day. Even with long thermal underwear, heavy flannel shirts, and trousers, a good pair of waterproof work boots, and a warm pair of gloves, it was still unmercifully cold. It was not uncommon for the crew to use an empty fifty-five-gallon steel drum and build a fire in it to keep their hands warm. These were the conditions that Les Marino, Kenny Anderson, and the rest of the crew were working under when they started this project in the winter of 1960. Needless to say, accuracy is an important part of the overall survey criteria. With Kenny Anderson performing the transit work and Les Marino carrying out the complex calculations required, the work that was taking place was being done in a professional and proficient manner.

The U.S. Route #495 project proceeded, in spite of the cold and snowy winter conditions that the survey crew had to work under. The long winter was wearisome but it eventually turned into spring and before they knew it, summer weather was again upon this illustrious survey crew. With the boundaries laid out and the interchange dimensions properly calculated, this would now allow the road-building construction crews to begin their portion of the excavation work on the project.

It should not come as a surprise as it did not take long for the people in the road-building and land surveying industry to recognize the excellent engineering work that was being performed by Les Marino and his crew. It was at this time that the work being carried out by Les Marino caught the eye of the road-building contractor who was performing the actual building of the road and the interchange at this U.S. Route #495 Chelmsford, Massachusetts location. Campinelli & Cardi Construction was the primary road-building contractor performing the majority of the road-building work at this location. As a result of excellent engineering calculations and a diligent work ethic, the primary owner of the company, Rico Cardi approached Les Marino and asked him if he would consider coming to work as a road-building foreman for his company.

In addition to receiving an offer to become a road-building foreman, another survey and engineering company, Vancouver Associates, which was quite prominent in the engineering and road surveying industry, also had their eyes on Les Marino. Walter Corsano, the owner of Vancouver Associates Engineering came forward and spoke to Les about possibly becoming a survey party crew chief for his company. Les listened as Walter Corsano made an offer to Les that he hoped would entice him to leave the Unites Engineering Company and come to work for him.

The simple fact that Les Marino had arrived in the United States of America from Cheiti Italy in 1957 and within a couple of short years, his hard work and analytical approach to solving problems had become well known in the surveying and road-building industry was not astonishing. The offers were coming in left and right for this smart young man. It was his time to shine and to move up in this construction and engineering-related world that he so loved and had become proficient and entrenched in. It was, furthermore a world of opportunity that had opened up for him. After giving his options considerable thought and weighing his possibilities, Les came up with a decision.

Les informed Walter Corsano, the owner of Vancouver Associates Engineering Company that although he had made him an attractive offer, he was going to have to pass as he had decided to proceed in a different direction. Les thanked Walter again and let him know just how much he appreciated his interest. For Les, the decision to move into another aspect of the construction world was not an amazing resolution to this situation. Les and his good friend Kenny Anderson had discussed the options that were presented to him; they both agreed that the future held many opportunities and that venturing into road-building would only strengthen his overall knowledge and understanding of both the road-building and engineering fields.

As for Rico Cardi, the primary principal of the Campanelli & Cardi Construction Company, Les informed him that he would come to work for his company as a foreman overseeing the road-building work that was taking place at the project in Chelmsford, Massachusetts. Les made the move from surveying to road-building which proved also to be a beneficial move with regard to his income. The move to begin working for Campanelli and Cardi Construction Company as a road-building foreman came to fruition in the spring of 1961.

1961 would prove to be a fruitful and prosperous year for both Les Marino and Kenny Anderson. Les made his move and began working as a road-building foreman for the Campanelli & Cardi Construction Company. As Les moved on from Unites Engineering Company as the survey party crew chief, this vacancy opened the door for young Mr. Anderson to move into the position that Les Marino had held as the survey party crew chief. The managers at Unites Engineering Company knew that although he was quite young, Kenny Anderson had the ability to run his own survey crew. Therefore, at not yet 21 years old, Kenny Anderson was now running his own survey crew on one of the major highway projects going on in the New England region.

****

Les Marino and Kenny Anderson remained very close friends. As a matter of fact, their friendship became stronger as they both advanced and continued to make a name for themselves in the survey and road-building industries. They would get together almost every Sunday afternoon, as Les's wife Anna Maria, would make a special Sunday dinner feast. Anna Maria had become quite fond of Kenny Anderson; she would make sure that Les invited Kenny over for Sunday dinner as often as possible.

Anna Maria Marino had become quite the cook and homemaker since arriving back in the country of her birth. She and Les had settled comfortably in Cambridge, Massachusetts. As they lived in Cambridge, this allowed Anna Maria to be closer to the 'Latanzi' side of the family which were her American cousins. It made the transition for Anna Maria's and Les's move to America just a little bit easier for them as she had her family and cousins close by, although the change from Italy to the United States would be an ongoing adaption. With the addition of their baby girl Laura to the family, Les, and Anna Maria seemed to be adjusting quite well to their American lifestyle.

Sunday was a family day and a chance for Les Marino to relax a little bit from his hectic weekly work schedule. Working as a road-building foreman for Campanelli and Cardi Road Builders all day long was a little different from his duties as a surveyor party crew chief. The road-building work on the Chelmsford Route #495 project included a considerable amount of overtime and additional responsibilities for Les, this made him an extremely busy individual.

Spending time with his family on Sunday and getting together with his very good friend, Kenny Anderson was a special time for Les. Anna Maria would put together a fabulous Sunday dinner. The meal would always start with some type of pasta and that wonderful 'ragu' (tomato gravy) that would accompany the pasta. Naturally, there were some plump and juicy meatballs and sausages to go with the pasta dish, then would come a leg of lamb, a top sirloin roast, or a roasted chicken. The main dish would then be followed by a wonderful garden salad. Italians normally finish dinner with salad as it helps cleanse the palate. This Sunday meal was a suitable feast for these hardworking men.

Kenny Anderson did not have a father that he could consult with during this time in his life. Someone that he could confide in and get proper direction from. Yes, his mom had done a great job with raising Kenny and his younger brother Dick, but that older, 'mature' male guidance when you are in need of some direction just wasn't there for him. It was his relationship with Les Marino that helped fill that void. Although they were technically equals when it came to the work that they were involved with, Les also provided that 'big brother' counseling for Kenny. It was during one of the Sunday afternoon get-togethers that Les, knowing full well how smart Kenny was, urged him to further his knowledge by taking some evening college courses and additionally develop his engineering and management skills. Kenny listened intently to Les's suggestion and decided that what he was talking about made perfect sense to him. Not long after this discussion, Kenny took the advice of his friend and decided to take some evening college courses to enhance his knowledge and skills, as Les suggested.

It was during this hectic time in his life that Les Marino began to absorb the true understanding of how in the United States of America, if you worked hard and made a concentrated effort with regard to the duties that you were performing, you would then be rewarded for your endeavors. It was also a tremendous period of learning for Les Marino. Being the intelligent and observant person that he was, he realized that by picking up on little idiosyncrasies from the people that he came in contact with in the course of his work, he could learn from them. He also learned that with regard to people that he came in contact with, you should only emulate the good and disregard the bad. He had tremendous discipline and focus but it was throughout this time frame that he honed his skills as a leader and someone that could figure things out that others seemed to struggle with. He became the person that others relied upon to get things done and to solve problems. Les truly understood that in the deep unwritten wisdom of life, there were many lessons to be learned that could not be taught.

It was the Sunday dinner get-togethers, with Kenny Anderson, that helped both Les and Kenny to develop a rapport, mutual trust, and an in-depth understanding of one another. A connection had been born from that simple act of kindness that Kenny showed to Les that first day that they worked together in the survey crew on the Braintree Route #3 highway project. Although they truly came from different worlds, they embraced their ethnic and cultural differences and established a two-way communication system that would lead them down an inevitable path that would join their individual strengths and forces forever.

Although there were many similarities relating to surveying and road-building, there was also a clear distinction relating to the efforts of a surveyor, as they were considerably less demanding physically than those of a road builder. The road builder needed to deal a little bit more forcefully with the people that they were working with. The road-building foreman also accepted the fact that he had to accept that a bit more prodding and motivation were needed for the laborers working on a road to get their work done than the engineers working in a survey crew. Therefore, an element of 'toughness' had to be developed and quite frankly, it was required at times to get the road-building work accomplished. The combination of intelligence and toughness proved to be a winning blend for Les Marino. It was established early on that he was not going to tolerate any incompetence or ignorance of the job functions from the people who were working under him. Les developed respect and reverence from everyone who was working on the job site in Chelmsford, Massachusetts.

During the course of a day's work, it was not uncommon to see Les take someone aside and explain to them, in no uncertain terms, that they needed to pay more attention to what they were doing and that they had to get the job done the right way and the most efficient way. If you looked closely, during one of those 'conversations' you just might see the veins in his muscular neck get ridged and red, along with his dark brown eyes bulging from their sockets just a bit, as he conducted his little 'talk'. He did not tolerate ineptness or incompetence. He demanded a complete and dedicated effort from each and every person during the time that they were working for him. He had become a task master which was how he got things accomplished. Les was getting the job done, quickly and efficiently and it seemed only natural that he developed his management and leadership skills right along with his understanding of road-building.

Les applied this aptitude in all aspects of the work that he was involved with. His intellect, diligence, and intuition made money for the Campanelli and Cardi Road-Building Company. He had become a force to be reckoned with and that force was getting stronger and more skillful as each day passed. In addition to his abundance of fortitude and strength, Les also developed a very strong understanding of exactly how the American way of 'free enterprise' worked and that this concept was undoubtedly the only true form of incentive that was required to survive in this New World that he had become so fond of.

Kenny Anderson had become one of the youngest and smartest survey party crew chiefs in Massachusetts. His ability to absorb knowledge had become even more evident as he excelled in his evening college studies. Strength and intelligence, along with an unwavering dedication to one another had surely developed between the period or 1959 and 1962 for Les Marino and Kenny Anderson. That fateful day in August of 1959 when a 'smart ass' junior rod man tried to buffalo the new survey party crew chief and was rebuffed by a notion of kindness and an act of civility by the young transit man in the crew; well, you might say that day was a somewhat historic one, as it became the start of an undying loyalty and friendship that would last a lifetime for Les Marino and Kenny Anderson. The future looked bright for these two guys, as different and as opposite as they might be, but it still looked quite bright!

Chapter Two
Hard Work Will Always
Produce the Best Results

1962–1963

*The best gift you can give someone is a good example***—Kenny Anderson**

Boxborough, Massachusetts
1526 Massachusetts Avenue
Route #495-Job Site Work Trailer
Monday, 22 October 1962
6:41 a.m.

The air was quite crisp on this fall morning, the sun had not quite risen, the smudge pots were still burning brightly next to the black and yellow saw horse near the entrance to the driveway. The green 1960 Ford F-150 pick-up truck, with the white 'Suburban Construction' lettering on the side doors, pulled up in front of the office trailer. After the dust had cleared, Les Marino took his foot off of the clutch and then put the emergency brake on as he and Kenny Anderson got out of the vehicle. They had gotten to the job site before the Project Superintendent Sam Melei. Les Marino reached into his pocket and got the key out to open the office trailer door. As they stepped inside the chilly office trailer, Kenny Anderson flipped the light switch on the wall and the fluorescent light bulbs began to hum and slowly brighten. Les turned to Kenny and said, "Well, this is where you'll work, but let's wait until Sam gets here though, so that he can officially welcome you to the company, he's the Super so let him tell you what the owner George Curly told him to tell you."

Kenny looked at Les and said, "Yeah, I know what I've got to do but I'll let Sam tell me anyway."

It was Kenny Anderson's first day working for Suburban Construction Company. He had remained at Unites Engineering as a survey party crew chief on the Chelmsford Route #495 road project after Les went to work for Campanelli & Cardi Road Builders. Campanelli & Cardi's section of road that included the Route #3 and the Route #495 interchange was close to finishing up when Les was approached by George Curly, the owner of Suburban Construction Company that had successfully won the bid to build a section of U.S. Route # 495 and the interchange of State Route #111 in Boxborough, Massachusetts. Les jumped ship and left Campanelli & Cardi and went to work as a road-building foreman for Suburban Construction in April of 1962.

In the late summer of 1962, during one of their Sunday dinner get-togethers, Les mentioned to Kenny that the company he was working for, Suburban Construction, was in need of a resident engineer to handle overseeing the road layout, profiles, curves, and cross-sections. He also let Kenny know that his duties as an engineer would also include compliance with contract specifications and getting involved in the quantities, submittals, and anything relating to the subcontractors that would be working on the project. This was a big move for Kenny as he would be venturing into a whole different aspect of construction work, but Kenny didn't even have to give it a second thought, as he knew that by taking this position, it would again, allow him to work with Les as they had when they were surveyors back in 1959 when they met on the Route #3 Braintree, MA project.

The U.S. Route #495 road project, when completed, would become the second longest 'auxiliary' highway (connecting road) in the entire United States Interstate Highway Road system, as it totaled 120 miles of road. The building of U.S. Route #495 began in the late 1950s and would not be completed until the late 1960s. The building of U.S. Route #495 roadway along with the extension of U.S. Route #90 (Massachusetts Turnpike) from Weston, Massachusetts through Auburndale, Newton, and Watertown to downtown Boston, the building of U.S. Route #93 from New Hampshire to downtown Boston and the construction of U.S. Route #95 from Westwood, Massachusetts to the Rhode Island border where all new roads that were being built simultaneously.

These four very large road-building projects were only part of the numerous miles of highway that were being built throughout the entire United States of America. This massive country-wide highway system that was being built would rival the road system of any civilized nation in the world. The 1960s was a very good time to be involved in the road-building industry.

****

Not long after Les and Kenny had entered the construction office trailer, a cloud of dust again rose up in the parking area outside as Sam Melei, the job superintendent abruptly pulled into the yard, jumped out of his pick-up truck, and headed for the steps to the trailer. Sam roared into the office trailer like a small tornado! He was short and stout and was as fiery as a lit stick of dynamite. Not known for his congeniality, Sam turned to Les and gruffly mumbled, "This is the kid that's gonna be the engineer?"

Les looked at Sam and nodded his head and said, "Yeah, this is Kenny Anderson." Kenny just stood there, trying to get a read on Sam. Les had told Kenny that Sam was not the most pleasant person in the world, but he was a damn good superintendent that knew how to build roads. Sam had worked for Perini Construction before George Curly, the owner of Suburban Construction, stole him away from Perini. Sam had also worked on the building of Route 128 back in the early 1950s; he knew his stuff when it came to road-building.

Sam, with his impatient attitude, looked at Kenny and said to him, "You were a surveyor, right?"

Kenny, getting a little anxious, answered Sam. "Yeah, I was a survey party crew chief on the Chelmsford section of Route 495 that Campanelli & Cardi built."

Sam then said, "Oh yeah, Les told me that you're kind of young, how old are you?" Kenny was getting just a bit perturbed by Sam's interrogation.

"I'll be 21 soon," he replied to Sam.

With a bit of surprise in his eyes, Sam replied, "And you were a survey party crew chief?"

At this point, Les was getting a little concerned at Sam's line of questioning as he blurted out, "Sam, I talked to George Curly about Kenny and Kenny sat down with George as well, he knows what he has to do. I've got to get things going with my crew; do you need me around anymore?"

Sam looked at Les and said, "No, you can go, and don't forget, you're getting a load of gravel later this morning, so make sure you've got the dozer ready." Les rolled his eyes a bit, as he turned and left the trailer. Sam spun around and pointed toward the drafting table in the middle of the office trailer and said to Kenny, "There's the drawings, take a look at them and get used to what's going on around here. I'm going to go and make sure that everyone is working, it's Monday morning, no telling what happened over the weekend with these guys." Sam, in a huff, darted toward the trailer door and headed out to his pick-up truck, a small mushroom cloud seemed to follow him as he sped out of the driveway and drove off to the job site. Kenny, a little bewildered, was wondering what just happened.

****

Kenny Anderson settled into his new position as the engineer on the Boxborough section of U.S. Route #495 that was being built. He spent much of his time in the job site trailer doing 'take-offs' and calculating quantities relating to the work that had been done on the job. He did get to spend some time in the field, on the job itself, checking boundaries and making sure that the road built thus far had the correct line and grade. His duties as the job site engineer encompassed many responsibilities. He was busy but not as overwhelmed as he initially thought he might be. Heck, the toughest part of his job was dealing with Sam Melei, the cantankerous project superintendent. Sam roared around the project like a pending catastrophe; Kenny wondered if Sam had a life other than being a road-building superintendent. He seemed to cause more confusion than a wild herd of buffaloes stampeding across the infield of Fenway Park!

One of the best parts of working on this job for Kenny was that he got to spend some time with his buddy Les. Even though they were involved with different aspects of the project, the two friends had developed a companionship that rivaled that of Laurel & Hardy, Abbot & Costello, or the Wright Brothers. Les and Kenny, would, when possible, have coffee or lunch together. As Les had a company pick-up truck, he would often give Kenny a ride to and from work. They seemed to make an effort to spend time together and when they were with each other, they usually talked shop. Kenny would ask Les questions about what he was involved with and Les would offer information so that Kenny could gather an understanding of all facets of the road-building work.

The times that Les would give Kenny a ride to and from work were a good time for them to spend together as they would brainstorm different subjects and issues that might be pertinent. However, the truth be told, it was also a tad inconvenient, as Les would rendezvous with Kenny at various intersecting places which were, at times, a nuisance for both. Kenny had been with Suburban Construction for a while now; his duties did warrant the need for a pick-up truck to perform his field duties. In order to get around the job, he would have to borrow Sam Melei's pick-up truck. Kenny had mentioned this to Sam a couple of times, that he needed his own pick-up truck, but the conversation seemed to fall on deaf ears.

It was during the construction of the U.S. Route #495 section of highway in Boxborough, Massachusetts while working for Suburban Construction that both Les and Kenny began to expand their horizons with regard to the different segments and characteristics of construction activities that were involved in the building of a roadway. In addition to blasting rock and moving dirt, there was also the installation of drainage pipes, culverts, and structures that needed to be built and put in place so that the highway could be completed. The different types of work that they were involved with did in fact broaden both Les and Kenny's horizons.

Fall turned into winter on the Boxborough project; in spite of the cold and snow, the work progressed. The crew had been cut back a little as was customary during the winter months. It was not uncommon for road-building contractors to lay off all of their employees for the winter, and shut the job down, and begin again in the spring. However, the road section that they were working on was almost complete, and with the amount of road-building work that was going on in the Greater Boston area the owner of the Suburban Construction Company, George Curly felt that he had a really good crew and if he let them go for the winter, he just might not get them back in the spring.

Suburban Construction had just won the bid to construct another section of U.S. Route #495. This portion of the road to be built was in Attleboro, Massachusetts, and was scheduled to start in late spring of 1963. Keeping the crew together was important, for continuity, when it came to the experience and knowledge of the guys that he had working on the Boxborough U.S. Route #495 project.

It was a really busy time for Les as he had been 'blessed' with the birth of his second child in 1962, a beautiful little girl that Les and Anna Maria named Lorraine. The birth of his second child seemed to cultivate and pollinate the seeds of growth and success that had been planted when Les began his journey in the United States of America.

Although Les was a family man, who fully understood his responsibilities, it was still necessary to take a few moments to just 'ease up' and enjoy his surroundings. Therefore, Les and Kenny would stay late every once in a while, and have a couple of beers with some of the construction guys in the office trailer. They would joke and laugh a little, but they also talked shop about the job making sure that things were going as they should. Les had become a pretty astute road-building foreman. His leadership skills were clearly evident as the project was ahead of schedule and the work that was being done had caught the eye of the irascible owner of Suburban Construction Company, George Curly.

To say that George Curly was tough might be an understatement. He was notorious for his 'job site dramatics', he would roar onto the project in his black 1962, Cadillac Sedan Deville, with dust and rocks flying and a heavy cloud of commotion surrounding his presence. The primary target when he got out of his car was usually the project superintendent, Sam Melei. George Curly would search out Sam and proceed to dress him down for whatever purpose he deemed necessary. It might be the lack of production, the fact that a piece of equipment wasn't working or just to make everyone in the area know that he was on the job and for them to start busting their asses!

George would not stay long, he was like a dive bomber, and he'd swoop in with guns blaring and release his torpedoes in whichever direction he thought necessary to cause as much pandemonium as possible. Unfortunately, the aftermath of his surgical strike on the job site had more fallout than the attack itself. As soon as that big black Cadillac roared off, then the aftershock would take place. Sam Melei would start with whoever was closest to him and then proceed to rattle and shake just about every living soul on the project. Sam's infamous rants were legendary. Quite honestly, the whole scenario of George Curly showing up and tossing grenades all over the place and then, upon his departure, Sam Melei following up with a strafing of any and all objects within firing range, had become somewhat melodramatic. The dog and pony show put on by these two individuals became redundant and counterproductive.

As the owner of the company and someone who depended on the pride, integrity, and workmanship of the craftsmen on the job, George Curly also understood that when you humiliate people, they just might shut down on you and not produce. Therefore, the stage theatrics used regarding temper tantrums and spontaneous eruptions of emotions needed a counterpart to offset the damage done.

George knew talent when he saw it. Trying his best to create a favorable mix between borderline psychotic behavior and that of a dubious business owner, he did his best to achieve plausibility when it was required. Knowing that he had a diamond in the rough with Les Marino, George would make sure that he instilled a certain amount of fear as well as respect when it came to cultivating talent. A good rider knows that if you keep kicking the horse, he's going to eventually buck you off, therefore, a civilized conversation with a sprinkling of gratitude added in would keep his subjects productive, which was his objective all along. The same held true with George Curly's handling of young Kenny Anderson. Knowing that there was a significant amount of importance involved with the correct measurements and quantities calculated which would ultimately equate to payment and subsequent profits, he would bark and growl at Kenny but he never would bite him.

The involvement that Les Marino and Kenny Anderson would have during the time that they spent working for George Curly at Suburban Construction Company would significantly impact their future actions and beliefs when it came to how a construction company should be owned, operated, and managed. George Curly was clearly from the school that taught how it's better to be feared than loved. Finding that balance, that stabilization of respect and reverence that would create an atmosphere of loyalty, productivity, and allegiance was beginning to take shape in the minds of Les Marino and Kenny Anderson. Les and Kenny both understood that the owner of the company has every right to be demanding and to push his employees so that it is advantageous to the bottom line of his company. However, the principles of democracy and free enterprise must also be taken into consideration when it comes to owning and operating a business. Les Marino's family had lived through the 'Mussolini' experiment with fascism in Italy during World War Two. Dictatorship and fascism proved to be the wrong way to run a country and it sure would not work with the running of a business. The future owners of the Modern Continental Construction Company were learning many lessons in both business and human nature as they worked toward an ideal that would eventually prove to be successful for them both.

****

Chapter Three
Rational and Understanding

1963–1964

The only way to get ahead is to be smarter today
than you were yesterday—Les Marino

Attleboro, Massachusetts
Proposed Exit #5 South Main Street
U.S. Route #495 Project
Monday, 29 July 1963
1:09 p.m.

The ironworkers who were working for Suburban Construction's subcontractor Owen J. McGarrahan Steel Erectors were setting steel beams in place on the section of the bridge that spanned South Main Street on the new section of U.S. Route #495 in Attleboro, Massachusetts. The bridge that was being built went over Main Street which was the existing Local Route #152.

The steel beam was being hoisted, as the ironworker on the ground held tightly to the 'tag-line' that was attached at the end of the beam to keep it stable. The crane swung the heavy load in the direction of the ironworker that was standing on the left concrete bridge abutment. The agile guy grabbed the end of the beam with his right hand as he signaled the crane operator to swing the load a little to the right with his left hand, then he signaled for it to be lowered a bit as the ironworker standing on the opposite concrete abutment reached out to grasp the swinging beam. With both ends of the beam securely in hand by the two ironworkers, the load was slowly lowered into place. The mobile crane that was being used to hoist the steel beam was sitting in the precise area on the job site where Les Marino had to navigate the D 7 Caterpillar bulldozer so that he could push the big pile of gravel that had recently been delivered to the project. Confusion reigned at this busy section of the project.

This new section of U.S. Route #495 roadway which was being built in Attleboro had two bridges that needed to be built. The coordination of the work being performed by the bridge building subcontractors fell upon Kenny Anderson who was Suburban Construction Companies engineer on this project, just like he was on the Boxborough section of Route #495 roadway that he worked on when he was first hired by Suburban Construction in 1962. It was the same scene but at a different time and location.

Les Marino did not want to pull rank or interfere with the setting of the steel beams, but he had his portion of work, responsibilities, and deadlines to maintain as well. Howie Bordelaise, the D 7 bulldozer operator got out of the cab of the dozer and immediately began to pack some tobacco into his pipe. As he lit the pipe, a cloud of smoke began to rise in the air, Les Marino approached Howie. They had become friends while working on the Boxborough project, Howie was a very good dozer operator. He also operated the road grader when necessary. Les said to Howie, "We need to get this matter resolved pretty damn fast or we are all going to get our asses chewed out by George Curly when he shows up on the job later this afternoon."

Howie, who kept puffing away on his pipe, and looked like he was sending smoke signals to the Mohawk tribe, replied to Les, "I think I can get the dozer by the crane without causing any problems?"

Les, looking a little surprised and with a faint glimmer of hope in his eyes, said to Howie, "Let's take a quick look to make sure." Just as they were about to walk over to where the crane was situated, Kenny Anderson pulled up in Sam Melei's pick-up truck.

Kenny jumped out of Sam's truck and approached Les and Howie with a smile on his face, "What are you going to do, push the crane out of the way with the bulldozer."

Les began to laugh and replied, "If I have to, I will!"

Kenny and Howie began to laugh and then Kenny said to Les, "I talked to the McGarrahan Steel Erector people and I let them know that we need to have access where the crane is because we have to move some gravel. They told me that they would be done and would move the crane out of the way by 1:30 this afternoon."

Les, had a look of frustration on his face as he replied to Kenny, "They still have to lower the boom of the crane and pick up the outriggers before they can move it, you mean to tell me that they will have it moved within the next twenty minutes?"

Kenny, with a little fire in his eyes, said, "Yes it will be moved, sit tight for a couple of minutes." Just as he finished his sentence, the crane began to lower its boom, and the oiler; the guy that drove the crane, started lifting one of the outriggers and took the wood dunnage out so that the crane could be moved. The crisis had been averted. Kenny, did in fact, get the job done.

Les, with a surprised look on his face, turned to Howie and said, "Let's go and move some gravel."

****

This job in Attleboro was not quite as large for Suburban Construction Company as the Boxborough project had been. However, it was somewhat more involved than the Boxborough project as this Attleboro Project involved two cloverleaf exit ramps, a couple of bridges, and a section of sanitary sewer pipe that needed to be relocated and installed.

Suburban Construction Company primarily performs the earth-moving and grading operations on this type of road-building project. They would usually subcontract the steel erection and the building of the concrete structures that were required on the job. However, on this particular project, George Curly decided to expand the operations of his company and to get involved with the drainage and sewer pipe work as there was a considerable amount of this type of work on the Attleboro Project. Getting involved in different aspects of work would require a separate set of knowledge and skills.

When Les Marino and Kenny Anderson were both involved with land surveying and road design, they had opportunities to get involved with sewer and drainage pipe arrangement. They did not have experience in the actual placement of the pipe but they were familiar with the process. It was on one of the afternoon visits to the Attleboro Project that George Curly took both Kenny Anderson and Les Marino aside and began to question them about the portion of sewer and drainage pipe work on the job that would need to be performed. Les mentioned to George that a couple of the laborers who were working in his crew had experience laying both sewer and drain pipes. George indicated that when he bid on the job, he had included what he considered a reasonable amount of money for the segment of sewer and drain pipework that had to be performed on this job.

George Curly, as much as he chastised and ridiculed Sam Melei, every time he showed up at the job site, he also understood that Sam was his project superintendent and that he did have great confidence and a positive comfort level with Sam. However, he did find himself conversing and colluding with Les and Kenny on numerous occasions. This time he was interested in their input regarding the pipe work that needed to be done on the job. It never hurt to get a second opinion, although George Curly, who considered himself somewhat of a know-it-all, seldom took the second opinions that he received to heart.

****

It was on this highway project in Attleboro, Massachusetts that Les Marino met the Commonwealth of Massachusetts Commissioner of Public Works. The commissioner's name was Jack Riciardi. He was a bright and charismatic individual who had been appointed to this prominent post by Massachusetts Governor John Volpe in 1960. Commissioner Riciardi was the youngest public works commissioner to ever be appointed to this position in the history of the Commonwealth of Massachusetts. A registered professional engineer with a significant background in civil engineering, Jack Riciardi was fortunate enough to be in office during the time that the most significant portion of the United States Highway building initiative was taking place in Massachusetts. Commissioner Riciardi was attending a meeting at the Department of Public Works District Office in Attleboro when he asked to be given a tour of the Suburban Construction Company Route #495 project that was taking place close by.

The commissioner's arrival at the job site was an unannounced visit. He figured that as long as he was in the area he might as well take a look at the highway work that was going on. He fully understood that the success of these projects was an important part of his own accomplishments and his eventual legacy, and was a direct reflection of his guidance and leadership.

It just so happened that this afternoon, Kenny Anderson had taken Sam Melei's pick-up truck to Fall River, Massachusetts as he had to drop off some architectural drawings and he was going to put fuel in Sam's truck on the way

42

back. Therefore, Sam was stuck in the office trailer as he was going over the employee payroll and time cards from last week.

When Commissioner Riciardi showed up at the Attleboro job site with his entourage in tow, it was Les Marino that greeted him. Commissioner Riciardi introduced himself and asked if Les would be kind enough to show him around the job site. Les, not being one to get involved in anything, but his own designated duties, felt that it was really not his responsibility to usher the commissioner of public works on a guided tour of the project. However, knowing that Kenny had Sam's truck and was not on the job this afternoon and understanding that the Superintendent Sam Melei, was not around either, as he was in the office trailer, Les felt obliged to help out. So, off they went to look at what was taking place on the job site; Les, reluctantly became the tour guide.

The jaunt around the job site did not take all that long. The funny thing is that something unexpected occurred. Les Marino and Jack Riciardi seemed to hit things off famously. Their Italian heritage and common interests, along with the fact that both were accomplished civil engineers and former land surveyors made the commissioner's visit somewhat interesting for Les Marino.

The beginning of a friendship took place when Les Marino met Jack Riciardi, on that fateful day in Attleboro. A spur-of-the-moment rendezvous took place in an unusual manner that would prove to be a valuable encounter for both individuals later on down the road. It's funny how a random, chance meeting that was undoubtedly somewhat of a tedious duty at the time for both participants, turned out to be such a fortuitous event.

Jack Riciardi thanked Les Marino for spending time with him and showing him around the job site. Jack was impressed with the accomplishments that Suburban Construction had made thus far on the project. He wished Les well as he headed off with his entourage following him. As quickly as he had shown up at the job site, he left in the same manner.

The traffic coming back from Fall River for Kenny Anderson was brutal on this late summer afternoon in 1963. An accident had taken place which really messed things up. The traffic was stop-and-go and the longer he was stuck in traffic, the more agitated Kenny was becoming. He knew full well that Sam Melei would be taking a conniption fit being stuck in the office all afternoon. Kenny also understood that the lack of him having a company pick-up truck of his own was the primary reason that this incident was taking place. It seemed that whenever he had to do an errand or go someplace, he had to beg

Sam to use his truck. Kenny had mentioned his need for a company truck of his own many times to Sam. This time, when George Curly came to the job site Kenny vowed that he would approach George Curly and ask him for his own company pick-up truck.

The traffic finally let up and Kenny made his way back to the job site office trailer anticipating a go-around with 'Sam the screamer' when he did get back. As he pulled into the yard where the office trailer was located, Kenny noticed the big black 1962 Cadillac Sedan Deville parked in front of the office trailer. He pulled Sam's truck into the yard and parked next to George Curly's Cadillac, the hair on the back of Kenny's neck began to bristle as he knew he was in for a 'battle royale'. He entered the trailer and sure enough, Sam started the ruckus, "Geez kid, where the hell have you been, you've been gone all afternoon. I've been stuck here in the office and not able to get to the job site?" Kenny's face was turning red as he just stood there.

No sooner had Sam finished when George Curly, with fire in his eyes, began, "I don't pay you to go joy riding, what did you do go visit a titty bar or something? Come over here let me smell your breath!"

At this point, Kenny was beside himself with anger, he replied to both of them, "I was stuck in traffic, there was an accident that messed things up. If I had my own company pick-up truck, you could have taken your truck and checked the job site, don't blame me for this shit." Now that he was good and pissed off, Kenny went on, "I've been here for almost two years, and I bust my ass for you every day. I deserve to have my own pick-up truck, George, when am I going to get one?"

George was all lit up as he came back at Kenny with, "You ungrateful bastard, you're lucky you've got a job, let alone a pick-up truck. Hell, you'll get one when I'm good and ready."

Kenny, who by now figured he had had enough, let George know, "George, you can take your company pick-up truck and stick it right up your ass, I'm done, I quit!"

****

Les gave Kenny a ride home after the big blowout. Kenny had calmed down a little after he quit and stormed out of the trailer. Les understood Kenny's frustration. They talked as they drove home; Les told Kenny that he would talk to Walter Corsano at Vancouver Associates, the survey company that had offered Les a job as a survey crew party chief a while back when he was working on the Chelmsford section of Route #495. He'd ask Walter to take Kenny on as a survey party chief. With all the work that was going on in the Boston area, it wouldn't be hard to hook on somewhere. In the meantime, it would be a good thing to take a little break from Suburban Construction and George Curly's tantrums for a while. Another chapter had closed for Les and Kenny, at least for now.

Chapter Four
Back by Popular Demand

1965–1967

Instinct is untaught ability—Kenny Anderson

Foxborough, Massachusetts
U.S. Route #495 interchange at Route #126
Friday, 23 April 1964
9:29 a.m.

The big spruce tree fell with a thud as it hit the ground; within a few seconds, a mighty oak tree gave a cracking sound as it tumbled to the ground as well. The roar of chainsaws could be heard for miles as the tree-cutting crew buzzed through the area. The 'clearing and grubbing' portion of this new project had begun a few days ago. Another section of U.S. Route #495 had begun to be built in Foxborough, Massachusetts. This was the third section of U.S. Route #495 that Suburban Construction was to build. However, it was the first section of the highway that the new project superintendent Les Marino would be in charge of.

Les stood next to his pick-up truck as he watched the tree-cutting crew fell the big trees. The lead tree cutters were followed up by a 'harvesting' crew that trimmed the branches from the trees and cut them into movable lengths so that they could be picked up by the skidder as the logs were then placed on a lumber truck to be taken to a sawmill. It was a busy operation that required precision and coordination.

****

The skills of Les Marino had been recognized and well understood by the owner of Suburban Construction Company, Mr. George Curly. Les got his promotion after the completion of the Attleboro, Massachusetts Project. Suburban Construction had another project that was going on at U.S. Route 95 in Wrentham, Massachusetts. George Curly left Sam Melei as the project superintendent in Wrentham and appointed Les Marino the project superintendent in Foxborough. However, the only way Les Marino would stay on as a project manager with Suburban Construction Company was if George Curly hired back Kenny Anderson as the project engineer. George Curly succumbed to Les's wishes and hired Kenny Anderson back to work on the project. Kenny's return to work for Suburban Construction would make him the highest-paid engineer on the Suburban payroll. The dynamic duo was back together after a short breakup. Kenny Anderson had gone to work with Walter Corsano at Vancouver Associates as a survey party crew chief after leaving Suburban Construction but the truth be told, he missed the road-building atmosphere and was glad when the opportunity arose for him to return. He was delighted to get back into the hectic routine of road-building. He was also thrilled that he finally got the pick-up truck that was the bone of contention that caused his departure from the Attleboro Project.

There were numerous pieces of heavy equipment on this job site in Foxborough, Massachusetts. Between the bulldozers, front-end loaders, backhoes, and graders, there was a need for a full-time master mechanic on the project. It was on the Foxborough section of U.S. Route #495 that Les Marino and Kenny Anderson became friendly with Aldo Morrelli, the Suburban master mechanic. The work being performed by Suburban Construction Company included union labor only. The equipment operators were all part of the International Union of Operating Engineers (IUOE) Local #4. There were also union members from the laborers union and any other union trades that were used on the project such as carpenters, cement finishers, electricians, and ironworkers.

Aldo Morelli was a member of IUOE Local #4; he had been an equipment operator, a very good equipment operator, who seemed to not only know how to run a piece of machinery, but he also fully understood how that piece of equipment actually functioned. He recognized the inner workings of the machine, how its engine operated, and most importantly, how to fix it if it had mechanical problems. Because of his wisdom relating to the intricacies of how a piece of heavy equipment performed and operated, he subsequently became a 'master mechanic'. Aldo seemed to have the uncanny ability to just listen to a piece of equipment to understand what might be wrong with it and what needed to be done to fix it. Aldo would prove to be an important figure with regard to keeping a fleet of heavy equipment operating to maximize its productivity and performance.

Les and Kenny had become associated with and somewhat friendly with many individuals during their time working as surveyors and road builders. Many of the people that they befriended were tradesmen who were good at what they did. It was understood that in order to have a productive operation, a certain amount of ability and loyalty had to take place. Although both Les and Kenny were hard drivers who demanded the best from those they worked with, there was also a fair amount of understanding, honesty, and objectivity when it came to the direction and work orders that were given to these workers. Kenny Anderson and Les Marino realized that to be successful, you needed to surround yourself with 'good' people, the kind of people who thought the way they did and had the same work ethic and drive that they did. The mold was being created that would be the template of future performance and actions associated with working for Les Marino and Kenny Anderson.

****

The road work that began on the Foxborough section of U.S. Route #495 in late April 1964 proceeded on schedule with a minimal number of problems and issues. The productivity of this project was a clear reflection of the leadership abilities of Les Marino and the superb engineering work of Kenny Anderson. It was a mild winter with a light amount of precipitation which allowed for the excavation and grading work to proceed and for the project to move forward in a positive and very productive manner.

****

It was during January of 1965 that an interesting situation took place for Les Marino. There was a change in political climate as there was a revamping of administrations in the Massachusetts State House. As a result of this political revision, the Commonwealth of Massachusetts Commissioner of

Public Works, Jack Riciardi retired from his position and became a private citizen again.

As a registered professional engineer and a civil engineer by trade, Jack Riciardi decided that he wanted to venture into land surveying and engineering work. Jack recalled the conversation that he had with Les Marino on the Attleboro section of Route #495 when he visited that project. As a result of their conversation, he made it a point to contact Les and discuss his idea of starting a survey company to take advantage of the many opportunities that were currently available for land surveying and engineering companies in Massachusetts.

Jack Riciardi met with Les Marino in early 1965 and made a proposal to Les. Jack wanted to start the surveying business but he needed some guidance and assistance in the actual logistics relating to bidding and acquiring engineering work. Therefore, Jack suggested that Les become a partner in the survey and engineering company that he was forming. Les was very interested in this venture. However, he had recently been promoted to project superintendent with Suburban Construction Company and did not want to jeopardize his position as a road builder. Les offered a compromise with regard to the development of the new entity; he agreed to be a partner in the survey and engineering company but he would not work in the field as a surveyor. Les indicated that he would assist with the hiring of competent surveyors and help with the bidding work and the organization of the field operations. After careful negotiations, a partnership was formed and Geodetic Engineering Company was born.

A busy man just became busier. With a wife and two daughters, a full-time job as a project superintendent for a road-building company, and now a partner in a land surveying and engineering company, Les Marino was firing on all cylinders.

It was during this 'hectic' time in his life that Les began to lean on his good friend and counterpart, Kenny Anderson. Although his duties were many as the project engineer, Kenny began to take on more responsibility with regard to the road work. Kenny became a road-building foreman to go along with his engineering obligations; Kenny was picking up the slack and making the project superintendent job just a bit less stressful for Les Marino.

Geodetic Engineering Company immediately picked up survey contracts that were part of the massive road-building programs that were taking place in

Massachusetts. In order to keep his end of the partnership with Jack Riciardi, Les agreed to create the survey crews that were needed to perform the work. Les talked with Kenny and came up with the idea to grab their old friend Paul Tibbets, who was the rod man in the original survey party that Les and Kenny started working together back in 1959, the infamous 'what time do you want to take your lunch break' fiasco. Paul Tibbets had become a survey party chief and was working for a rival survey and engineering company.

Les approached Paul Tibbets and offered him a position with Geodetic Engineering; Paul gladly accepted the offer as survey party crew chief. Les also asked Paul Tibbets if he could bring along a good transit operator, Paul suggested that they hire George Gardner as the transit man. George had been working with Paul Tibbets for a couple of years. Paul vouched for George Gardner and indicated that he was a good man and would be beneficial to the formation of a new survey crew. The survey crews were formed and work progressed smoothly for Geodetic Engineering Company.

****

The Sunday dinner get-togethers continued for Les and Kenny, although they may have been a bit more animated than the original get-togethers as Les's two girls, Laura and Lorraine, were now a big part of his life and they made sure that they got their share of attention from their dad on Sunday afternoons. In spite of the interruptions, Les and Kenny got to spend some quality time and had a chance to discuss things that were taking place in both of their lives. Although there were numerous issues taking place that affected both Les and Kenny, work and family, the long-ago scenario that played out on the first day that they both met on that survey job on Route #3 in Braintree never was forgotten. It had been six years and during their time together, the bond, friendship, and affection that they had for each other only became stronger.

It was during one of the Sunday dinner feasts in late 1965 that Les and Kenny began to toss around the idea of the two of them starting their own construction company. It was a vision, a passing fancy that got the two of them excited, but at that particular time, it was only a positive idea, a distant dream. Les and Kenny knew that in order to pursue their dream of starting a construction company they both needed to gather as much knowledge, information, and understanding relating to all aspects of the various types of operations that they were both involved with in order for this dream of theirs to have any chance of being successful.

Throughout this time frame, Les Marino got actively involved in the bidding process associated with contract work for Geodetic Engineering Company. He became quite adept at figuring out pricing and time frames associated with various types of jobs. The same held true for Kenny Anderson as he got more acquainted with the different work that Suburban Construction was involved with. This would include blasting operations, culvert, and drainage pipework, the setting of curb stone, and the creation of sidewalks. There were also asphalt paving work and concrete structure building operations that went along with the road work that was taking place. Getting to understand quantities, costs, and applications were very important. In order for any business to be successful, it would take the ability to recognize how exactly the work would be performed, how much it would cost, and how long it would take for it to be completed. These were all the ingredients necessary to create a successful company.

The wheels were turning in the heads of Les and Kenny. The idea of creating a construction company of their very own was more than just a pleasant thought and a pipe dream, it was something that they both wanted. The wheels were turning and the gears were moving.

****

The work had progressed famously on the Foxborough project, in spite of the constant turmoil that was created every time the owner of Suburban Construction Company, George Curly showed up at the project. His job site theatrics and drama had not subsided. There always seemed to be an air of 'distrust' when George Curly would go through his job site rant. He never seemed to portray a feeling of faith or confidence with the people that he had working for him. Les and Kenny both felt that his antics alone were a major reason to get away and start their own company.

One of the principal attributes that could be associated with the work ethic of Les Marino was the fact that although he was working for someone that he had very little confidence in and did not have any other incentive other than a good-paying job and the position as project superintendent, he went out of his way to come up with ideas and ways to save the company money and to make more profit for the owner. Part of the mystique of his success was that Les seemed to come up with ways to get things done that were somewhat unconventional, but ultimately profitable.

Les and Kenny would usually have lunch together and spend a few minutes going over what had taken place on the project. The two of them had spoken quite often about their idea of starting a construction company of their own. They would go over what the issues might be that would confront them as business owners. The biggest obstacle to overcome was to actually take the big step and incorporate and start the business. It would take more than just the fortitude to go forward. The ability to actually bid work and secure a contract was somewhat difficult for a start-up company, especially a company with no work history or experience.

It was after a particularly intense 'go-around' with George Curly, that when Les got back to the office trailer that afternoon he confronted Kenny, and he said to him, "The time has come, let's make our move and incorporate the business."

Kenny had a look of surprise on his face and replied to Les, "I've spoken to the lawyer. He told me that we need to give him a $300.00 check to incorporate the business."

Les looked at Kenny and said, "I'll bring you a check tomorrow morning." The move had been made, the dream that they had both been talking about for quite some time was about to come true.

The next morning when Les went to the job site, he went into the trailer and took Kenny aside, he said to him, "Here's the check, it is blank so put the information in that the lawyer tells you to."

Kenny looked at Les with a bit of apprehension in his eyes as he said, "You're sure you want to go through with this?"

Les, with a touch of sarcasm, replied, "Most definitely."

The ownership of the business had been discussed by Les and Kenny; they both figured that together they could make things happen. However, looking at the 'big picture' of somewhere down the road, they thought they might need to have someone involved with the company who understood heavy equipment and had a strong union background. Naturally, they immediately thought of Aldo Morrelli, the master mechanic on the job. They both approached Aldo with their idea; he was somewhat tentative when asked. Les explained that the ownership in the company would be Les-75%, Kenny-15%, and Aldo-10%.

Aldo gave a puzzled look to both Les and Kenny and then, in a low sort of whisper, he replied, "I don't think so. I've got a good job now and don't want to take any chances." Les and Kenny looked at each other and realized that it would just be the two of them. They then proceeded with the ownership of the new company being Les-75% and Kenny-25%.

The ownership of the company had been established; the only thing left was to give this company a name. Les liked the name 'Continental Construction Company'; he said he also liked the name 'American Construction Company'.

One of the subcontractors on the Foxborough job was making a cement pour for one of the bridge abutments on the job. Kenny let Les know that as soon as he got the subcontractor going with the bridge pour, he would head over to the lawyer's office in Mattapan to get the company incorporated. Kenny got the concrete pour going and then went to the lawyer's office. Kenny met with the lawyer and told him the names that they wanted to use to name the business. This was a big moment. However, because the cement pour was taking place on the job, Kenny could not stay around and wait for the lawyer to come back with the completed documents. Kenny went back to the job to make sure that the concrete pour for the bridge abutment was completed without any issues or problems.

The next morning bright and early, Kenny Anderson went to the lawyer's office to pick up the incorporation papers and the related documents. When Kenny got to the lawyer's office, he found out that the two names that Les wanted, Continental and American were both already taken. Therefore, the lawyer took it upon himself to name the company which he duly named 'Modern Continental Construction Company, Incorporated'.

When Kenny got to the construction office trailer in Foxborough, Les was waiting inside for him. Kenny parked his truck in the yard and went into the trailer. Les was standing there with a look of anticipation, he said to Kenny, "So, how did you make out?"

Kenny had a timid look on his face; the timid look turned into a painful look as he showed Les the papers and told him the name, "Modern Continental Construction Company, Incorporated."

Kenny was standing behind the drafting table in the office trailer when Les looked at the company name, he turned red in the face and said, "What did you do? How could you name the company that?" He then proceeded to chase Kenny around the office in a fit of anger!

****

The ability to come up with ideas that would save time and money had become almost second nature to both Les Marino and Kenny Anderson. Their combined efforts had saved George Curly quite a bit of money on the Foxborough project. Many times, in order to get things done, Les and Kenny would have to go 'toe to toe' with the Commonwealth of Massachusetts engineering representative on the job site, whose name was Willie McCabe. Willie was a skeptic by nature, as he always thought that he was getting the wool pulled over his eyes, or somehow being bamboozled by either Les or Kenny whenever he dealt with either one of them.

There was a specific incident that took place on the job when the excavation of a hillside needed to be removed to create the proper road grade, the material that was found in this hillside was a specific material that could be considered 'bank run gravel'. This find created an interesting situation. There was a 'line item' that required the Commonwealth of Massachusetts, by contract to pay the road builder for all 'bank run' gravel that was brought to the job site and spread as a sub-base for the roadway. As Les had found the material on the job site and as it had to be removed to bring that section of road to the proper grade, this material would usually have to be trucked off-site at the expense of the contractor.

It was Les's contention that this material could be used on a different section of the job as acceptable sub-base gravel and that the Commonwealth would have to pay the noted 'line item' as required by the contract for the material that was moved and spread.

This particular situation became a bone of contention as Willie McCabe the Commonwealth's engineer did not believe that the material was acceptable as 'bank run' gravel. Les had Kenny come up with the proper definition of 'bank run' gravel which stated that 'the material must consist of scrabbled stone, sand, dirt and round pebbles'. According to Les, the material that he had come across clearly met those specifications. An argument proceeded to take place. As this heated argument was going on, up roars George Curly in his big black Cadillac Sedan Deville. George stepped out of his car and approached

Les and Willie McCabe. Les was immediately pleased, as he figured he had got an ally in George. Les, breathed a slight sigh of relief.

Willie McCabe proceeded to explain the situation to George and made it a point to show him the gravel samples that he had collected from the hillside. Les knew full well that George was no friend of Willie McCabe's as they had had their own share of go-around on the project. George looked quickly at the material, then took some of this questionable grit in his hand and felt the texture. George looked as if he was thinking and then, giving the impression that he had a piece of shit in his hand, he took the handful of gravel and with a flair of a circus ringmaster, he proceeded to throw it on the ground as he turned to Willie McCabe and stated, "You're right, Willie, that stuff is garbage, no way can it be considered as bank run gravel."

Les looked at George with fire coming from his eyes, he tensed up as those infamous neck veins began to protrude and turn scarlet as he then blurted out, "You've got to be kidding me, you are siding with him?"

George kind of smiled and replied, "Well, he does seem to be right about it."

Les was livid, he could not contain his anger as he looked at George and told him, "Well, you're as stupid as he is!"

George Curly looked at Les with utter surprise, "What did you call me?"

Les looked at George and with complete contempt, he again replied, "I said that you're as stupid as he is. I don't know how you can run a company, with your stupidity, and you couldn't run an ant farm being as dumb as you are." Les, with his eye twitching and his face as crimson as holly berries, continued, "You don't deserve to have someone like me working for you, you don't realize just how much I care about what takes place and that I continuously make the effort to save you money." He then proceeded to shout in George Curly's face, "You dumb bastard, I quit!"

****

This time it was Kenny's turn to give Les a ride home. Les could not believe that the owner of the company would go against his own project manager and side with the Commonwealth's engineer in a situation that could save his company a considerable amount of money; it just didn't make sense to him. Les eventually regained his composure but he still had a very hard time understanding what took place. He knew that he could not work for someone that did not have his back.

Les discussed the matter with Kenny and decided that he would start to look at work for Modern Continental Construction Company. He let Kenny know that until he came up with a job that they both could work on, Kenny should stay on with Suburban Construction Company. Kenny agreed and let Les know that he would help him with looking at proposals and assist in whatever way possible in getting this company going.

It was the spring of 1967; under unfavorable circumstances, and not being identified at the time to them both, the launching of an empire had taken place, they just didn't know about it yet!

Chapter Five
It's Not Easy Starting a Business

1967–1969
*Do the thing you fear most and the death
of fear will be certain—Les Marino*

Peabody, Massachusetts
Intersection of Pleasant Street & Holton Street
Wednesday, 14 June 1967
8:25 a.m.

The big, noisy, cement truck with the words 'Wakefield Redi-Mix Concrete' painted in bright red lettering on the side of the gray rotating drum, was just turning the corner from Holton Street onto Pleasant Street when Kenny Anderson first caught sight of it. Just a bit apprehensive, he immediately put down the shovel that he had in his left hand and motioned to the cement truck driver to pull onto the left side of the street. Les Marino was energetically spreading gravel with a rake as the cement truck pulled up beside where he was busily working. The curb stone had been set in place and the wooden forms and bracing were built and properly arranged. A fibrous, felt expansion joint stuck up from the gravel bed in the middle of the first section of sidewalk that was about to be poured. It was a warm and clear day with just a few wispy, stray cumulous clouds lazily drifting along in the sky just above the section of Peabody, Massachusetts that would one day be remembered as the place that was the beginning of a dream.

****

It had taken just a little bit longer than they had anticipated but the first section of the pedestrian sidewalk was ready for the concrete to be poured into the forms that would make it a completed sidewalk and the beginning of a successful project for the newly formed Modern Continental Construction Company, Incorporated.

The work was quite tedious and laborious as it was all performed by hand. The grading of the terrain, the excavation for the curb stone, and the actual installation of the curb stone itself were all performed with hand tools and a lot of back-breaking labor. The amount of the contract with the City of Peabody Massachusetts was $10,483.00. The scope of work to be performed included the engineering and layout of the pedestrian sidewalk, the marking with wooden stacks and plastic flagging. The excavation of the existing grass and dirt, the sub-base of gravel, the wooden slates used to form the sidewalk grid, the excavation and installation of granite curb stone, and the pouring and final finishing of the concrete. The estimated time to complete the project was four weeks.

Contrary to the many erroneous declarations that the very first job ever performed by Modern Continental Construction Company, Inc. was the sidewalk job in Peabody, Massachusetts, it was not their first job.

The actual first job performed by 'Modern Continental' was the paving of a residential driveway in Malden, Massachusetts. This first job was performed for a former fellow Suburban Construction Company employee that Les Marino and Kenny Anderson had worked with on the Foxborough, Massachusetts U.S. Route #495 project when they both worked for Suburban Construction Company. The ironic thing about the 'first job' was that it did not come out very well. The guy who they did the paving job for was not happy at all with the outcome. It's a good thing that back in 1967, they did not have 'Angies List' available as the guy that they did the driveway paving job for would surely have given them a bad 'online' review that probably would have sunk the company before it ever got going.

In all actuality, getting the sidewalk job in Peabody almost didn't happen as well. The formation of, and the subsequent operation of a construction company takes numerous moving parts to actually get it in motion. The first and probably most important part was 'working capital'. Fortunately, a very frugal and economically minded Anna Maria Marino, Les's wife, was astute enough to put aside in a bank account quite a bit of the hard-earned money that Les had earned working as a surveyor, a road-building foreman and project superintendent. Thirty-five thousand dollars to be exact! Following his leaving

Suburban Construction Company in a huff after the squabble over the use of the bank run gravel, Les concentrated on bidding work for the newly created Modern Continental Construction Company, but to no avail. No one would trust a company that had no experience or a 'track record'. But he kept trying!

It was a combination of luck and humility that allowed the acquisition of that first real job in Peabody Massachusetts to take place. Using the 'liquid capital' that they had on hand, thanks to Anna Maria Marino, a 'cash' bid bond was used for the Peabody sidewalk bid. When the bid opening took place, Modern Continental was a low bidder with a price of $10,483.00. Mass Construction Company came in as second bidder with a price of $11,691.00 which was about a 10% difference or savings for the City of Peabody. However, the ugly fact that Modern Continental Construction Company had no previous experience with building municipal sidewalks came into contention. The City of Peabody engineer and the ultimate decision maker as to who would receive the contract was named Alan Taubert. He was aware of the extensive background and experience that the two principals Les and Kenny had with regard to construction, engineering, and road-building, but he had an obligation to the taxpayers of the City of Peabody with regard to the stability and probability of the company actually completing the work in a timely manner and within the budget appropriated for the work. He had a concern that they might not be able to complete the work.

As a required 'precaution', Alan Taubert approached the owner of the second-place bidder, Mass Construction Company, Eddy Vozzella, and asked him if he had a concern about the City of Peabody awarding the sidewalk contract to Modern Continental Construction Company. Eddy Vozzella contemplated the question, and after giving it a quick thought, he realized that his company had an abundance of work on hand, as his reply to Alan Taubert was, "Let them have the job."

It has been overheard numerous times and for many years since by friends and acquaintances of Eddy Vozzella the owner of Mass Construction Company as he lamented, "Why did I ever let them have that sidewalk job in Peabody, look at what they've become!"

Upon being awarded their first actual contract for the sidewalk job in Peabody, Massachusetts Les Marino let Kenny Anderson know that the time had come for him to leave Suburban Construction Company and to start working with Les in their own company. Kenny had moved up the ladder at

Suburban Construction Company after Les left the company. He had become the project superintendent on the U.S. Route #495 project in Foxborough, Massachusetts. George Curly had come to depend on Kenny Anderson as he proved to be a very competent project superintendent. As a matter of fact, Suburban Construction Company had just secured a rather large road-building contract for building a section of I-684 in Westchester, New York. Rumor had it that George Curly wanted Kenny Anderson to be the project superintended on that big project.

George Curly had made one of his quick visits, with a properly timed strafing and surgical strike on the job site, and was about to leave when Kenny Anderson called out from the job site office trailer for George to hold on a minute before he took off. Kenny nervously approached George's big black Cadillac with a certain amount of anxiety. Kenny placed his hands on the door of the Cadillac as George rolled the driver's window down. Kenny shyly looked George in the eyes as he told him, "Les Marino and I started a construction company and we just got awarded our first contract, I'm going to be leaving and going to work with him."

George looked at Kenny with venom coming out of his eyes as he blurted out, "You'll probably be back in a week begging for your job back, you two idiots will never make it, go ahead, leave what do I care." George was so pissed off that before Kenny could step back from the side of the car, George jammed the car in reverse, stepped on the gas, and proceeded to run over Kenny's foot as he backed out of the yard. Kenny jumped around the yard howling in pain as George sped away!

****

The sidewalk job in Peabody was an exercise in perseverance for Les and Kenny, as they worked side by side with one another to get the job done. Needless to say, the budget was limited with regard to equipment and materials for the project. The actual work was all performed by hand. No heavy equipment or machinery was used to complete the job. A wheelbarrow, shovels, rakes, crowbars, and various hand tools were the only equipment used on the project. The excavating and grading of the actual section of the sidewalk was not all that difficult. However, the sections of granite curbstones proved to be a challenge. With each section of granite curbstone weighing an estimated

400 plus pounds, muscling these babies into position was not an easy task. After a couple of days of back-breaking lifting and shoving, Les and Kenny looked at each other and understood that as tough and strong as they both were, they both began to cry 'uncle' after a couple of days of torture. Kenny looked at Les and let him know that although they had not carried any extra money for hired help, Kenny mentioned that he could get his buddy John Malm to come to work for them for a day or two just to set the curbstones in place. Les, with a look of distress and perhaps just a touch of gratitude, reluctantly agreed. It would be recorded for history's sake, that John Malm, the lifelong friend and confidant of Kenny Anderson became the very first employee of the Modern Continental Construction Company on the Peabody, Massachusetts sidewalk project.

****

After the Peabody sidewalk job was completed, things did not just fall into place and takeoff for this fledgling company. The road forward for Modern Continental was laced with numerous speed bumps and potholes. Les and Kenny put quite a bit of time and effort into the company regarding visits to potential job sites and in spite of a lot of hard work and effort relating to calculating measurements and quantities, the bids that were submitted were not all winners. Later in 1967, a first-place bid was recorded in Reading Massachusetts for the installation of a drainage pipe in the amount of $30,000.00. However, the town engineer for Reading was not as considerate as the City of Peabody engineer as he refused to recognize Modern Continental Construction Company as a viable entity and recommended that the second-place bidder be awarded the project.

Fortunately, for Modern Continental, it had established a 'track record' in the City of Peabody because of its successful sidewalk project. They were now accepted and allowed to bid work in the City of Peabody which proved to be a beneficial opportunity for these two young and aggressive entrepreneurs. They were able to pick up two more small bids in Peabody, one for a sanitary sewer project and another for drainage work. Alan Taubert, the City of Peabody engineer would prove to be a staunch supporter of Modern Continental and would provide them with a positive performance rating that showed his respect for their hard work, and their useful contributions to the City of Peabody.

With three successful municipal projects under their belt and a feeling of confidence, Les and Kenny worked together to create a triumphant set of numbers that allowed them to be the low bidder on a $68,000.00 drainage pipe project in the Town of Wellesley, Massachusetts. They even included the use of mechanized equipment for this project, a first for the company. However, the line item for equipment was limited. Therefore, the money spent on equipment would have to include a versatile piece of machinery that could perform numerous duties. Les and Kenny agreed that the best piece of equipment for the job would be a Gradall. This machine could both dig and grade which was a plus. However, equipment rental companies did not freely provide credit for companies that did not have references or liquid assets available to them. This was just another hurdle in their ongoing establishment of credibility and trustworthiness.

It was at this time, the fall of 1967, when the development of the company was in its infancy that an unsuspecting benefactor entered the picture. The old adage of 'you're only as good as your reputation' certainly came into play in this scenario as word back got to George Curly the owner of Suburban Construction Company, the former employer of Les Marino and Kenny Anderson that they were in need of renting a Gradall, but were running into obstacles. George, although still a bit stung by the departure of these two renegades, called them and offered to rent them one of his Gradalls. Les and Kenny humbly accepted his offer and were grateful for this act of decency on his part. The use of the Gradall on the Wellesley job proved productive at first, but although it was a versatile piece of equipment, it still had its limitations as it really was not a true excavator. Therefore, the need for a machine that could provide more pure excavation activity came into play. Les and Kenny sent the Gradall back to George Curly with a very big thank you to him for his kindness.

It was in early 1968, during the Wellesley project that Les and Kenny were introduced to Stan Fitts.

He was the owner of Clark-Wilcox Equipment Company which was located in Cambridge, Massachusetts. Stan Fitts allowed Les and Kenny to try using a 'dynahoe' on the project. This was a unique piece of heavy equipment that had a backhoe on one end of the machine and a front-end loader on the other end. A truly versatile piece of equipment that would solve all of their problems. Stan Fitts had great foresight as he recognized a good hard work ethic in both Les and Kenny which led him to believe that these boys were going to be successful. He gave them a line of credit which was a very positive factor at this stage of growth for the company the project in Wellesley, Massachusetts involved a considerable amount of earth-moving. As much as they tried to avoid it, they had two options with regard to moving dirt; option one, they could rent a dump truck which meant that you hired by the day a dump truck with the driver. Option two, they could purchase their own dump truck, knowing that if they hired a dump truck with a driver, the truck and driver would sit around half of the time doing nothing, which was sure to frost the asses of both Les and Kenny, so option two was the lessor of the two evils.

It was during their fourth municipal project less than two years after starting the business that Modern Continental purchased their first dump truck, a 1956 Diamond 'T' ten-wheel dump truck. Kenny Anderson was the first company truck driver.

The project in Wellesley was completed in the spring of 1968. It did not take long for the up-and-coming contractor that had begun to establish themselves as a company that could dig dirt and lay pipe, to win another bid in, you guessed it, the City of Peabody Massachusetts. This job was a municipal sewer project for just a tad over $100,000.00. Although they had begun to blossom, they still kept grounded and continued to perform the majority of the work themselves. Kenny would operate the dynahoe and Les would install the pipe. Kenny and Les would share driving the Diamond 'T' dump truck, but the truth be known, Les had trouble getting the truck out of first gear; he was not a very good truck driver.

John Malm, the company's first employee, who had been working for the company off and on since the first Peabody job, left to join the U.S. Army in 1968. His leaving allowed for the hiring of the first full-time laborer. Joe Ricci, a laborer who had worked with Les and Kenny at Suburban Construction. He became the first full-time field employee of the company. Joe Ricci worked with Les and Kenny laying pipe and performing whatever jobs were required. Joe also had a background in blasting and explosives, which would prove to be beneficial as the company moved forward.

Joe Ricci was surely a one-of-a-kind type of guy; an 'old salt' that had been around construction work since the end of World War Two. He had spent some time working for C.J. Maney Company, a contractor that performed excavation, railroad, and road work. He then went to work for Suburban Construction Company as a laborer. He understood the business and was a good worker. He had gotten married not long ago to a girl who was a bit reluctant to tie the knot with him. She had become pregnant by Joe but still had her concerns if he was the guy to settle down with as he most certainly had a wild side to him. In an effort to entice the young lady to marry him, Joe agreed that when the child was born, no matter what the sex might be, he would name the child after her. She thought about it for a while and although she was a little apprehensive, she agreed to marry him.

Not long after Joe and his bride Susan got married, their little bundle of joy arrived. The child was a healthy baby 'boy!' True to his word, the little boy was christened with the name 'Susan Samuel Ricci'. Yes, long before the country singer Johnny Cash got the idea to write the song 'a boy named Sue', Joe Ricci had already done it! Many years later, Joe Ricci, the very first employee of Modern Continental Construction Company was still working for the company when his son had begun his first year of college. Joe's son wanted to earn some money for the summer, so he asked his dad if he could work at Modern Continental. Joe Ricci asked Les and Kenny if his son could have a job working for the company for the summer. They agreed, and young 'Susan Samuel Ricci' was hired as a laborer for the summer months. By the time he had gotten older, it was agreed that the boy would go by the name of 'Sam' rather than Susan. However, when young 'Susan—Sam Ricci' received his first paycheck that summer, the labor foreman who was handing out the paychecks on the job noticed that he had a check in his hand that was made payable to 'Susan Ricci'. The foreman figured it must be a mistake. The foreman looked at young 'Sam Ricci' and said to him, "Hey, this check I've got says that it's payable to 'Susan Ricci', is that you Sam?"

With a bright red face and a hesitant reply, he said, "Yeah, that's me." Well, it did not take long for the word to get around the job site that Modern Continental had 'a boy named Sue' working for the company!

The sewer job in Peabody went through the summer of 1968 into the fall. The company had kind of established itself as an entity that would take on just about any kind of work and be successful at it. Kenny Anderson became somewhat adept as a machine operator, as the company dynahoe got a very good workout from him. The work taking place necessitated another purchase by the company; it was in the summer of 1968 that Modern Continental Construction Company, Inc. purchased their first company pick-up truck, a 1963 Chevrolet C-10. It was when the purchase of this pick-up truck took place that the idea to have the company trucks painted bright yellow came about. Having foresight that eventually there would be a whole fleet of company trucks running around the roadways, Les wanted to be able to spot the company trucks from far away, therefore, going forward, a bright yellow paint would be used to identify all company trucks and equipment. By using this bright yellow color, Les had achieved his objective of observing each and every vehicle!

It was in the late fall of 1968 that a mysterious phone call was made to Kenny Anderson by Joe Rosenfeld, who was the owner of Rosenfeld Concrete Company. Rosenfeld Concrete Company was the primary concrete supplier to Suburban Construction Company on many of their road-building projects. Joe Rosenfeld knew Kenny and Les from his interaction with them when they were working for Suburban Construction. Joe Rosenfeld mentioned to Kenny that one of his customers, Corio Construction Company, had been awarded a pretty big sewer job in Worcester, Massachusetts, and that the owner, Pat Corio had concerns about some of the work on the project. Joe Rosenfeld suggested that Les and Kenny should give Pat Corio a call to see if they could help him out.

The call was made to Pat Corio; it appeared that his company had in fact been awarded a large contract to install a new section of sanitary sewer in the Salem Square section of Worcester, Massachusetts. This new section of sewer system that was to be installed, would tie into an existing city trunk line that was very deep. As sewer systems are designed on a 'gravity' method, this particular section of sewer pipe to be installed in the Salem Square section of Worcester was approximately 50 feet deep. Excavating at this depth concerned Pat Corio.

Heck, excavating a trench and installing a sewer pipe 50 feet below the street, downright terrified Pat Corio. He made no bones about it when he talked with Les and Kenny. Pat Corio indicated that the section of work in the Salem Square portion of the job was estimated to be about $500,000 worth of work. Being presented with the opportunity to perform work in the amount of $500,000 and not having to post a bond or any collateral, would be a 'Godsend' for Modern Continental Construction Company. Normally, a bond would be required to perform this amount of work but as Pat Corio's company had already provided the bond to the City of Worcester, this alleviated Modern Continental from this financial surety and bonding obligation.

After carefully reviewing the situation and the circumstances associated with taking on the work in this section of the sewer project, and feeling somewhat confident that they could actually get the work done, Les and Kenny, knowing full well that this venture would most likely either make or break the company, they agreed to take on the job. With a roll of the dice and taking a huge gamble that they could actually pull this caper off, Les and Kenny put on their scuba tanks, flippers, and goggles, and proceeded to dive head-first into the fifty-foot-deep abyss!

Chapter Six
Deep Thought and Reflection

1969–1972

The difference between ordinary and
extraordinary is that little extra—Kenny Anderson

Worcester, Massachusetts
Salem Square
Monday, 6 January 1969
9:27 a.m.

The frozen ground did not pose a problem for the 30-H Bucyrus-Erie hydraulic excavator as Kenny Anderson dug the bucket into the ground. The soil was hard but not difficult to dig. The trench was getting deeper but the reach of the bucket and dipper on this backhoe only went so far, which in this case was not nearly far enough. Getting deeper was not going to be possible with this machine. Kenny looked at Les from the cab of the backhoe with a look of disgust on his face as he pointed out, "I think we've got a problem?"

Les was looking at the material that Kenny had just dug from the trench as he shouted back, "You can't go any deeper?"

Kenny got out of the backhoe, and walked over to where Les was standing, and replied, "We're going to need a machine that can get us down to grade." They both stared into the open trench and pondered the situation as a gust of cold air swept through the section of Salem Square in downtown Worcester that had been the center of attention for the past few days. When they took on this beast of a job, they knew that there would be problems, but the problems seemed to be taking place a lot earlier than anticipated.

Les confirmed what they both knew, "There's no machine with the reach that we need."

Kenny who had been deep in thought, turned to Les, with a wide-eyed look on his face that said, "I think I just solved the problem. We could use a crane with a drag line!"

Les looked at Kenny with a quizzical expression and said, "That just might work; it just might."

****

They had begun the job just before the end of the year. The layout and preparation work took a couple of days. They were lucky that there had not been any bad weather thus far. Starting a job at this time of year was never easy, but a job like this with such a deep cut was almost suicidal. The problem was that they basically had no choice. Les Marino and Kenny Anderson had bet it all on this project. They knew that a successful outcome was critical if they were to go forward as a viable entity. An awful lot of eyes were on these two persistent characters. The heavy betting money was on failure and not success. These two reactionaries had completed a couple of simple projects but had not actually delved into the real world of 'must-win' territory that would prove if they were for real, or just another flash-in-the-pan operation. Solving the problem of how to dig deep enough for them to set the sewer pipe was only one of the many obstacles that seemed to be rearing their ugly head. How to procure the right machine, and how not to blow the budget by spending lots of money on acquiring it, was also an issue that they had to deal with.

They got through the day in Worcester digging and moving dirt as best they could. On their way home from Worcester that evening, both Les and Kenny decided to take a moment and try to figure out, first of all, who had a crane with a dragline available and second, how would they pay for it. Les thought for a minute and then let Kenny know that Suburban Construction had an 'American 797' crane with a dragline bucket. Kenny remembered the piece of equipment. The trouble was would George Curly come to their aid again, as he had on the Wellesley job when he rented them his Gradall? They could only try and ask him, nothing ventured, nothing gained. When they got home from work, Kenny called George Curly and explained their situation to him. George listened to Kenny and when he was through telling him his tale of woe, George let Kenny know that the 'American 797' crane was actively working and that he couldn't let it go. Kenny reluctantly understood and thanked George for his time.

After he hung up the phone with George Curly, Kenny called Les to let him know about the situation with Suburban and that the crane wasn't available. About a half hour after his phone call with Les, Kenny got a call from George Curly; he let Kenny know that he had made other arrangements and was now able to free up the 'American 797' crane and that he could let Les and Kenny use the crane in Worcester, and that he would also provide the crane operator, 'Peewee' to go along with the crane. Kenny inquired about how much he wanted for the rental of the machine and George let him know that they could work something out, but to first see if the crane could actually do the job that they wanted it to. Kenny hung up the phone and quickly called Les to let him know that they would be able to get the crane from Suburban Construction.

The use of a crane with a dragline bucket proved to be the right decision and it worked like a charm. Well, the crane with the dragline bucket worked like a charm that was until the next ugly mug stuck their face out of the dirt and spit at Les and Kenny. This time it was a vein of rock that caused concern. At a depth of just under thirty feet, there was a deposit of what geologists like to call 'glacial till', but in fact, it was a large section of granite rock that would need to be blasted from the trench. Removing the rock from the trench area would slow things down. However, on the positive side of things, working with solid rock in the trench would create a stable environment to work in as the rock walls would prevent the soil from collapsing into the open trench. Kind of a lose-win situation. The rock being blasted and removed might slow things down a bit but the ultimate result would be a safer place to work when they eventually had to set the sewer pipe into place.

The hiring of the Peabody job of Modern Continental's first employee, Joe Ricci as a laborer turned out to be a very good gesture. Joe knew how to blast and would be able to drill the holes and load the dynamite to remove the rock at the bottom of the trench in Worcester. Therefore, the hiring of a blasting company to remove the rock would not be necessary and be a big savings. Through their connection with Stan Fitts at the Clark-Wilcox Equipment Company they were able to rent a drill rig and compressor to use to remove the rock. The process was somewhat slow but effective. Joe Ricci would drill the holes in the rock all day long and then at the end of the day, he would load the holes with dynamite and blast the rock. As soon as the days blasting was completed, Peewee, the operator of the crane with the dragline bucket would remove the broken rock from the trench area.

To say that the area around Salem Square in Worcester was in disarray would be to a certain degree, like saying the Titanic had a slight leak. The turmoil that was taking place in that section of Worcester looked somewhat like Berlin Germany did during April 1945. The street was torn up, there were piles of rock and dirt everywhere, there was a crane with its boom sticking up in the air, and an assortment of compressors, drills, and excavation equipment scattered all over the area. In spite of the commotion that was taking place, progress was being made.

When the proper depth had been obtained for the installation of the sewer pipe, the next set of concerns came into play. Using a crane to set pipe was not an efficient way to perform the task. This is when another 'bright idea' came to the minds of Les Marino and Kenny Anderson. The dynahoe was the best piece of equipment to use for spreading the crushed stone bedding and for the setting of each individual piece of sewer pipe. The question was how do we get the dynahoe down 50 feet into the trench? The answer was simple, you use the crane to lower it down the hole.

The idea to use the 'American 797' crane on his project proved to be just another one of those 'ace up the sleeve' moves that Les Marino and Kenny Anderson would become famous for. The crane had been positioned in a strategic way to maximize the excavation capabilities of the machine. However, in order to hoist the dynahoe and lower it into the open trench, the crane would have to be repositioned to increase its safe lifting capacity. Therefore, the crane had to be moved down the street so that it would be adjacent to the trench at a perpendicular angle. When it was time to move the machine, 'Peewee' the operator began to walk the machine down the street. 'Peewee' sat in the cab of the crane and slowly moved down the side of the road. The size of the crane and the small section of road there was to travel on made it a very tight fit.

Unfortunately, in his haste to reposition the crane, Peewee did not take into consideration that on the right side of the machine, there was a row of city parking meters. The view from the right side of the crane was partially obscured for 'Peewee', as he did not see or hear the snapping at the base of each parking meter as they snapped like match sticks, as the counterweight on the rear side of the crane began to clip the parking meters, the meters just seemed to explode as they were so abruptly rooted from their seemingly secure base. As each parking meter abruptly and resoundingly crashed to the ground, the cash box on the side of the meter opened and the coins flew out in every direction onto the street.

As the crane approached the place that it needed to be positioned, Les Marino and Kenny Anderson looked in awe, as down the road they saw all the parking meters that had been busted and destroyed. Les motioned to 'Peewee' to look at what he had done. 'Peewee' looked back at Les with a shit-eating grin on his face and just shrugged his shoulders. Les looked at Kenny and told him to get an empty bucket. Les and Kenny proceeded to pick up each and every one of the coins that were on the ground and put them in the bucket. They then gave the bucket full of coins to the city traffic department. Even though they made the effort to pick up the coins, the City of Worcester still charged Modern Continental for the cost of replacing and repairing the broken parking meters.

Not only did they use the crane to lower the dynahoe into the deep hole, as the blasting had caused an irregular grade in the bottom of the trench, but some calibration of the final subsurface needed to be accomplished, as such, a small bulldozer was also lowered by the crane into the pit as well so that it could effectively and properly grade the bottom of the trench.

It was in the late spring of 1969 when the accomplishment of not only digging a 50-foot trench was completed but also the installation of the new sewer pipe took place. The final connection was made from the new sewer pipe into the existing sewer line in Salem Square in Worcester, which completed Modern Continental's portion of the project. What had been considered a difficult and almost impossible job to perform had been not only effectively been carried out, but it was done in a reasonable time frame that pleased everyone involved. Corio Construction Company was able to keep its reputation intact with its bonding company as the job was completed without any hardship to the surety company. The City of Worcester had its sewer system updated as required by their contractual obligations and Modern Continental Construction Company Incorporated had completed a $500,000.00 portion of work with a profit of $240,000.00. A tremendous accomplishment for the fledgling company that was still wet behind the ears. An achievement that basically put this new company on the map.

The profit earned on the Salem Square Worcester project would now allow Modern Continental Construction Company to acquire a surety line of credit that would allow them to bid work in the six hundred-thousand-dollar range. A relationship was formed with the surety agent that provided bonding for Suburban Construction Company. The bonding people were impressed with the work performed and the profit margin relating to the work completed on the Salem Square Worcester, Massachusetts project. The success of the Worcester project opened the door to a whole new arena for the company. The work that they would bid now would set them apart from the 'little' guys that they had been constantly running up against.

In the final analysis, the decision to take the gamble and perform the deep-cut sewer job in Worcester was a stroke of genius for Les Marino and Kenny Anderson. They bucked the odds and did something that almost everyone thought they would fail at. Taking a chance and being successful would be a trait that these two guys would live by for many years to come. One disappointing incident did take place just before the job in Worcester was completed, in late March of 1969, at the age of 66 years old, Kenny Anderson's mother, Lulu 'Elizabeth' Anderson passed away. Kenny Anderson was now an orphan.

Within a month of the completion of the Worcester job, Modern Continental was a successful bidder on a new sewer installation project in Burlington, Massachusetts. No rest for the weary. The company also made a decision to open an office location and to hire their first 'non-construction worker' employee which was an office and clerical person, a girl of all trades was hired to take care of accounts payable, payroll, and all related office duties. The location of Modern Continental Construction Company's first office was 426 Cambridge Street Cambridge, Massachusetts. The office was a two-room unit, one room was used for accounting and bill paying and the other office was used by Les and Kenny as an engineering room with a drafting table for the many sets of plans that they would be looking at relating to placing bids to acquire more work. These two guys did it all, they did the construction work during the day and then, after working all day, they went back to the office to look at drawings and bid more work.

As Modern Continental got into larger projects, they became acquainted with the many engineering firms that were hired by the municipalities to oversee the work and to act as their representative for the city, towns, or awarding authority that was responsible for the contract. There were many different engineering firms back in the late 1960s and early 1970s, Camp Dresser & McKee Fay, Spofford & Thorndike, Metcalf & Eddy, Weston & Sampson, and Tighe & Bond were just a few of the names of the engineering companies. These engineering firms would have a representative on-site to oversee the work that was being performed to make sure that the contract specifications were being adhered to and that the materials used on the project were as described in the contract.

Not long after acquiring the sewer job in Burlington, Modern Continental was successful in acquiring a project in Wilmington, Massachusetts. As soon as the company had more than one job working simultaneously, it was necessary to expand the workforce. Although Les and Kenny were still actively involved, as Kenny Anderson was the primary company equipment operator and Les Marino was the primary project superintendent, the need to hire another supervisory employee was inevitable. It was when the project in Wilmington, Massachusetts was about to commence that another milestone was met in the company as Cosmo Pallazola was hired to be a project superintendent. Cosmo had been working for Suburban Construction Company as a superintendent when Les and Kenny approached him to come to work for them at Modern Continental.

It was on the Wilmington, Massachusetts project that as a result of a nasty section of excavated trench, a series of boulders were encountered. Not an established vein of buried rock that would have shown on the project drawings, as prior to the project a company would perform 'drill borings' to identify if any rock existed. What was unexpectedly identified were random boulders that were too large for the excavator to lift and move. This slowed down the progress of the pipe installation crew. There was a need to have Joe Ricci at the scene to perform the blasting of the boulders to reduce them to pulverized stone so that the backhoe could dig them out. For established sections of underground rock that are encountered, there are conventional ways to calculate the removal. There is blast hole diameter, specific gravity, and the number of explosives used per each individual milli-second delay are taken into consideration. However, when you run into a boulder, you're not sure exactly how big it is or how deep it goes into the ground. There are no scientific calculations that can be taken into consideration when blasting a boulder.

Joe Ricci arrived on the job site with a small compressor and a hand-held pneumatic drill. He took a look at the boulder and made his best 'guestimate' of its actual size, seeing that it was partially buried in the ground. He drilled a couple of holes and shoved in a few sticks of dynamite. He told everyone to back off as he tied in his 'lead line' to the blasting caps and hooked it up to his rack-bar blasting machine—he yelled 'fire in the hole' as he pushed the plunger down on the blasting box. Well, as mentioned, the blasting of random boulders is not an exact science. After a very loud 'boom' and a shaking of the ground, much like the great San Francisco earthquake, a cloud of dust and smoke rose from the site in the form of a mushroom. Along with the rising cloud of smoke and dust were a considerable number of little rocks and stones that proceeded to fly in every direction imaginable. Joe Ricci initially had a look of amazement and awe on his face when the immediate reaction to the blast took place, this look of amazement and awe quickly turned into a look of horror as the rocks flew and the ground shook violently. Joe's only response was, "Oh, shit!"

After the smoke cleared and all employees were accounted for, Cosmo Pallazola, looked at Joe Ricci and said, "I think you might have overloaded that one, Joe?"

Joe Ricci, still somewhat dumbfounded, looked back at Cosmo and said, "Yeah, maybe a little." The good news was that the large boulder that had once been in the trench and was impeding production, no longer existed and the backhoe didn't have to move it. The bad news was, that the little yellow wood-frame cottage that was about 50 feet from the site of the explosion looked like it was about to fall down. It was a good thing that it was a calm day, as a good gust of wind might have knocked the little house over.

As things began to calm down, Cosmo Pallazola, noticed from the corner of his eye, that the front door of the little yellow house was rattling, Cosmo gave a quizzical look in the direction of the little yellow cottage. He then heard some noise coming from behind the rattling door. Cosmo sauntered over to the little yellow cottage and started to climb the three wooden stairs that led to the door. His first step on the bottom stair caused him to realize that the stairs were loose and very uneven. As he climbed the stairs, he listened closely to what was a woman's voice behind the door. Apparently, she heard Cosmo on the other side of the door as she spoke in a loud voice "Is someone out there?"

Cosmo, a little concerned at this point, answered the voice by saying, "Yes, I'm from the construction crew."

The woman behind the door said in a trembling voice, "I can't open the door, can you help me." Cosmo proceeded to grab a hold of the doorknob and gave it a good yank; it did not move.

Cosmo looked over his shoulder and yelled to Joe Ricci, "Joe, come here and give me a hand." Joe climbed the stairs to the front door and together with Cosmo pulled on the door knob and with a good hard tug, they got the door open. The woman standing there was a small, frail lady, about 65 years old and in somewhat of a state of shock.

She thanked Cosmo and Joe for their help opening the front door and then said, "I don't know what happened, I was sitting here watching television and then a very loud boom occurred and the house shook violently. Do you think it was one of those new jet airplanes breaking the sound barrier and causing a sonic boom?"

Cosmo looked at Joe and then in a sheepish voice replied, "It could have been."

Joe Ricci, feeling a little squeamish and uncomfortable, told the little old lady, "Ma'am, the problem might have come from our construction work, if you don't mind, I'll get some tools and fix your door so that it opens and closes properly."

The woman smiled at Joe and said, "Well, that would be very polite of you to do that." Cosmo looked at Joe and started to walk away as he figured Joe Ricci caused the problem, let him fix it.

In late 1969, after giving considerable contemplation to a project that looked to be a nice piece of work for the company, Les and Kenny put their heads together and came up with what they thought would be a very good price for the job. The job in question was another sewer installation project, but this one was a little more involved as it required that the pipeline that would be installed had to go under a main section of railroad track that was owned by the Boston & Maine Railroad Company. This would be an intricate project that would prove to be beneficial to the growth of the company.

The project in question was for the City of Woburn, Massachusetts, and was part of the sanitary sewer initiative that was originally put in place by Governor John Volpe in the mid-1960s. The objective was to convert communities from septic systems to municipal sanitary sewer systems. This project was to take place in the East Woburn, Massachusetts section in the Montvale Avenue area.

The bid opening took place in Woburn City Hall. The engineering firm that was the representative for the City of Woburn was Camp, Dresser & McKee (CDM). The resident engineer for CDM on this project would be Donald Breeda. The bid opening took place and Modern Continental Construction Company was the successful low bidder on the project. The Woburn sanitary sewer project would begin in late 1969.

It was in the spring of 1970 when the sewer project in Woburn progressed down Montvale Avenue and came closer to the Boston & Maine Railroad Line, a meeting had to take place with all involved parties. This meeting would include, Modern Continental Construction Company, the representative from the engineering firm, Camp, Dresser & McKee, a City of Woburn Public Works official, and public safety officials, including the police and fire departments. This meeting took place at the Boston & Maine Railroad headquarters which was at Ironhorse Park in North Billerica, Massachusetts.

The start of the Woburn sewer project meant that Modern Continental would now have three projects running simultaneously. The Burlington and Wilmington jobs were both finishing up when the Woburn project commenced. As the company was straight out, it was necessary for both Les Marino and Kenny Anderson to spend time on all three projects. However, to get the Woburn job started off correctly, Les Marino would be the project superintendent with Kenny Anderson running most of the heavy equipment on the job.

The Woburn sewer project ran from east to west down Montvale Avenue from the Stoneham, Massachusetts border toward the Goodyear School. It was just past the Goodyear School that the Boston & Maine Railroad tracks, a mainline that carried both passenger and freight trains, had to have the sewer pipe installed under the existing railroad tracks.

Back in the early days of the railroad, when the existence of a railroad track in a community meant that civilization had come to town when all of the big railroad tycoons invested their money in what was at that time progress. The railroad companies demanded that they be given complete control and that any and all encumbrances or impediments to their growth be taken out of the equation. Therefore, railroads became untouchable conglomerates that dictated what and when anything would take place within their realm or sphere of influence. Railroad 'easements' were created that basically allowed any railroad track that was in existence to have an imaginary line run down the middle of their railroad track and then 50 feet on both sides, from the center of the railroad track, became the territory that was controlled by the railroad. Encroaching on this 50-foot easement was not something that any of the railroads readily accepted. If any type of operations were to be conducted within that 50-foot railroad easement, the controlling railroad line dictated exactly what could be done and when and how it would take place. Railroads had become their own governing entity that everyone, including states and municipalities, had to contend with. And the railroads did not make it easy for anyone to deal with them. The railroads called the shots and that was that!

The Boston & Maine Railroad appointed a project manager to oversee the work that would be performed within their railroad easement, his name was John Scalli. In order to perform work within a railroad easement, specific necessities had to be adhered to. One of the prerequisites was that certain insurance limits and language had to be provided. The railroad companies precluded that a 'railroad protective' policy had to be put in place. The language and requirements associated with a 'railroad protective' insurance policy had been created in the 'heyday' of the railroads and had specific language and limits that in essence required that anyone performing work within the railroad right of way' of a functioning railroad had to protect the railroad from any liability and physical damage to the railroad property. This protection also included that if the railroad itself made any mistakes or breached protocol, it would be covered by the contractor performing work on the right of way. In essence, it was a pretty big deal to be able to perform work with a railroad, and the railroad was completely protected from any precarious or fortuitous events that might take place.

John Scalli was the railroad project manager and the person who would be on-site to make sure that the railroad's property and interests were properly protected. John Scalli would also schedule the 'flagmen' who were Boston & Maine Railroad employees who stood on the railroad tracks with a red flag to slow down any oncoming trains when they approached the affected area.

In order to install a pipeline under an existing railroad track, it took a specified process which is known as 'pipe jacking'. This procedure includes the excavation of a 'jacking pit' and a 'receiving pit'. The pipeline is installed up to the jacking pit and then a cylindrical steel tubing, which comes in small sections and is pushed by force with a hydraulic jack into the soil. Then when the cylindrical section is impaled in the soil, the earth material within the cylindrical tube is removed, which creates an opening. A new section of cylindrical steel pipe is then welded to the existing tube and the process is repeated with the tube being pushed further under the sections of railroad track. It is a slow, tedious process that requires accuracy to ensure that the direction that the tube is being pushed will align with the receiving pit on the opposite side of the railroad tracks. Once the steel tubing is installed and the earth is removed from inside of the tubing you have a conduit to install the sewer pipe. When the calculations are completed and it is confirmed that the pipe may be installed, the pipe must be connected and then the gravity portion of the process comes into play. As sewer lines are gravity systems, there must be a proper pitch and slope so that the sewerage can flow properly.

As noted, the process of installing a sewer pipe correctly in a jacking sleeve is a tedious operation. When the actual installation of the sewer pipe took place in the section of the sleeve that was installed under the railroad track, Les Marino was present to make sure that the pipe was correctly installed. Once the pipe is put in place, concrete must be poured around the sewer pipe to keep it in place in the steel tube sleeve. It was during this complicated procedure that a problem occurred. The sewer pipe had been secured and the proper grade and pitch were established when the liquid concrete that encompassed the new sewer pipe caused the sewer pipe to begin to float.

The procedure was well underway when Les realized that the pipe was floating and that some of the liquid concrete had to be removed from under the sewer pipe so that it would not float. Throwing caution to the wind and understanding full well that he would be putting himself in harm's way, Les Marino proceeded to crawl into the steel tube and with his bare hands, he began to pull concrete out from under the sewer pipe so that it would not float. After, what seemed like a perilously long period of time, out of everyone's sight, as he was within the steel tubing, Les Marino crawled out of the opening, with his arms covered in concrete, as he exclaimed that the pipe was no longer floating and that it was now stabilized.

This courageous and bold action taken by Les Marino to correct the problem that took place with the floating sewer pipe would have its consequences. Not long after cleaning the liquid cement from his arms, a severe redness began to form, as it became quite evident that the chemicals and the lye in the cement mixture had seriously burned his arms. An immediate trip to Winchester Hospital took place as Les needed prompt attention for his wounds.

It would take almost a month for Les Marino's wounds to heal on his arms. The burns to his skin would leave permanent scars on the strong muscular biceps of the feisty guy who seized the opportunity to correct a mistake, as he would now, like a badge of honor, wear the telltale scars on his arms to remind him of that valiant gesture in Woburn, Massachusetts.

The project in Woburn would indeed prove to be a success for Modern Continental Construction Company. As a result of the effort made by the company, a lasting relationship was formed with both John Scalli the Boston & Maine Railroad Project Manager, and with Don Breeda, the resident engineer for Camp, Dresser & McKee Engineering firm. Both men held Les Marino and Kenny Anderson in the highest regard and respected them for their tremendous work ethic.

The ability of Les Marino and Kenny Anderson to establish and maintain relationships with the people that they worked with over the years seemed almost uncanny. They were always truly sincere and genuinely trustworthy in their conversations and actions. The question has been asked, how did Les Marino and Kenny Anderson create a company that became successful and prosperous; well, one of the answers would surely be that they both maintained an aurora of genuine honesty and integrity in all of their actions and conversations. An almost simplistic and candid approach to communications, 'what you saw was what you got with both of them'. There was never any phoniness or artificial sincerity, both men shot from the hip and lived with the consequences. It's very probable that many people may have found their way of communicating to be somewhat blunt and to the point, but then again isn't that just another way of being honest and truthful?

As a result of establishing a positive relationship with John Scalli from the Boston & Maine Railroad Company, some site work at the Boston & Maine Ironhorse Railroad yard in Billerica was made available to Modern Continental. John Scalli was able to provide a negotiated contract to Modern Continental Construction to provide the installation of drainage piping and the grading of land along with the creation of a storage yard and parking area at the North Billerica, Massachusetts location. This work and other Boston &

Maine Railroad work would be assigned to Modern Continental over the many years that they maintained a relationship with John Scalli.

****

As the company prospered and grew, the necessity to establish a bona fide office location with accounting and clerical people became essential. In the fall of 1970, an office location was secured at 905 Main Street in Cambridge, Massachusetts. This office facility had a total of five rooms and was on the second floor above a car rental office. It was at this time that the company office manager Edna Hughes was hired. Edna would become an important part of the growth of Modern Continental Construction Company. She was a 'no-nonsense' lady who was tougher than most Marine Corp Drill Sergeants at Paris Island, South Carolina. She was as dedicated as they come, a woman who ruled with an iron hand. The trend or you might call it a 'movement' had begun with the hiring of Edna Hughes. The need to surround themselves with 'like-thinking people' and to create a company that worked much like a military organization as the chain of command and the need to instill a discipline that encouraged loyalty and faithfulness was important to both Les Marino and Kenny Anderson.

It was under the 37th president of the United States of America, President Richard M. Nixon that the Environmental Protection Agency was formed. This government organization was charged with cleaning up the pollution and the overall environment of the country. One of the very first tasks that the newly appointed Secretary of the Environmental Protection Agency (EPA), William Ruckelhaus committed to was the separation of combined sewer and drainage systems that were creating pollution of our nation's oceans and harbors.

When sewerage systems were first designed at the turn of the century, it was common to have drain pipes that siphoned rainwater off roadways to empty into existing sewer pipes. This type of system would become overtaxed when a heavy rainstorm took place as the amount of combined rainwater and sewerage would become too much for the wastewater treatment plants to handle. When one of the heavy rain storms took place the treatment facility would just open its sluice gates and let the untreated, combined water and sewerage to just enter the ocean and harbor. This was the primary cause of polluted harbors and waterways around the country.

To alleviate this problem, the separation of storm drains and sewer pipes became a top priority for the EPA. This was a tremendous opportunity for contractors like Modern Continental. The fact that many communities were already installing new sewer systems to replace septic systems and now the new EPA was about to make the pot of gold at the end of the rainbow only bigger!

It was in early 1971 that Modern Continental acquired a large sewer project in Billerica, Massachusetts and simultaneously, they also acquired a large sewer contract in Nashua, New Hampshire. Kenny Anderson would run the Billerica project and Cosmo Pallazola would be in charge of the Nashua, New Hampshire project.

The relationship with Stan Fitts at the Clark-Wilcox Equipment Company only became stronger as the need for equipment became essential to perform the excavation of the trenches to install all of the pipes that needed to be put in the ground. Bucyrus-Erie backhoes and Terrex front-end loaders were showing up like Easter Eggs on the various Modern Continental job sites.

****

All work and no play can be a problem. Since 1969, Les Marino and Kenny Anderson had been hitting it very hard with regard to working and growing their company. Neither one had so much as taken a day off or made an effort to enjoy some downtime in the past couple of years. Even their Sunday dinner get-togethers would ultimately turn into a work session as they talked and planned constantly. As the Christmas and New Year's holidays approached in 1971, Les spoke to Kenny and let him know that he had been in touch with his brother Luciano in Cheiti Italy, and that he was going to go back to Italy for a couple of days to visit his family. He also let Kenny know that there may very well be a business opportunity for Modern Continental Construction Company to perform some joint venture work in Europe with Les's father's construction company. Les then asked Ken if he'd like to accompany him over to Italy for a couple of days. As both Les and Kenny needed a little break, they agreed to travel together to Chieti Italy to celebrate Christmas. The trip would be a four-day excursion. With aspirations of becoming an international conglomerate, they boarded the plane and flew to Italy.

Les's brother Luciano met them at the airport. On the ride from the airport to Les's father's house, Luciano filled Les and Kenny in about the possibilities that were available to them. It appeared that Luciano was in need of a joint venture partner as the work that his company wanted to pursue was not something that their bonding company was ready to approve unless there was another deep pocket involved. Les knew that the relationship with his own bonding company may be jeopardized as well if he were to start getting involved with performing joint venture work in Europe. Nonetheless, Les and Kenny would listen to what Luciano had to offer.

The reunion with his family was very emotional for Les. He had not seen his family in many years; he was eager to catch up with what was going on in their lives. Kenny Anderson was accepted with open arms by Les's family. It was good to spend time together with family and to just relax for a couple of days. They celebrated an old-fashioned Christmas; Les' mother provided them with a true Christmas Eve feast fit for royalty. Christmas day was another day of feasting. Lots of talking, laughing, and the sipping of homemade wine took place.

The day after Christmas, Les, Kenny, and Luciano traveled to a potential work area that involved the Monti-Casino Edison Electric Company. There was some work that would be bid that involved the building of a power plant in the Monti-Casino area as that particular section of Italy was still being rebuilt after World War Two. The other area that Luciano Marino was interested in getting involved with included a housing development in East Germany. After reviewing the work and the circumstances surrounding the possibilities, Les informed Luciano that he had some concerns about dealing with a communist country; Les did not feel that there would be any recourse if they did not make progress payments. Who could they complain to if they weren't paid?

Ultimately, it was a pleasant trip, a joyful holiday, and a wonderful family reunion but the possibility of Modern Continental Construction Company getting involved in any joint venture work in Italy, or East Germany at this particular juncture of the development of the company was not possible. Les and Kenny traveled back to the United States of America well-rested and ready to jump right back into the mix of things with their aspirations of becoming an international conglomerate put on permanent hold.

In early 1972, another job was acquired in Stoughton, Massachusetts. This project would be overseen by the newly retired army sergeant who had been the actual first employee of Modern Continental Construction Company, Kenny Anderson's very good friend, John Malm. The project in Stoughton, Massachusetts included a piece of land that would be used as a staging area and the location that the job site trailer would be placed at.

The piece of land in Stoughton was something that Les Marino thought might be a good place to establish a maintenance facility to maintain and repair the trucks and equipment that the company had accumulated. When the Nashua, New Hampshire job started, two more dump trucks were purchased. These two dump trucks were a pair of B-81 Mack trucks. They were the equivalent of a team of Clydesdale Horses as these trucks were real workhorses.

With the help and assistance of Stan Fitts, Modern Continental Construction Company outright purchased the piece of land in Stoughton, Massachusetts, and created a shop/maintenance facility that would also be used to store materials and necessary equipment that was being used by the company on various job sites. Gerry Houle became the first 'master mechanic' for the company as he now had a fleet of trucks and equipment to look after.

With four projects working at the same time along with a sizable workforce and a substantial amount of equipment to keep busy, Les Marino now dedicated the majority of his time to looking at plans and bidding new work to keep everyone and everything busy. He did, however, visit the projects on a daily basis to make sure that production was being met and that the jobs were staffed properly. Kenny Anderson was running work and heavy equipment and made sure that production and problems were all managed properly.

It was late fall in 1972, as a matter of fact, it was the day after Thanksgiving that Les Marino traveled to Nashua, New Hampshire. It was a very brisk day with a serious chill in the air. Knowing full well that the company could not afford to keep a full workforce through the upcoming cold months as production on the job would diminish considerably because of foul weather. With the winter about to set in, which would seriously impede production, Les felt that it was time to make some cutbacks to keep things 'lean' for the winter months that were right around the corner. A day that is known commercially and for retail shopping stores as a day that brings in customers and revenue 'black Friday' would henceforth, in the history of Modern Continental

Construction Company be known as 'black Friday' for a completely different reason. This 'black Friday' would be a day that Les would go to the jobs that were working and make necessary cutbacks for the upcoming winter. A few of the guys were going to be losing their jobs, which would surely be a 'black Friday' for them.

The Nashua, New Hampshire job had a very unique feature, as a new sewer pipe had to be laid in the ground at the bottom of the Merrimac River. This was no easy task as a 'coffer dam' had to be installed which basically means that you build a dirt road in the river and then dig through the dirt road that you built to install the pipeline. Then when the pipe is in place, you proceed to remove the dirt road and put the river back to its original condition. This was the first job that Modern Continental Construction Company had to perform the construction of a 'coffer dam' to install a pipeline. There would be many more to come.

On the Nashua New Hampshire project, there was a pair of brothers who were working as laborers and they both also helped out with the blasting operations that were taking place on this project. Jessy and Billy Abbot were their names. Jessy was the older of the two and was married with three children. Brother Billy was the younger brother who had recently gotten married to his childhood sweetheart, Sharon. Billy and Sharon Abbot did not have any children.

When Les showed up on the Nashua, New Hampshire job site, he proceeded to converse with Cosmo Pallazola the project superintendent. Les let Cosmo know what his intentions were with regard to cutting back the workforce. Cosmo asked Les if he wanted him to let the guys go. Les told Cosmo that he would in fact do the deed as it was his company. There was a total of nine men working on the job and it was Les's intention to let two of the guys go. One of the guys that Les intended to let go was Jessy Abbot. The word traveled quickly around the job site about who was going to be laid off. When younger brother Billy found out that his big brother Jessy was being dismissed, he immediately approached Les Marino. Billy went up to Les and told him, "Les, what are you doing? My brother Jessy has a wife and three kids, he needs this job, you can't let him go."

Les, thought for a moment about the decision to let Jessy Abbot go, and with a look of compassion, he turned to Billy Abbot and said, "You're absolutely right, Billy, I can't let your brother Jessy go, (pause) you'll have to take his place, I'll lay you off instead of him."

Billy Abbot just smiled and said, "Good move, Les, but please bring me back to work as soon as you can!"

Although the crew on the Nashua, New Hampshire job had been cut back the day after Thanksgiving, the job continued. It got cold and miserable very quickly as winter approached. There was ice forming on the banks of the Merrimack River and the wind blew as if it was being funneled down a very large wind tunnel right into the faces of the guys that were still working on the job.

This particular project included a section of sewer pipe that was a 'trunk' line, meaning that it would pick up numerous smaller pipes that would empty into the larger section of pipe which would bring the material to the sewerage treatment plant. The cement sewer pipe that needed to be installed for this particular section of the trunk line was an extremely large, 108-inch diameter pipe, which equates to a conduit that is nine feet wide.

The backhoe that was the machine of choice on this job was a Bucyrus-Erie-40 H. The '40-H' was a fine machine to use to dig, lift, and set the smaller diameter pipe. However, with the huge 108-inch diameter pipes, the '40-H' just did not have the lifting capacity. The need for a much larger machine was in order. The problem was that there wasn't a backhoe with that kind of lifting capacity. The difficult terrain and the proximity to the trench limited the use of a conventional crane with a boom that would be the logical choice to lift something as big as a 108-inch cement pipe.

The dilemma that faced Modern Continental Construction Company at this juncture of the project should have been recognized when the calculations were being made to bid on the job. Needless to say, this specific element and detail of the job had escaped both Les Marino and Kenny Anderson when they put together the pricing for the bid. It made them think that maybe this omission may have been the reason why they were the low bidder by such a small amount. Apparently, the other bidders must have factored in the cost of a much bigger machine for this section of work.

It was Friday afternoon when this quandary came to light. Kenny Anderson thought about the situation for a day, well actually it kept him awake for most of the weekend. This problem even took up the majority of their Sunday afternoon dinner together at Les's house. It was not until he got back on the job on Monday morning that the picture became much clearer to Kenny. He looked at the Bucyrus-Erie-40-H backhoe. The machine had an arm (boom) that extended about twenty feet from the cab of the machine. At the end of the boom was attached a 'dipper' arm with the digging bucket attached. The dipper arm and the attached bucket extended another twenty feet from the boom arm. Kenny imagined that if he took the 'dipper' arm and the bucket off of the machine and just left the twenty-foot section of boom, this would drastically increase the lifting capacity of the machine. With an ice-cold wind whipping across the frozen ground, Kenny assembled a crew to proceed with his idea and to alter the backhoe as he envisioned. With the short boom arm only and a cable rigged to the machine, an attempt was made to lift one of the jumbo sewer pipes.

With his fingers crossed, Kenny Anderson climbed into the cab of the backhoe; he ever so gently lifted the massive pipe and slowly began to swing the load in a semi-circle to check for balance and to see if the counterweight of the machine would handle the load. His idea, although somewhat unconventional, was a complete success! Kenny put the enormous pipe back on the ground and hustled over to the job site office trailer. With a big grin on his face, and an expression akin to the cat that ate the canary, Kenny expeditiously dialed the phone and got Les on the other end of the line. He proceeded to let him know what transpired and that the problem had been solved. Les let Kenny know that he was thrilled that his 'brainstorm' of success and that this method would expedite the completion of the job and keep them within budget. The two amigos strike again!

Chapter Seven
Events Are Moving Very Fast

1973–1974

The first rule of survival—pay attention!—Les Marino

Boston, Massachusetts
Atlantic Avenue, the waterfront
Thursday, 2 February 1973
9:57 a.m.

It was an abnormally warm day in Boston for this time of year. The temperature had just crept past 50 degrees. The crew that was shoveling the stone pile next to the harbor was working in shirt sleeves. The seagulls around the harbor were in full flight on this spring-like morning. These flying monsters posed a two-fold problem as they would randomly dive bomb the guys in search of food and then, these flying 'dodos' would release giant splatters that if they hit you, you would be drenched in a sticky, smelly, white mess. The wearing of hard hats was a true necessity with these flying menaces.

John Malm, the project superintendent was looking at the set of blueprints for the job that were spread across the hood of his bright yellow 1971 Chevrolet pick-up truck. There was a lime green, Terrex front-end loader that was moving past John Malm's parked truck, carrying a length of cement drainage pipe that was hanging from the hook that was welded on the top of his loader bucket. Bob Bates, the front-end loader operator was in a hurry to deliver the piece of pipe to the waiting Bucyrus-Erie 40-H backhoe that was digging inside of a section of steel sheeting that was adjacent to the sidewalk that wound its way precariously toward the harbor. Bob Bates, the loader operator, was one of the many new additions to the Modern Continental workforce in the past few months. The Boston Harbor project on Atlantic Avenue was just one of many jobs that Modern Continental had going in early 1973.

The Boston Harbor project was another one of the many Environmental Protection Agency projects that were being performed in an effort to clean up the polluted Boston Harbor. The separation of storm drains and sewer pipes was the majority of the work that needed to be accomplished on this somewhat involved job. There was also a provision in the contract to remove a section of dilapidated concrete wharf on the waterfront and to replace it with a new portion of cement pier.

The removal of the old, rundown wharf was to be accomplished by blasting the section of concrete that was in need of destruction. One of the new employees that Modern Continental had hired for this job was Larry Pooler who was referred to with lenient reverence as 'the Preacher'. He was a combination laborer/blaster, much like the job that Joe Ricci performed for the company. How he got the handle 'Preacher' no one seemed to know.

The 'Preacher' had experience as a blaster that primarily related to removing 'high bottom' rock in the bottom of a pipe trench, or much like Joe Ricci, he would also blast any boulders that posed an obstacle to digging a trench and installing a pipeline. On this infamous day, a completely new meaning to the term, 'fire in the hole' was about to take place.

The removal of a crumbling concrete pier was something that 'the Preacher' would have to learn by trial and error. This type of operation was not exactly a common impediment in the normal scope of excavation work. Much the same as removing a vein of ledge, the process involved with getting rid of an old concrete pier was to drill holes and load dynamite. Unfortunately, there was also a critical factor that needed to be taken into consideration. And apparently, was not? The constant turmoil associated with salt water washing up against buried concrete, along with the perpetual high and low tide cycles that had transpired over the many years that this barrier had been in place desperately needed to be considered. Although it was not visible to the eye, the portion of the concrete pier that was below the low tide mark was terribly eroded and decayed, which ultimately compromised the subsurface condition. The holes were drilled and the dynamite was loaded. What seemed like a simple operation was about to take place. Needless to say, all applicable safety precautions were contemplated and taken into consideration.

However, during the early 1970s, the Commonwealth of Massachusetts Department of Public Safety did not really have a whole lot of rules, regulations, or restrictions in place when it came to the application and use of explosives. Not that it would have made any difference. The use of a warning horn to let the general public and the pedestrians and passersby that were in the vicinity of the area know that a blast was about to take place didn't seem necessary, after all, it was just a simple little piece of old worn-out concrete that was going to be displaced and removed.

Well, let's put it this way, after the little 'fiasco' that took place with the removal of the decayed concrete pier on Boston Harbor that day, a whole new set of rules and regulations relating to blasting in the downtown section of the city of Boston were about to be put into place. As a matter of fact, henceforth from this legendary atrocity, absolutely no blasting would ever be allowed to take place in the downtown section of the city of Boston, ever again!

On this spring-like day, the city was a beehive of activity as many of the city's inhabitants and working people who were stuck inside during the bitter cold days prior to this 'fluke' of a warm day, were happily out and about walking along the picturesque waterfront. However, when 'the preacher' so rudely jammed down the plunger to his blasting box, the result would forever be remembered. At first, there was no reaction at all, it was as if the blast was a dud and didn't go off. Something that was unknown to 'the preacher' and to every other poor sole within a half mile of the broken pier, the combination of salt water and deteriorated chemicals in the rotted cement in the bottom of the drilled blast holes caused a delayed reaction, A violent firestorm began to ignite in the pit of the pier, a very bright, orange flash of burning light was observed and then, after the inferno that was set ablaze, it was immediately followed by an ear-piercing boom and an eruption that showered the area with a combination of water, cement, sand, sea shells and various sizes of concrete objects that flew in every direction imaginable!

To the absolute amazement of everyone, including God almighty himself, there were no serious injuries or damage. However, it was necessary that a change of undergarments take place for almost everyone who was in the sphere of influence relating to this ghastly explosion. The cleanup, well that was a whole separate matter!

Work was plentiful in the New England area, now that the Environmental Protection Agency (EPA) had released a number of contracts that would involve the separation of existing combined drain and sewer systems throughout the New England region. In order to participate in this target-rich environment, some negotiations had to take place with the bonding company that was providing the company with a surety line of credit.

The surety company's bonding agent was Bob Herterich who was one of the principals of the Herterich-Foley Insurance Agency that was located on Federal Street in Boston. Bob Herterich had also been the bonding agent for Suburban Construction Company, the organization that Les Marino and Kenny Anderson had worked for in their salad days.

Bob Herterich was a dapper gent, well-dressed and dignified. He had an interesting background; he had served under Four Star General George S. Patton in the Third Army, Company 'B' of the 378th Infantry Division during the Battle of the Bulge in World War Two. He was a decorated war veteran who took advantage of the GI Bill after the war to attend college. He excelled in financial and surety applications and upon entering the surety field, he proceeded to develop some very strong relationships with numerous bonding companies. His relationship with the bonding people proved to be quite beneficial for Modern Continental Construction Company. The establishment of a surety line of credit with the bonding company was basically a lifeline for any contractor. Without the capacity to bid work, a contractor could not survive. The intriguing factor associated with a surety line of credit is that it becomes extremely imperative that the contractor remains profitable and that the work performed by the contractor is performed in a professional manner with no encumbrances that would adversely affect the surety company. The bottom line is that in order for a company to grow, it must remain profitable, and professional in all aspects of its operations.

How a surety line of credit was established, involved profitability, cash on hand, and tangible assets. The combination of these variables would determine how much work could be bid and the type of work that a company could pursue. It wasn't just that a company had acquired a certain amount of work, it was imperative that the work be profitable. The profitability of the company included many factors. One such factor was the actual management of the company. The addition of Edna Hughes as the company office manager was something that the bonding people encouraged as the previous clerical person who was working for Modern Continental before Edna Hughes was hired had not been trustworthy and had pulled an unscrupulous act.

In their haste to concentrate on acquiring work and executing the contracts that they had obtained, Les and Kenny kind of left the workings of the office to the person that they had first put in charge. When she was hired, she seemed capable and competent. Unfortunately, they did not take into consideration her honesty and loyalty. The bills were being paid and the employees got a paycheck every week. The problem was this young lady was taking advantage of the two guys that she was working for as she would write herself a paycheck each week and in her devious way, she would first ask Les to sign her paycheck. Then when she got Kenny all alone, she would ask Kenny to sign her check. She was taking advantage of a couple of nice guys by snookering them into each signing a check for her. What the little urchin was doing was writing herself two paychecks each week without letting Les or Kenny knowing what she was up to. It was by pure chance that they found out what she was pulling. Les had signed her paycheck and then after Kenny had signed her check for the same week, Les and Kenny were working on a bid when Kenny mentioned to Les that he got ink all over his hand from signing her paycheck. Les looked at Kenny with a quizzical expression on his face as he told Kenny that earlier in the afternoon, he had also signed her weekly paycheck. Immediately, they knew what was going on as they learned that they had both been signing her weekly paycheck for a couple of months. The jig was up as Les and Kenny proceeded to approach her with uncertain veracity as they got a tearful confession out of her, which coerced them into immediately firing her.

A valuable lesson was learned from the double paycheck incident. Putting all of their attention into acquiring work and figuring out the costs related to bidding on construction work was counterproductive if controls were not in place regarding the paying of bills and the writing of paychecks. Someone honest and loyal had to take control of the office. The hiring of Edna Hughes satisfied all of these objectives.

Edna Hughes was a determined woman and an experienced manager. Her references and the positive comments from former employers showed that Edna would be a smart and responsible office manager. She was a war bride, originally from Vicksburg, Mississippi. She had met her husband Jim when he was training to become an Army Air Corps fighter pilot in the Second World War. Jim Hughes was from Brockton, Massachusetts, and eventually became a 'hellcat F6F' fighter pilot. He flew many combat missions during the Second World War. When the war was over, Jim took his war bride Edna home with him to Massachusetts where they eventually settled down. Edna was a no nonsense, buxom lady who spoke with a heavy Southern accent and could hold her own with any foul-mouth-construction person who might try to get the better of her. Honesty and loyalty would prove to be her two best traits. Frugal, thrifty, and economical would also be positive attributes that she possessed. Edna spent the company money as if it were her own. Not long after she took over the office, Edna hired Fran Pelrine as the company payroll clerk. Fran was another valuable asset to the office staff as she was proficient and skillful with regard to figuring out pay rates, taxes, and withholding tables associated with issuing weekly payroll checks. It was also at this time that Edna decided that the company should have a full-time receptionist. Roseanne DiCarlo was hired to fulfill what would become an important position in the company. As a result of the paycheck issue, a strict check singing protocol was also initiated to avoid any future 'double dipping' incidents.

The pieces to the big jigsaw puzzle known as 'a successful business' were slowly being put into place, one by one. It was one thing to bid and acquire lucrative work. It was another very important factor to control just where that money went and how it was spent. Just like they say in the old road-building business, you needed to make sure that you had both 'line and grade' to be triumphant.

A positive relationship with the surety and bonding people was in place as a surety line of credit allowed Modern Continental to bid and obtain construction work. The situation with the office and clerical portion of the business had been addressed and fine-tuned to prevent any future malfeasance, crime, or misconduct. The operations associated with the maintenance, servicing, and control of the company's heavy equipment, dump trucks, and vehicles, along with having a place to store materials and tools were in place at the shop location in Stoughton, Massachusetts. The master mechanic Gerry Houle in conjunction with Stan Fitts from Clark-Wilcox Equipment Company was successfully keeping the equipment in working order.

There were another couple of pieces to the puzzle that needed to be put in place for the company to prosper and flourish. Although, neither Les Marino nor Kenny Anderson had ever formally attended business school, they both understood that for a company to grow and thrive, it had to surround itself with professionals that would protect the company from legal and financial ruin. Therefore, the importance of developing a positive and mutually rewarding relationship with a law firm and a certified public accounting company had to also take place.

It was in early 1973 that the accounting firm of Darmondy & Merlino became associated with Modern Continental Construction Company as did the State Street Boston law firm of Snyder, Tepper & Berlin. Frank Merlino was the certified public accountant who took control of the financial aspects associated with the company and it was Herman Snyder the lawyer who developed a relationship with Les Marino and Kenny Anderson. Although, as a true sign of the respect and honor that Les Marino held for Attorney Herman Snyder, he would always call him 'Mister Synder' although Mr. Snyder would always tell Les to call him 'Herman', Les would call him nothing, but Mr. Snyder.

For now, the jigsaw puzzle pieces were being put in place, there were still a couple of pieces that still needed to be found, but the picture was beginning to come into view. Les would often profess that for a company to be successful you needed to have the blessed trinity, a good bonding agent, accountant, and lawyer. Those pieces of the puzzle were now in place.

In addition to the Boston Harbor project that was actively working, there was the Nashua, New Hampshire sewer job that was taking place as well as a contract that was acquired in Manchester New Hampshire. This new job in Manchester, New Hampshire was being run by a new project superintendent named, Dale Flynn. This project involved quite a few concrete structures that needed to be built on-site. A major amount of this work would be performed by carpenters. Dale Flynn was a carpenter by trade. It was through Dale Flynn that the company hired a crew of carpenters who were very competent and closely affiliated with him.

The addition of Dale Flynn to the company brought with it a number of new carpenters that belong with him to the Jehovah's Witnesses congregation. These guys were very good carpenters who had an excellent work ethic and really knew their stuff. This addition to Modern Continental proved to be quite beneficial as it solidified a segment of the company's carpentry operations that were increasingly becoming more frequent. It was kind of interesting that these carpenters, who were also very religious guys, would profess that 'their true boss was a carpenter' meaning Jesus Christ's profession was a carpenter. Dale Flynn was the guy who would lead his fellow carpenters on weekends as they would get together and build many of the 'Kingdom Halls' that were springing up all over New England in the early 1970s. They would basically perform the old 'barn raisings' as a group of skilled craftsmen would get together on a weekend and put up a new church.

It was also during this time frame that Cosmo Pallazola, the superintendent who was running the Nashua, New Hampshire project, became friendly with one of the laborers on his job named Manny Valentim. Manny lived in New Bedford, Massachusetts; he was originally from the Azores in Portugal. He was a dedicated worker. Cosmo's friendship with Manny Valentim, opened the door for his two brothers Mack and Joe to come to work for the company, and eventually the 'Valentim' connection to Fall River and New Bedford, Massachusetts would lead to a constant stream of very good Portuguese workers coming to work for Modern Continental Construction Company.

It was the early influx into the company of the 'Dale Flynn and Manny Valentim' people that created a core group of workers that would establish a skillful work ethic and an experienced workforce that would be the backbone of Modern Continental Construction Company. Having an established and seasoned group of people who understood the concept of working hard and accomplishing a lot in the course of the day was a very positive aspect of the company's growth. These guys understood the concept of 'an honest day's work for an honest day's pay'.

Unfortunately, with rapid growth also come problems. It was on the Nashua, New Hampshire project that an ill-fated accident took place. When a cement pipe is installed, there are two sides to the pipe, the 'bell section' or the female section, and the 'narrow section' or the male part of the pipe. The bell part usually has a rubber 'O' ring or gasket to keep the pipe in place and to prevent any leaking. As the male end is put into the bell section, sometimes the rubber gasket might get squashed or severed during the process. This is most often not noticed or identified until the groundwater leaks in through the compromised gasket. When water leaks into the pipe system, the leaking water will often build up in the manholes and the lower level of the pipe. Therefore, a patching crew will enter the manhole and apply hydraulic waterproof cement to stop the leaks. However, before you can perform any patching, you need to get the water out of the manhole and pipe. Therefore, a pump will be put into the manhole to pump the excess water out of the system. In this particular incident, instead of using a submersible electric pump to take the water out, an inexperienced laborer used a gasoline-powered pump to take the excess water out of the manhole.

The worker who put the gasoline-powered pump into the manhole had every intent of just removing the excess water that had entered the system. When the leaking water was almost gone, he let the foreman know that the water level was down so that someone could enter the system and patch the leaking pipes with hydraulic cement. Unknown to the laborer who put the gasoline pump in the manhole, there was already someone in the pipeline performing patchwork that he didn't know about. Although the gasoline-powered pump was only operating for a few minutes before the laborer became aware that there was someone working in the system, it was too late. The carbon monoxide had already taken its toll as the worker patching the pipe was overcome and could not get out of the system. He became asphyxiated and succumbed to the fumes. It was the first accident that would take place with the company. It was an avoidable situation that could have been avoided with proper communication and the right type of pump.

Things were moving kind of fast, the work that the Environmental Protection Agency was putting out to bid was coming fast and furious. In just a four-week span, Modern Continental Construction Company picked up three EPA sewer-related projects in the State of Maine.

Not long after the incident that took place, on the Nashua, New Hampshire sewer project, another event took place on the Manchester, New Hampshire job. A portion of the pipe needed to be placed under a section of the existing roadway. To accomplish the placement of pipe under the roadway, a 'jacking' crew was hired as a subcontractor on the job. The subcontractor dug a jacking pit and began the operations associated with jacking the pipe under the roadway. This subcontractor was using a different method than had been previously used when a section of pipe needed to be installed under the B & M Railroad in Woburn, Massachusetts. The jacking project where Les Marino had to remove some liquid concrete from under the pipe to prevent it from floating when he incurred burns to his arms from the chemicals and lye in the cement. This method being used had the subcontractor digging into the existing clay soil and then placing a section of sleeve after the clay had been removed.

The subcontractor was digging an open tunnel under the roadway into existing clay soil. It was an extremely bitter cold day when the worker was performing the digging. He had opened a pretty deep section of the unprotected excavated tunnel when it became lunchtime. The only explanation as to why this worker would spend his lunchtime sitting in an unprotected tunnel consisting of clay is that it was much warmer in the tunnel than it was outside. The worker was eating his lunch when a large section of heavy wet clay peeled off of the tunnel roof and landed right on top of the poor guy while he was eating his lunch. He was crushed and killed instantly by the weight of the clay.

Within a month, two fatal accidents had taken place that would adversely affect the company as it severely impacted the workforce and took a toll on everyone associated with the two projects. Was the growth of the company too rapid? It was evident that appropriate safety measures were not in place or not being followed properly. The tragic events made everyone realize that life is short and that working in the construction field can be dangerous and costly if you were not careful.

Chapter Eight
Heading 'Down East' for a While

1974–1975

An idea a day will hopefully keep the sheriff away—**Kenny Anderson**

Lewiston, Maine
Big Chuck's Gentlemen's Club
Thursday, 20 September 1974
8:25 p.m.

The six guys sitting in a row next to the stage have been drinking beer since a little after six o'clock. They were blowing off a little steam after spending the past four days knee-deep in mud and crushed stone. In spite of the name on the door, 'Big Chuck's Gentlemen's Club', these guys were far from gentlemen. The Modern Continental boys were cheering on the young lady that's on stage, as she was just about to let her two massive 'cupcakes' to be set free from their tight restraints. A cat call goes up and a couple of high shrilled whistles. It was worth the three-song wait until she treated the boys to what they were so impatiently waiting for. The smell of stale smoke, cheap beer, sweat, and perfume lingered in the air of this dingy barroom.

As the young lady danced on stage, one of her fellow compatriots approached Al Medeiros, who was sitting on the end seat where his buddies were grouped together. She sat next to Al and reached down and slowly rubbed her hand along the top of his inner thigh as she leaned in and whispered in his ear.

This group of Modern Continental employees that were sitting together just received their weekly paychecks this afternoon, when the job shut down for the day. Kenny Anderson, who was overseeing the three jobs that were simultaneously taking place in Maine, made the Lewiston job his last stop of the day. He dropped the weekly paychecks off at the Winslow and Waterville jobs earlier that afternoon.

Kenny had supper with the guys at the motel. The woman who owned the motel was an elderly widow who was so excited and appreciative that the company was renting her rooms by the week that she offered to cook the guy's supper on Thursday nights. Kenny picked up the food for her and she prepared what he brought her. Tonight, she made a big pot roast for the guys with all the 'fixins'. The boys were very thankful to get a nice, home-cooked meal once a week. These guys were all living away from home, the rest of the nights they ate out at Mcdonald's or someplace cheap with big helpings. After their home-cooked meal, and having all cashed their paychecks, the boys decided to take in some local 'attractions' over at Big Chuck's. Kenny decided to join the boys for a couple of beers.

Kenny, who was living away from home during the week, just like the guys that were working for him, looked forward to the home-cooked meal on Thursday nights. The hectic pace that must be kept to keep three projects working and making money took its toll, even on the energetic and hard-driving Kenny Anderson. Spending a few minutes enjoying a good, home-cooked meal and then having a couple of beers with the boys, kind of took the sting off things for this ambitious guy.

The music was loud and the atmosphere charged, with lights flashing and a considerable amount of naked skin being exposed as well at Big Chick's Gentlemen's Club this evening. Al Medeiros was deep in conversation with the little showgirl who was erotically whispering in his ear. Kenny looked over at Al as he saw him take out a twenty-dollar bill and hand it to the young lady who was hanging all over him. Al sported a big grin as she got up and walked away. Kenny leaned over to Al and asked, "Where is she going?"

Al replied, "She told me to meet her in a minute back near the men's room, she had to go backstage for something." Kenny nodded with approval as Al got up and headed back toward the secluded area in the back of the club, where the young lady told Al to meet her.

By now, the dancing girl on the stage who let her 'cupcakes' out a few songs ago was now very slowly starting to shimmy out of her 'G' string. All of the guy's eyes were glued on her, that is except Kenny Anderson's eyes. Like the 'older brother' to all of his men, Kenny was looking out for Al Medeiros who was standing all alone down by the men's room. Kenny got up and headed toward Al who was standing there with a look of frustration on his face. As Kenny approached Al, he asked him, "Where did she go?"

Al, who looked confused, answered, "I have no idea, and she took my money." Kenny looked pissed off knowing that the little 'chippy' just fleeced Al out of his hard-earned twenty bucks!

Kenny and Al headed toward the bar where 'Big Chuck' himself was sitting. Big Chuck was situated at the end of the bar near the entrance. He had a big fat Phillies Blunt cigar sticking out of the corner of his mouth, with a steady stream of smoke circling above his fat bald head. Although there was a major distraction going on as the girl on the stage had finished taking everything off, one of the guys looked over and noticed that Al and Kenny were in a heated discussion with Big Chuck. As Kenny so politely asked Big Chuck where the girl with Al's twenty dollars had gone, the boys on the stage got up to see what was going on. At the same time that the boys started to head over to where Kenny and Al were, Big Chuck's bouncers who were spread out around the club, began to walk in the same direction.

Kenny Anderson's face turned bright red as he explained to Big Chuck in no uncertain terms that one of his guys was 'fleeced' by one of Big Chuck's girls and that his guy wanted his money back. It appeared that Al Medeiros had, in all good faith, which included his twenty-dollar bill, negotiated a transaction of an intimate nature with the young girl, and the enticing little angel did not fulfill her part of the transaction.

Tempers began to flair as Big Chuck refused to acknowledge that one of his upstanding, young entertainers would entice someone in any way, shape, or form with regard to the transaction that was discussed. This debate was going nowhere, Kenny looked at his boys and felt compelled to protect them as the feeling was quite mutual with his men as they stood their ground next to Kenny.

At this point, Big Chuck's guys started to move toward the Modern Continental Contingent, a clear standoff was taking place as the two groups shuffled and stared each other down. It looked like an old-fashioned 'donnybrook' was about to commence. Just as the two groups were about to mix it up, in through the side door walked three of Lewiston's 'finest', two patrolmen and a lieutenant. Kenny Anderson blurted out to Big Chuck, "What's the matter, you got to call the cops to fight your battles." The lieutenant put up his two hands and made a gesture for everyone to calm down.

He then asked, "So, what's going on here?" Big Chuck looked at the lieutenant and began to accuse Kenny and the Modern Continental boys of causing a ruckus and being disorderly.

The lieutenant looked inquisitively over at Kenny and then said, "Hey, I know you, you're the guy that's running the construction job that's going on all over town."

Kenny, with a look of sarcasm, responded, "Yeah, and I'm the guy that's been hiring all of your cops to do details and putting lots of cash in their pockets." The lieutenant raised his eyebrows and then stepped back and looked at Big Chuck, as he motioned for him to step aside so that he could 'chat' with him. The lieutenant secretly whispered to Big Chuck, who listened intently and then reluctantly nodded and slowly stepped away. Big Chuck gradually reached into his pocket and took out a twenty-dollar bill, and then reluctantly handed it to Al Medeiros.

The lieutenant, with a look of apprehension, then looked at Kenny and said, "Will that work?"

Kenny paused, and then nodded and turned to the Modern Continental boys and told them, "Let's go find an honest place to go drink and spend our money." The crisis had been averted. The only one still pissed off about the whole thing was Al Medeiros as he never got what he bargained for with his twenty dollars!

****

In 1974, Modern Continental Construction Company had shown a very big presence in what the locals called 'Little Canada'. Lewiston, Maine is a city that sits on the shores of the Androscoggin River. Lewiston is one of the oldest cities in the State of Maine. Lewiston, Maine even has a slight distinction as it once was the site of a professional boxing heavyweight title fight which took place between champion Cassius Clay (later known as Mohammed Ali) against the challenger Sonny (the Bear) Liston. The match took place on 25 May 1965 and will forever be remembered as the shortest championship fight in history and the most controversial, as it lasted only 1 minute and 45 seconds with Mohammed Ali knocking out Sonny Liston with his infamous 'anchor punch' as the victor.

Lewiston, Maine was settled back in the 1770s. Although the city is an old one, it was just getting an updated sewer system in 1974 which was part of the EPA's effort to clean up the shores of the Androscoggin River. This project involved the installation of an 84-inch sewer main that was the primary trunk line that led to the new sewerage treatment plant that was also being built.

In addition to the Lewiston, Maine project, there were also projects taking place in Winslow, Maine, and one in Waterville, Maine. All of the projects noted were being overseen and managed by Kenny Anderson. He would spend his time between each job making sure that production expectations were being properly met, and that the materials and equipment needed to perform the work were adequately supplied to each project.

Once a week, Les Marino would venture from the Cambridge, Massachusetts office up to Maine to see how things were going and on occasion deliver the weekly paychecks. Les liked to keep his finger on the pulse of all projects and to physically view and observe what was taking place. Very often he would interject ideas, or suggest techniques that might enhance the progress of the jobs.

The timing and the proximity of the three concurrent projects prompted Modern Continental to invest in a couple of company vehicles. It was in the fall of 1973 that both Les Marino and Kenny Anderson obtained their first company vehicles. Les picked a 1974 Cadillac Sedan Deville and Kenny chose a 1973 Pontiac Grand Safari Station Wagon, as his ride of choice. It was a milestone in the company's history, the acquisition of company vehicles for both Les and Kenny.

The new projects that were taking place in Maine were also a historic time for the company as it was during these projects that allowed the Durkin family to begin working for Modern Continental Construction Company. Billy Durkin Senior who was the father of the three boys, was a carpenter by trade. His sons, Billy Jr. and Rodney were pipe foremen. Billy Jr. and Rodney both ran pipe-laying crews and the younger brother Brian would eventually work at the shop in Stoughton, Massachusetts as a parts runner and all-around mechanics helper.

It was during the Maine projects that Superintendent Jerry Joy started working for the company as he took over the daily operations of the Waterville, Maine project. It was on the Winslow, Maine project that brought Superintendent Bob Pottle back to Maine as he had been working on the Nashua, New Hampshire job helping Cosmo Pallazola. Bob Pottle was originally from Maine and still lived in the Portland area. Paul Ladakakis also joined the company in Lewiston, Maine as a pipe foreman and a blaster. Paul was a 'colorful' individual who eventually would become the primary blaster for the company. Joe Ricci also performed some blasting activities but he had been promoted to a foremen's role which would limit some of his blasting duties.

The relationship that Les Marino and Kenny Anderson had established when they worked on the Woburn, Massachusetts sewer project with Don Breeda, the resident engineer for Camp, Dresser & McKee was rekindled as Don Breeda had been promoted to vice president of Camp, Dresser & McKee and had been assigned to oversee the numerous sewer-related projects that were taking place in the State of Maine. Don Breeda was the person that was responsible for the three jobs that Modern Continental Construction Company was performing in Maine. He had resident engineers on each project that answered directly to him. Having established a working relationship with Don Breeda on the Woburn, Massachusetts project proved to be beneficial, as it made negotiations just a bit more civil than they might have been if the resident engineers were not familiar with the way Modern Continental Construction Company performed, with their hard-driving and expeditious manner that they were becoming famous for.

Since their first job in 1967 which involved putting in sidewalks and curb stones in Peabody, Massachusetts, the standards and mission statement of the company had not changed. Hard work, with a diligent effort by all involved, along with ingenious techniques and unconventional methods of execution proved to sustain the company as it instilled, in everyone who got involved with the company, a sense of pride and accomplishment.

A conscientious group of employees, coupled with excellent management personnel was just a part of the company's success. The professional equipment operators and the ability to keep the machines in top-notch working condition added to the productivity of the company. The capability of the support staff to expedite the logistics involved with the successful launching of the start of the project proved vital to the overall accomplishments of the organization. However, the ability of Les Marino and Kenny Anderson to ingrain in the mindset of every person that they were involved with the traits that they both possessed, which were flat-out honesty, sincerity, and trust, proved to be the single most valuable asset that made this company different from any other.

The growth of the company by 1974 was somewhat phenomenal, as within a relatively short period of time, the workforce of Les Marino and Kenny Anderson had blossomed into a group of over forty employees. In addition to a solid workforce of 'field' employees, there was also a support staff of office and clerical people along with mechanical and equipment repair and service personnel.

However, as mentioned previously, along with growth come 'growing pains'. Although work was plentiful with the Environmental Protection Agency releasing more and more sewer and environmentally sensitive projects, the ability to continue to obtain the work was always a challenge. Surety companies are conservative by nature. The bonding people, although they were ecstatic at the accomplishments accrued to date by Modern Continental Construction Company, were in no hurry to jeopardize their financial stability by constantly increasing the per-job and aggregate limits of the surety capacity of the company. In layman's terms, they were getting a little 'gun shy' with extending large limits of credit to a company that was not quite five years old.

This little 'hiccup' in the growth of the company did not sit well with either Les Marino or Kenny Anderson. They had done their job by moving the company forward in a positive and profitable manner. It was time to have a 'sit down' with the dapper and suave bonding agency representative, Mr. Herterich. A meeting was scheduled that would involve, Les and Kenny along with the various bonding company representatives which would take place at the Modern Continental office location at 905 Main Street in Cambridge, Massachusetts.

As mentioned, the office at 905 Main Street was much bigger than the original two-room office, but it was not big or opulent by any nature. However, there was one room at this location that was a bit capable of hosting a meeting of this type. When the location was acquired, Les Marino established his office which was to the immediate left of the entrance to the place. This was not an overly large room and it was far from lavishly decorated, but there was one item that kind of signified what might take place to the individual that attended a meeting in this room if it did not go to the liking of the primary occupant. Directly behind the desk of Les Marino, painted in very bright and realistic colors was a portrait of a large bull, with numerous swords and spears stuck in the beast with the blood flowing profusely from the carcass as the bull fought not to die. The immediate viewing of this Matador's conquest, and the subsequent, somewhat subliminal message that this painting depicted, might create an intimidation factor to anyone that observed it hanging on the wall.

Apparently, the image that the picture behind Les Marino's desk instilled in the participants that sat in the meeting created the results expected, because after a slightly intense gathering of the powers-to-be, it was established that if the current work on hand, could show continued progress and profitability, the capacity to bid work would be increased. This was exactly what Les and Kenny were looking for. With renewed vigor, Kenny Anderson jumped in his 1973 Pontiac Grand Safari Station Wagon and headed back to Maine with every intent of moving the three projects along in an expeditious manner and achieving what was necessary to increase the company's bonding capacity. A challenge had been presented to young Mr. Anderson, his immediate response to this challenge, would, no doubt, prove to positively impact the future of the company!

Chapter Nine
A Game Changer!

1975–1977

Necessity is the mother of invention—**Les Marino**

Haverhill, Massachusetts
Town Hall-4 Summer Street
Tuesday, 11 March 1975
10:03 a.m.

The patina shown on the old wooden table situated at the front of the room would lead you to believe that this instrument is a holdover from the Puritan Days. The three gentlemen seated at the table were slightly fidgeting and trying their best to remain patient as the clerk delivered the bundle of sealed envelopes to them. It was a couple of minutes past the deadline of 10:00 a.m. which meant that it was time to open the sealed bids that had been submitted regarding the sanitary sewer project that will update the City of Haverhill Massachusetts aged combined drainage and sewer systems. This particular contract was one of the more substantial Environmental Protection Agency projects that would soon be performed in one of Massachusetts' largest cities. The engineering firm of Camp, Dresser & McKee, would be overseeing the construction activities associated with this project, had estimated the cost to complete this work should be in the $6.2 million range.

Ben Hudson, the City of Haverhill Engineer, cleared his throat with a slightly stifled cough as he announced, "The acceptance of sealed bids, relating to the advertised City of Haverhill sanitary sewer project is officially closed." He went on to declare, "We will now begin the process of identifying and announcing the results of each sealed bid." Don Breeda, the vice president of the Camp, Dresser & McKee Engineering firm was sitting to the left of the Haverhill City Engineer, Ben Hudson.

Don Breeda picked up the first package on the top of the pile and then took a sterling silver letter opener and slit the seal of the manilla envelope and handed it to Ben Hudson. Mr. Hudson took out the bid documents and passed them down to the gentleman at the far end of the table who was the city solicitor, he looked over the bid bond and checked to make sure that it was official and legal, as he then handed the papers back to Ben Hudson, who stammered ever so slightly, as he announced, "The first bid is from Methuen Construction Company and is in the amount of $6,423,251.00." Don Breeda wrote the stated numbers at the top of a yellow-lined pad of paper. The bid-opening process continued. Mr. Hudson stated, "The next bid is from P. Gioioso & Sons and is in the amount of $6,398,980.00." Don Breeda quickly jotted the figures down as the next envelope was opened and the bid was announced, "This next bid is from Cimbro Construction Company and is in the amount of $6,501,873.00." The old and somewhat drab room in Haverhill City Hall was deadly silent as the nerve-wracking process of determining, who the low bidder for this envious project would soon be.

****

Kenny Anderson sat in the second to last row of folding chairs that had been set up in the City of Haverhill engineering conference room for this affair. He was anxiously and intently staring at the front of the room as the slow and tedious bid-opening process continued. Kenny had kept up his end of the bargain, as the three projects that he had been responsible for in the State of Maine had been expeditiously and profitably completed. With the successful completion of these jobs, the bonding company had agreed to allow Modern Continental Construction Company to bid, by far, the largest project that they had ever pursued. This is, in some measure, a calculated risk that the bonding company was taking, as Modern Continental was already pushing their capacity limits, as they had two jobs currently working for the Boston Redevelopment Authority in the city of Boston as well as a sewer project in Billerica, Massachusetts, a water main installation contract in Concord, New Hampshire, an ocean pipeline outfall project in New London, Connecticut and a sanitary sewer project in Bellows Falls, Vermont. So far, 1975 had already started off as a very busy year. The addition of a six million-dollar contract would surely test the limits of durability for this rapidly growing company.

106

Ben Hudson looked over at the pad of paper that Don Breeda had in front of him, as he checked to see what the results were thus far in the bidding process. Don Breeda slit the top of the next package and handed it to Ben Hudson, he looked quickly at the documents and then passed them to the city solicitor as they were properly checked and handed back. "This next bid is from J.F. White Contracting and is in the amount of $6,219,066.00." The figures were duly noted and the process continued. "The final bid is from Modern Continental Construction Company." The due diligence process was completed as the City of Haverhill Engineer Ben Hudson announced, "This bid is in the amount of $6,160,862.00." The numbers that came out of City Engineer Ben Hudson's mouth had not quite been completed when a loud cheer from the back of the room and an expression of 'Yes' was shouted by a very excited Kenneth L. Anderson!

****

Kenny Anderson could not get to the pay phone across the street from Haverhill City Hall fast enough; he shoved in the 30 cents that the operator asked for as she connected him to the Modern Continental office. Roseanne, the receptionist answered the phone in her perky, upbeat voice, "Modern Continental Construction Company, how can I help you?"

Kenny could barely contain himself as he excitedly stated, "Hi Roseanne, we got the bid in Haverhill! Can you connect me to Les please?"

Roseanne, with a reassuring reply, "That's great news, good job! Hold on a second, here's Les."

Les got on the phone and let Ken know just how great the news was, "Ken, Roseanne just told me, we got the bid! How much did we leave on the table?"

Kenny quickly shot back, "You're not going to believe this, we beat J.F White who was the next low bidder by less than sixty-thousand dollars!"

It took a while for the reality to sink in, but getting the 'big job' that they had been striving for since the company began, had finally taken place. This cast a whole new light on the future of the Modern Continental Construction Company. The bonding company was thankful that the bids were so close, this was reassuring that the numbers put together for this job were spot on, and very accurate, as the bid submitted by Modern Continental was pretty much the price that the engineer's estimate was for. Now the fun began; this job would no doubt, explore the creativity and experimental nature of the company as it would be challenged to accomplish the numerous different types of activities that were included in this contract. To be a little more specific, this citywide contract would include the crossing of, at times, turbulent, Merrimack River, an astounding three times with the installation of sewer pipes.

Not long before the bid was put together for the City of Haverhill job, Modern Continental was the successful bidder on two Boston Redevelopment Authority (BRA) projects that were taking place, one at Harrison Avenue and the other at Faneuil Hall. The acquisition of these two jobs in the city of Boston put the company in a position that it pretty much understood would eventually be inevitable. Pressure was being applied by the city of Boston's mayor, Kevin White's office, as well as city councilors and union protagonists that thought it 'prudent' that if Modern Continental Construction Company was to become involved with work in the city of Boston that they affiliate themselves with the various unions applicable to their work.

In early 1975, the Modern Continental Construction Company, Inc. signed formal agreements with the Boston chapters of the Operating Engineer's Union Local #4, the Laborer's Union Local #22, and the Carpenter's Union Local #723. The entrance into a 'union' environment put the company in a position that was an unspoken requirement if they were to continue acquiring work in the Greater Boston area. Boston has always been a union stronghold and the influence portrayed by the political climate that existed in the city made it much easier to succumb to the persuasions of dealing with unions, rather than to fight the system.

It was also, almost immediately after their entrance into the union habitat, that a long-time friend and associate of Les Marino and Kenny Anderson was hired by the company. Their old buddy from Suburban Construction Company and the guy that Les Marino held in such high esteem that he once actually had offered part ownership in Modern Continental to him, Aldo Morrelli, became the new master mechanic for Modern Continental Construction Company. The hiring of Aldo Morrelli caused a kind of a little shake-up at the Stoughton maintenance location. Although there was always a good solid working relationship with Stan Fitts from the Clark-Wilcox Equipment Company, the connection with the master mechanic Gerry Houle that Stan Fitts was involved in putting in place for Modern Continental seemed to cause some issues regarding the union presence of mechanics on job sites. Aldo Morrelli was a staunch union person who was obliged to follow union protocol with regard to equipment use and mechanics. Becoming a 'union' affiliated contractor was another step forward that helped Modern Continental to move ahead and climb a little higher up the ladder of success.

The mobilization for the Haverhill job was much akin to the preparations that took place for the invasion of Europe during World War Two. The troops had to be assembled and trained and the equipment had to be procured and mobilized. Much like landing in France, there would also be barges and tugboats involved in this massive operation. As the river crossings involved the numerous placements of pipelines in the bed of the Merrimack River, acquiring the proper system to perform this work would necessitate the development of a relationship with a marine construction affiliate that could provide Modern Continental with the mandatory amenities.

A total of five pipe crews would be put together to work on the Haverhill project. The standard pipe crew involved a foreman, two laborers, a backhoe, and a front-end loader. It could be possible to have one front-end loader feed two crews, but this would depend on the logistics and proximity of the crews. If they were close enough, then one loader could feed stone and deliver pipe to two crews. However, this was only possible if they were within reason, as having a crew sit and wait for pipe or stone to be delivered would be counterproductive.

A considerable amount of behind-the-scenes work had to be accomplished before the first shovel could be dug, or the first pipe installed. Prior to bidding on the job, the cost and availability associated with the various tangibles had to be determined. This would include the procurement of the 66-inch concrete pipe and the 48-inch ductile iron pipe that would be used on the project. The cost and availability of crushed stone, the establishment of a local concrete supplier, along with the delivery of the numerous manholes needed for the project, and finding a diesel fuel supplier to fuel the equipment in a timely manner, would also have to take place.

In addition to the five pipe crews, there would also be two carpentry crews that would be responsible for building the six siphon structures associated with the three river crossings. At each end of the pipe that crossed the river, a concrete structure had to be built. Dale Flynn and his carpentry people would be responsible for building these concrete siphon structures.

The need to acquire barges and a tugboat required that a long-time friend of Kenny Anderson's would be called upon. Arthur Fornier, who hailed from Charlestown, Massachusetts, owned steel-hulled spud barges and tugboats. Two steel-hulled barges that had 'spuds', which are long pipes that can be lowered into the river bed to stabilize the barge and keep it from moving, were leased along with a small, but quite powerful tugboat, named the 'Pushy' for the river activities. An earthen ramp was built for the 40-H, Bucyrus-Erie backhoe, to walk onto the barge and then the 'Pushy' tugboat would move the barge into position. The 'spuds' would be dropped to stabilize the barge and then the backhoe would dig from the end of the barge. The material that the backhoe dug from the river, would then be placed onto the adjacent barge, which had a 10-wheel dump truck sitting on the barge. When the dump truck was full, the 'Pushy' would move the barge to the earthen ramp and the dump truck would drive off and dump the material in a designated area. The process was efficient, but somewhat tedious, and a bit time-consuming.

When the trench was dug in the riverbed, the ductile iron pipe that was to be installed needed to be put in position so that the pipe could be properly installed into the trench in the riverbed. The process involved with verifying the actual location of the below-water trench and corroborating the proper depth, and the accuracy of the operations became the responsibility of the people that were hired to perform scuba diving in conjunction with the underwater functions. The marine company that Modern Continental Construction Company became involved with on this project was New England Divers, which was a specialty company that was located in Beverly, Massachusetts. The company was owned and operated by Jim Cahill, who was someone who was quite familiar with underwater diving, as he had been a United States Navy diver who got his training during World War Two. Jim Cahill had developed many unique applications with respect to construction underwater diving projects. This was the second project that New England Divers was involved with Modern Continental on, as they had been providing divers to assist with the New London, Connecticut project that involved the installation of steel pipe almost two miles offshore.

The New England Diver personnel go underwater in the Merrimack River to make sure that the trench being dug is accurate and to assist with the actual installation of the pipe into the trench. To get the pipe in position, a system was developed that involved wooden 'yokes' and empty 55-gallon steel drums.

The pipe is assembled on shore and then moved by the Bucyrus-Erie-30-B crawler crane that Modern Continental had recently purchased. The crane drags the pipe in a series of 'lift and move' cycles and slides it into the river. The pipe is floated into place and then the yokes are removed and the 55-gallon drums are removed in sequential order. The divers below the water guide the pipe into position. Once the pipe is secured in place, the process associated with bringing the excavated dirt back by dump truck onto the barge and placed on top of the submerged pipe begins. It takes a significant amount of collaboration, coordination, and synergism to successfully achieve this feat. Installing ductile iron pipes in the bottom of a river is not an easy task to complete. Kenny Anderson, with the help of a dedicated crew, made the process achievable.

In the course of events relating to this first Merrimack River crossing, the process that was being employed, and the techniques involved with tackling such a complex procedure of placing an underground section of pipe in the bed of a major waterway, were of much interest to numerous people. It was during the excavation and removal of the spoils activities that Kenny Anderson noticed that a group of interested individuals were kind of keeping hidden from the site but no doubt, extremely interested in how the project was commencing. After further scrutiny, Kenny realized just who this group of gawkers were. Kenny started to walk over to where they were basically hiding and called out to them. After realizing that they were identified, they reluctantly exposed themselves and timidly sauntered in the direction that Kenny was walking. As they grew closer, Kenny smiled and said, "Hey guys, we've got nothing to hide, if you want to take a closer look at what's going on, come with me and I'll give you a grand tour." The three J.F. White Contracting people, staunch competitors and second bidders on the project, just smiled and shook hands with Kenny and acknowledged his gracious invitation to get a closer look as to how, Modern Continental, was pulling off this difficult river crossing.

The fact that this project was a large one required that the engineering firm of Camp, Dresser & McKee (CDM) have a senior engineer on-site, which in this case was Modern Continental's old friend, the CDM vice president, Don Breeda. In addition to the senior engineer working on this project, there were three other inspectors that CDM had working on the job site. There was an awful lot of activity going on that required that each operation be closely monitored. As well as the project had been commencing and progressing thus far, problems do crop up on occasion. There were five pipe crews working, who were very productive. As some of the trenches being dug were deeper than the newly created Occupational Safety and Health Administration (OSHA) required (over five feet deep). Therefore, any trench dug deeper than five feet required that protection in the form of shoring be put in place to prevent a collapse of the material, which could cause severe harm or death if a 'cave-in' took place in an unprotected trench. Modern Continental was using steel trench boxes in their excavation work. The trench boxes had steel walls on each side and steel tube cross struts for stabilization. These OSHA-approved trench boxes would be pulled forward by the backhoe as the work progressed.

It was the Paul Ladakakis pipe crew that the CDM inspector decided to check. The inspector wanted to make sure that the proper grade was being maintained, as the pipe being installed was gravity-driven and required that a percentage of pitch be maintained for proper flow. This situation relating to grade and pitch had always been a concern with the installation of gravity sewer systems. However, recent technology had advanced so that a new device could be used to determine the proper pitch. This system was known as a 'LASER' (light amplification by stimulated emission of radiation) Beam, which involves the setup of this LASER Beam system inside of a manhole. The system which is a tube that is about four inches in diameter with a length of about twenty inches sits on a tripod and is calibrated to project a beam of light that automatically calculates the proper pitch that is entered into the system. As each pipe is installed, a target is set on the flange of the pipe and once the light beam is centered properly on the target, the pitch is correct. Unfortunately, the inspector who was checking the work performed by Paul Ladakakis's pipe crew did not 'trust' the use of a LASER Beam to determine the proper pitch. The CDM engineer decided to set up a conventional 'transit' instrument to check the proper elevation of the pipes that had been installed.

The CDM inspector did not communicate with the pipe foreman, Paul Ladakakis, as such, the inspector ventured into the trench area, just as the backhoe was pulling the trench box forward, as the inspector walked into the trench area, the protection was moved, which allowed the side of the open trench to collapse on to the inspector. The soil that collapsed on the inspector, did not bury him, but it did land on his leg and pinned him in a precarious position in the trench, which subsequently injured his leg. He was removed from the trench and taken to Holy Family Hospital in Haverhill, Massachusetts. He had a broken leg but otherwise was okay, but pretty shaken up. Another lack of communication issue caused an accident that could have been avoided.

Unfortunately, the downtown area of Haverhill and the surrounding neighborhoods that were affected by this massive pipe project looked like they were under attack by a foreign power. In this case, it was Kenny Anderson and his marauding band of renegade pipe layers that were the foreign entity. As much as they tried to keep the confusion to a minimum, there were road detours, piles of crushed stone, and dirt in numerous locations along with a lot of blocked driveways and quite a few pissed-off people in late 1975 in Haverhill, Massachusetts. The annual Christmas parade which was a community favorite for many years had to be canceled because it was not safe for pedestrians to congregate in the community as the sidewalks had been torn up, and many of the roads were unpassable. For the poor little kids in town, they definitely felt that the 'Grinch' stole Christmas, well in this scenario, the Grinch was the Modern Continental Construction Company. The New Year of 1976 was fast approaching, regrettably, this New Year was sure to only make more commotion for the people of Haverhill, as two more river crossings and another two miles of pipe, still needed to be installed before the project would be completed.

The end of 1975 was a bittersweet time for Les Marino and Kenny Anderson, they realized that this passing year was one that they would never forget, which made them a bit sad to see it end. Then again, the outlook for a new 1976 might be even better than the year that just ended. Les and Kenny celebrated the 1975–1976 holidays together as they had for so many years in the past. Their friendship was as solid as ever, as they wished each other 'Buon Anno' Happy New Year!

****

The second river crossing on the Haverhill job began right after the beginning of 1976. Working in the river with freezing conditions made it a little more precarious than the first crossing that took place during warm weather. The first winter challenge was to keep the barges and the tugboat from freezing in place on the river. The Merrimack River was a moving body of water but when a deep freeze took place, the flow of the river would come to a standstill and freeze any object in the river dead in place. Just such circumstances presented themselves in late January 1976. When the crew left the job on Friday, 22 January, the weather was getting cold. The crew made sure that the barges and the tugboat 'Pushy' were secured. However, a deep freeze swept into the Greater Boston area on Saturday dropping the temperature to a bone-chilling minus six degrees (-6) on the Merrimac River in Haverhill, Massachusetts. This rapid freeze and dire conditions caused concern for Kenny Anderson. Therefore, early on Sunday morning 24 January, Kenny decided to check the job site to make sure that everything was secured and stable.

Upon arriving at the job site, Kenny Anderson rode around the streets where the pipe crews had been working, as he checked the signs and barricades that were in place, to make sure that everything was alright. He then headed over to the river crossing area to check on the barges and the tugboat. Much to Kenny's amazement, when he got to the river crossing, he did not see the tugboat 'Pushy'? The barges were there but no tugboat. He immediately became concerned and drove to the Dunkin Donuts that was close by to use the pay phone. Kenny placed a call to Arthur Fornier, the owner of the tugboat, to see if for whatever reason he might have taken the tugboat from the job site. Arthur answered the phone and let Kenny know that he did not take the tugboat from the job; he then questioned Kenny as to why he would ask him that.

Kenny, more confused than ever let Arthur know that the boat was missing! Kenny hung up the phone with Arthur and immediately placed a call to the Haverhill Harbor Master, Red Clemens to see if he might have an idea as to what might be going on. Red Clemens proceeded to let Kenny know that since Saturday, the river had been frozen solid and nothing had moved on the waterway. After hanging the phone up with the harbor master, Kenny proceeded to call the police to let them know that the tugboat 'Pushy' had been stolen from the river. Kenny placed another call before he left Dunkin Donuts as he called Aldo Morelli the master mechanic to ask him if he might know anything. Aldo, let Kenny know that he was unaware of the whereabouts of the tugboat, but he did let Kenny know that with the temperature being so low, he had concerns for the backhoes on the job as the hydraulic fluid might freeze and cause damage to the equipment. He let Kenny know that he would meet him on the job site as soon as he could get there from his home in West Roxbury.

After hanging the phone up with Aldo Morelli, Kenny felt compelled to make one last call and bring Les up to date as to what was taking place, after all, they were in this together. Les, upon finding out that the barge was missing got a little excited and let Kenny know that he would meet him on the job as soon as possible. Kenny put the phone down and then decided to get a hot cup of coffee and a French Cruller and sit at the counter at Dunkin Donuts and compose himself as he waited for the Calvary to arrive.

It didn't take long for Aldo and Les to get to Haverhill as the traffic was quite light on this fridged Sunday morning. Kenny told everyone to meet him at the job site office trailer. When all interested parties were there, this included the harbor master, the sergeant of command who was on duty for the Haverhill police that morning, along with Les, Aldo, and Kenny, they decided to travel over to the river crossing and see if there might be any clues that could help them find the missing tugboat, 'Pushy'.

The freezing weather conditions did not make this an enjoyable journey as the assembled cast of characters slowly made their way down the icy river bank and onto the frozen barge that held the Bucyrus-Erie 40-H backhoe. Kenny let everyone know that the 'Pushy' had been tied off and secured to the barge on its starboard side. The wind was whipping down the Merrimack River like a run-away B & M Freight Train as everyone held their footing and pulled their overcoat collars up to help ease the pain of the biting cold. It was Kenny who ventured over to the starboard side of the barge and peered into the icy depths of the frozen Merrimack River.

The cold wind was making Kenny's eyes water as he looked intently beneath the hazy ice surface. Kenny squinted hard and then gave a slight, inaudible to the assembled group, sigh as he looked in awe at the tugboat 'Pushy' just below the ice. Kenny reluctantly turned to everyone and let them know, "I found the missing tugboat!"

Apparently, before the river had frozen over, the current became strong and the river depth increased. The tugboat, being tied off, listed to the side which allowed the boat to fill with the rushing water. As the water froze, the weight of the ice caused the boat to sink. The river froze over quickly which did not allow the boat to come back to the surface.

By Tuesday, 26 January the deep freeze had let up, which permitted the 40-H backhoe that was sitting on the barge, to break the surface of the frozen river. The New England Diver scuba diving crew that was working on the river crossing went into the water to assess the situation with the 'pushy'. After checking the conditions, it appeared that the tugboat was salvageable. The Bucyrus-Erie, 30-B crane that was being used to set the pipe in the river bed was moved into position, and the tugboat 'pushy' was raised from the depths of the river and pumped out. The appropriate repairs were made which put the tugboat back in service. The work to repair the tugboat caused a minor delay that set the timetable to complete the river crossing back just a little. The crew would now have to work overtime to make up for the lost time.

The excavation continued with the trench in the bottom of the river bed being dug to the proper grade, and the carpentry crew remained busy building the cement siphon structures located on each river bank. Preparation was being made for the ductile iron pipe that needed to be installed. The 40-H backhoe operator noticed that this section of the riverbed was not as easy to dig into as the first crossing. The New England Diver's crew that was checking the underwater elevations, noted that there were in fact, noticeable outcroppings of ledge present and that the desired depth could not be obtained by digging. No doubt, the ledge had to be removed. As the primary blaster, Paul Ladakakis was running a pipe installation crew; this meant that Joe Ricci would have to perform the necessary blasting work in the riverbed trench to achieve the proper grade.

Blasting ledge underwater was a whole new ballgame for Joe Ricci. The New England Diver crew that had worked on the Modern Continental New London, Connecticut sewer outfall system project had run into a similar situation. The use of 'conical' explosive charges was used in New London Connecticut, which produced a positive outcome. They suggested that 'conical', cone-shaped explosive charges be used in this 'high bottom' river trench situation as well. The Modern Continental Construction Company supplier of explosives at the time was 'Shea Explosives Company' from Quincy, Massachusetts. Jimmy Shea, the owner of the explosive supply company indicated that he would have to special order the 'conical' explosive charges that would be needed for the river crossing blasting. The explosives were soon delivered, and the 'conical' explosive charges were placed strategically in the 'high bottom' sections of the underwater trench.

'A conical' explosive charge is a cone-shaped charge that is primarily used in demolition applications as they are very high explosives that can penetrate metal and steel. When Jimmy Shea delivered the 'conical' explosives to Joe Ricci, he passed along the precautions that he knew about the product. He also mentioned to Joe Ricci that the power produced from the cone-shaped charge is purely kinetic in nature and that it has a significant secondary incendiary effect after penetration. Basically, what was said in layman's terms would be, these babies pack a major 'wallop' so be careful!

The charges were set and the area was cleared as Joe Ricci held the blasting detonation device in his hands. This time, a warning horn was blown, with three long signals. Warning bystanders and passersby of what was about to happen. Everyone, including Les Marino who was standing next to Kenny Anderson, waited in silent anticipation for the explosion to take place. Joe Ricci bellowed out, "Fire in the hole," as he twisted the detonation lever. Somewhat similar to the performance that was put on by his fellow blasting compatriot and former employee of Modern Continental 'the Preacher' on the Boston Harbor waterfront in February of 1973, a waterspout, proceeded to lift from the surface of the placid Merrimack River as if Poseidon himself was standing there with a trident in hand. As the eruption of water, rock, and silt were still airborne, Kenny Anderson turned to Les Marino and told him, "You just might want to get out of here pretty fast, as I'm sure the cops and the State police will be here soon!"

The Haverhill police did show up, along with the Massachusetts State Police and a couple of representatives from the State Fire Marshal's Office, along with numerous insurance adjusters. An investigation was conducted and it was determined that, as warned, the use of demolition grade 'conical' explosives was not the proper choice for this particular application. Modern Continental, although, performing their duties in an expeditious manner, where starting to cause some concerns with their insurance carrier.

The actual property damage, which was incurred as a result of Joe Ricci's aquatic spectacle, was relatively minor. A couple of cars that were parked in the area were hit with rocks and there was lots of mud and dirt that needed to be cleaned up, but all in all, under the circumstances, the situation could have been much worse, no one died!

The blasting did achieve the proper underwater trench level that was needed for the installation of the pipeline for the second river crossing. As a matter of fact, a considerable amount of crushed stone had to be placed in the open underwater trench to bring it back to the desired grade. The pipe was pulled into place using the same yoke and 55-gallon empty drum technique, and the 30-B Bucyrus-Erie crane pulled the floating pipe into position and the New England Diver crew made sure that the pipeline was properly installed and anchored in place.

****

The five pipe-laying crews working on the Haverhill project continued at a blistering pace. With the springtime weather improving production conditions, it was an all-out push to see which crew could install the most pipes. The pipe-laying foremen on the Haverhill job were Billy Durkin, Jr. Paul Ladakakis, Joe Valentim, Joe Rocha, and Dick Durand. These guys were getting things done, and expeditiously getting pipe in the ground. Needless to say, there was an awful lot of activity going on each day in the City of Haverhill. Dump trucks moving dirt, backhoes digging trenches and Terex front-end loaders zipping around as if an infestation of lime green bugs had overtaken the area.

The coordination of the Haverhill project was supervised by Kenny Anderson. Les Marino would visit the job site very often, to see how things were progressing and to observe what was going on. This was by far Modern Continental's biggest project. However, in addition to the Haverhill project, there were other jobs ongoing that needed attention as well. The growth of the company had gotten to a point where the addition of some key people was required to satisfy the staffing requirements that a company this size needed to maintain a competitive edge. It was during this timeframe that Les decided that although Kenny Anderson had been directly involved with the bidding process, he would need someone else to help him with the bidding work. Bruce Rapoza was brought on board to assist with chasing prices and securing subcontract costs for the upcoming bids. Bruce was a needed addition as Les and Kenny had been handling the crux of the bidding duties by themselves. Bruce had worked as a surveyor and most recently as an estimator and purchasing agent for a small construction company. He had just enough background to understand what needed to be done, yet he was still young enough to be properly molded so that he could properly learn just how Les Marino actually wanted things done, which was understandably, his way!

It was also during this time frame that another addition was made to the Modern Continental management staff as Brad Bumpus, was hired to work in the accounting department. Edna Hughes had her hands full with the daily accounts payable and receivable headaches. Brad Bumpus, had an accounting background, and he was attending Boston University, taking night courses, as he was in pursuit of a Master of Business Administration (MBA) degree. It was essential, that a true accounting person work with the numbers that needed to be prepared for Frank Merlino's accounting company when they performed the various audits that were necessary. Brad Bumpus had a very good head for business and numbers which was very helpful to Edna Hughes. Les also had visions of getting involved in some business operations that were not construction-related. Having Brad Bumpus involved as part of the company, would allow him to apply his business background and become the business development person that Les and Kenny had envisioned when they thought of eventually expanding the company operations. In addition to the accounting duties, Brad Bumpus also did quite a bit of research and analysis, which related to business opportunities that Modern Continental might consider eventually getting involved with.

Not long after Brad Bumpus was on board with Modern Continental, they decided to bid on the operation of the City of Boston Parking Garages. There were four city of Boston Public Garage facilities at that time that were put out annually for bid. The successful bidder would be responsible for the overall management associated with the daily operations of each particular parking facility. The city owned the parking garages, but did not operate them; they were operated and managed by a third-party administrator who paid the city a percentage of what the monthly receipts were. At that particular time, the mid to late 1970s, the parking garages were strictly cash operations, which generated immediate cash flow for Modern Continental. The construction portion of the business lived on monthly billing statements to the various construction entities, which hindered normal cash flow. Therefore, having a daily cash-based operation would prove beneficial, with regard to payroll and accounts payable situations.

Looking back, it seems somewhat uncanny how the addition of the people that were brought on board worked so well into the overall Modern Continental corporate structure. There was no formal training for new employees, no human resources department, it was basically, fly by the seat of your pants, keep your head down, and pay attention, as things happen very fast around here. As the philosophical Les Marino would often point out, "Success has many fathers, but failure is an orphan!" There was very little room for failure in this organization. The ability to achieve success in a reasonably short period of time showed how important the Modern Continental way of doing things would work its way into the mindset of each and every employee that worked for the company. The examples set by Les Marino and Kenny Anderson kind of summed up just how each employee was expected to perform their duties. The funny thing about this 'company doctrine' of hard work and diligence, it was accepted and included in the work ethic of every employee who was part of this Modern Continental 'phenomenon'.

****

The dirt was being moved and the pipe was being installed on the Haverhill job. Things were moving quickly and when things move too fast, problems occur. The company had a few of its own dump trucks on the job. They now owned the two B-81 Mack trucks, the old Diamond-T rig, and a relatively new Autocar ten-wheel dump truck. However, this was not enough trucks as each pipe crew needed a dump truck to move the dirt that was taken out of the trench and then to bring dirt and stone to the location. Therefore, it was necessary to hire a couple of ten-wheel dump trucks to keep up with the demand. It was one of the hired B-81 Mack dump trucks that had a Modern Continental driver that experienced a problem. The hired B-81 Mack truck that the employee was driving was an old machine. When this type of truck is loaded and it is climbing a hill, it requires dexterity and agility to keep the truck from losing power, and ultimately control of the vehicle. It was a bright summer morning in 1976, when the fully loaded hired B-81 Mack truck being operated by a Modern Continental driver, had an issue. The driver did not double clutch fast enough while climbing a hill, which unfortunately became a situation where the driver lost control of the massive truck that was fully loaded with crushed stone. The truck, being out of the control of the driver, quickly became a run-a-way monster as it came down the hill out of control and headed for disaster. The

120

careening truck, with its full load of crushed stone, savagely crashed into the unsuspecting bakery at the bottom of the hill.

The destruction was horrendous, as the dump truck, being fully loaded upon entering the building, fell through the floor into the basement of the bakery. The ovens were pushed out to the back of the building. The structural integrity of the building had been severely compromised, as after the crash, the building was being held up, strictly by the body of the dump truck that had crashed through the front of the building and was sitting in the basement. The driver of the dump truck died. It was confirmed that the driver died from a heart attack. The exact time of death could not be established, and it was not known if the heart attack happened before, or after the crash took place. Miraculously, no other deaths took place. There were a couple of minor injuries to a baker and a customer. The building was destroyed. This situation was not advantageous to the presence of Modern Continental Construction Company in the City of Haverhill. This accident created a serious situation for the company.

****

With the amount of work that was taking place, there would continuously be issues that arose relating to changed conditions on each project. A changed condition was basically something that was different from the original conditions that were specified in the bid documents and the contract. The changed condition could be that underground rock was encountered that was not identified, which would cost the contractor an additional expense from what was originally anticipated. There were also, conflicts with 'right of way' and easement situations that would mean that the direction of the pipeline might have to be altered or changed. When a changed condition occurred, a submittal to the engineering company had to be made so that proper payment could take place to compensate the contractor accordingly. Change orders were time-consuming and had to be documented in writing and had to be accurate and factual.

The preparation of change orders and submittals was sometimes a little more involved than the project manager on the job site might be familiar with. The amount of work constantly increasing, and the changed conditions escalating, it became evident that a qualified engineering person would need to be hired by the company to handle the numerous change orders and associated documentation necessary to substantiate proper payment for the additional work performed and to collect the additional money owed to the company.

Les and Kenny put out 'feelers' with the engineering people that they were friendly with in hopes of identifying a competent person that they could hire to take care of this growing problem. As luck would have it, someone who had been a resident engineer with the engineering firm of Metcalf & Eddy Associates was indeed available and quite qualified as he was a registered professional engineer. During the summer of 1976, Robert Wetherbee became a much-welcomed addition to the Modern Continental Construction Company's rapidly growing family. Bob Wetherbee was a regular shark when it came to chasing money that was owed for changed conditions. He had been the responsible person at Metcalf & Eddy Engineering Company, which reviewed the numerous submittals and change orders that were prepared relating to this very subject. He knew, chapter and verse, exactly how to write a powerful and factual changed conditions request for additional payment. Bob Wetherbee was a word master, with a golden touch when it came to chasing additional payments. As such, he immediately became a very busy and important man in the company.

****

It was during the late summer of 1976, that the third and final river crossing took place in Haverhill. Unlike the second river crossing, this section of the Merrimack River did not have a ledge in the trench area. The excavation was conducted with minimal difficulties. The work was falling behind somewhat so Kenny Anderson had the river crossing crew working seven days a week. The river had been turbulent as the summer had brought more than a couple of torrential downpours from passing thunderstorms. With a fatigued workforce, working continuously for numerous days in a row, they boisterously begged for a day off. Kenny, disinclined to grant them their wish, reluctantly relented and gave everyone Sunday off. It just so happened that prior to the day off, the pipeline had been moved into position in preparation for installation. The pipeline with the yokes and empty 55-gallon drums had been maneuvered into position, with a section of the serpent-like pipeline extended into the river. Sure enough, one of those supercell thunderstorms roared through the Merrimack Valley on Sunday evening, which disrupted the section of pipeline exposed in the river and dislodged the barrels and the yokes. The section of pipeline hanging in the river came loose and sunk. The benevolent Kenny Anderson who reluctantly gave his men the Sunday off had to work like hell to get the section of pipe that came loose back into position. A setback, that could have been avoided, now became a costly mistake.

The pipeline that had been installed by the five crews that were installing pipe in the Haverhill roadways had to be tested. The testing process involves air pressure being built up in sections and a timeframe established to acknowledge if over a period of time the pressure drops. If the pressure does drop, that means that the section pipe is leaking and that it needs to be repaired. Repairing involves, sending men into the manhole and pipeline to install hydraulic cement to repair the leaks. Since there were more than a couple of leaks in the system, there was a specific crew that worked in the pipeline just to fix any leaking pipes.

It was in the late fall of 1976 when the majority of pipeline installation work had been completed and the testing of the sections of the pipeline were being conducted. A particular section of pipe had been identified on Friday afternoon as showing some leaks. The pipe-fixing crew that worked in the manholes and pipeline indicated that they would tackle that section first thing Monday morning.

In 1976, technology with regard to halogen lights and battery-operated lanterns was not totally reliable or available. The use of open flame, kerosene burning 'Coleman' lanterns was the accepted norm back during that time period. It was early Monday morning when the pipe-fixing crew prepared to enter the manhole and begin their day's work. The manhole was opened and the first guy started down the ladder with the burning 'Coleman' lantern. When he got to the bottom of the ladder in the manhole, the flame mysteriously went out. The employee then took a book of matches out of his pocket. His partner was standing at the top of the manhole looking down and asking what was wrong. The guy in the manhole with the 'Coleman' lantern, lit the match, and no sooner had he struck the match on the striker pad, an insidious spark began to twinkle, and then an all-out 'boom' took place as the manhole exploded violently.

Apparently, over the weekend, one of the older cast iron natural gas mains that ran parallel to the sewer line that had been installed, cracked as a result of the changed subsurface ground conditions, and some natural gas had leaked in through the portions of the pipeline that were porous. As natural gas is heavier than air, the natural gas had sunken at the bottom of the manhole, causing no concerns. It was the disruption of the dormant gas that affected the flame in the 'Coleman' lantern and extinguished it. When the guy in the manhole lit the match to start the lantern again, the disrupted natural gas had been stirred and risen enough to create the explosion.

The employee in the manhole was severely burned as was the employee standing at the top of the manhole. The employee at the bottom of the manhole succumbed to his burns not long after his arrival at the hospital. The other guy that was standing at the top of the manhole received third-degree burns on his face and hands, the exposed parts of his body that were susceptible to the explosion. This was a devastating accident that caused concerns for everyone in the company. The project was shut down while a proper OSHA investigation was conducted.

In addition to the accident that had taken place on the Haverhill project, there were numerous incidents that took place on a couple of other Modern Continental Construction Company projects with regard to damaged utility lines. In the spring of 1977 on the Harrison Avenue Boston Project, New England Telephone Company ducts had been damaged while digging was taking place. At the Faneuil Hall project, a series of Boston Edison underground cables had been damaged by Modern Continentals digging causing power outages throughout the city.

The numerous accidents and damage that had been caused by Modern Continental Construction Company within the past year and a half, had caused the insurance company that provided the company with their general liability, workers' compensation, and auto coverage, some concerns. A pattern had been developing, that was not conducive to the safety, or the well-being of the employees, or the general public. The circumstances surrounding the problems that were taking place needed to be properly addressed and rectified.

In the late summer of 1977, with numerous jobs taking place and Modern Continental beginning to expand the company operations into related work that would increase the growth of the organization, the insurance company reluctantly decided to pull the pin!

As a result of a very poor safety record, Modern Continental Construction Company had been issued a cease and desist by their own insurance carrier. An ultimatum was given to Modern Continentals management, hire an in-house safety person to control your safety and liability claims issues, or we will not insure your company!

The high-speed growth that was taking place was quickly coming to a stop. Fix your problems before you go any further were the terms, conditions, and mandates set forth by the insurance people, stop the safety problems, now!

Chapter Ten
Be Safe Out There!

1977–1980

As a leader, you must constantly change to be effective—**Kenny Anderson**

Cambridge, Massachusetts
Modern Continental Construction Company, Inc.
Office Location 905 Main Street
Tuesday, 23 August 1977
2:19 p.m.

The trip up the flight of stairs was filled with anticipation, apprehension, and outright fear for Bill Shields. He read the name on the door and entered the office. The cheery receptionist looked effervescent as she addressed the tall stranger who entered. The young receptionist whose name was Roseanne, asked in a pert and professional voice, "How can I help you?"
The tall nervous guy answered, ever so cautiously, "Hi, I'm Bill Shields and I have an appointment to see Mrs. Edna Hughes for a job interview." He went on to say, "My appointment is at two-thirty, I'm a few minutes early."
Roseanne looked at the clock on her desk and replied, "Hold on a minute, let me see if she's available." Roseanne got up from behind her desk and scurried off toward the back of the office as she disappeared around a corner. A moment later, she promptly returned and let the waiting job candidate know that Edna would be right with him.

****

It has been a long and strange journey over the past couple of years for the ambitious job candidate named Bill Shields. At twenty-nine years old, he had already experienced more turmoil in his somewhat young life than most people

126

have experienced in a lifetime. At six foot two inches tall and weighing two hundred and ten pounds, he looked to be in good physical condition, but then again, sometimes looks could be deceiving.

At eighteen years old after graduating from Winchester, Massachusetts High School in 1966, Bill Shields became an apprentice ironworker in the Boston-based Local #7 Ironworkers Union. Bill's dad was an officer in the affiliated Riggers Union #607 which opened the door for Bill to enter the ironworkers apprentice program. During his tenure as an ironworker, he was involved with walking on steel beams on some of the more memorable skyscrapers in downtown Boston, the 52-story Prudential building, the 60-story John Hancock Tower, and the 42-story State Street high-rise office building known as the Boston Building. Having completed his three-year apprentice training in 1969, the journeyman ironworker spent time with Bethlehem Steel Corporation working on the twin bridges that cross the Savannah River from South Carolina to Georgia. Then worked his way back to the Boston area and worked as a foreman for the AB Maddison Company on the construction of the new Post Office Building in South Boston.

Bill settled down and married his young bride Maria in April of 1973 and not long after their marriage, in March of 1974, they welcomed their first child, a daughter named Kimberly. Life was going along just fine for Bill until that fateful day in July of 1974, when he fell three stories and got badly injured, breaking both of his arms. He spent a tentative time span with the unsettling knowledge that if the corrective surgeries that were being attempted on his left arm did not resolve the problems, it would have to be amputated. Fortunately, after the fourth round of corrective surgery, the orthopedic surgeon performed an experimental procedure that tied the tendons from his upper humerus bone with the radius and the lower ulna bone in his left arm, which prevented it from being amputated. However, the use of his left arm was severely diminished but the good news was that it was still attached to his shoulder.

The recovery and rehabilitation that took place after he broke his arms was a long, wearisome, and frustrating process. For the young, rugged ironworker, his most valuable asset, his raw strength, had been taken away from him. At twenty-six years old, his ironworker days were suddenly over. Sullen and somewhat dejected, this once productive worker was sidelined and out of a job. His love of the construction industry prompted him to refocus his efforts on finding work that would keep him involved in the field that he so loved. Having suffered a debilitating industrial accident, this experience led Bill in the direction of construction safety. With the relatively new Occupational Safety and Health Administration (OSHA) having recently been enacted and now monitoring the safety conditions in the construction industry, Bill looked to become familiar with the procedures and actions associated with this organization. At that time, the only higher education facility that was offering courses and training relating to OSHA was Fitchburg State University. Bill enrolled in classes and got a brief outlook as to what the OSHA organization was all about and what a contractor needed to understand in order to comply with the newly enacted safety statutes, rules, and regulations.

Armed with his experience and hands-on exposure in the world of construction and a brief course in OSHA taken at Fitchburg State University, Bill applied for the advertised position by Modern Continental Construction Company of their need for a 'company safety officer' that he recently observed in the *Boston Globe* 'want add' section of the newspaper. He now anxiously waited for Mrs. Edna Hughes to begin the interview process associated with this position.

****

Edna Hughes introduced herself to Bill Shields and then asked him to follow her into Mr. Marino's office. Upon entering the office of Les Marino, the bigger-than-life portrait of the raging bull with the swords and blood dripping from it caught the attention of Bill Shields. He immediately thought to himself, this guy must be out for blood with anyone that he comes in contact with. Les Marino was sitting behind his desk, he looked impatient and irritated. Also, in his office sitting on the sofa that was to his right was Bob Wetherbee. Edna introduced both Les and Bob and asked Bill to sit down in the chair in front of Mr. Marino's desk. Edna then handed a copy of Bill's resume to Les and Bob as she took a seat on the sofa next to Bob Wetherbee.

After they all quickly looked at the resume sheet that they were handed, a bevy of questions began to come forth from all three individuals. What experience do you have with writing and implementing a safety program for a heavy construction company? Are you familiar with the various exposures that are inherent to an excavation contractor? Do you know how to conduct an effective safety meeting and do you have experience with public speaking?

How are your communication and writing skills? Do you understand the relevant OSHA 1926 standards?

Feeling somewhat overwhelmed and challenged, Bill did his level-headed best to keep up with the answers to the many questions that he was being asked. Unfortunately, the answers did not seem to be coming fast enough, nor did the look on everyone's faces assure him that he was passing this baptism by fire. Quizzical looks and raised eyebrows seemed to be the only feedback that he was getting from this trio of examiners. But then, a glimmer of hope emerged as Les Marino looked at the bottom of the page and noticed a name that he was very familiar with. Les looked up from the resume and with a questioning look, then asked Bill Shields, "How do you know Walter Corsano from Vancouver Associates, you have him written down as a reference?"

Bill perked up as he quickly replied, "I worked for Walter as a surveyor in the summers when I was in high school, he was my older brother's best friend, and they went to Massachusetts Maritime Academy together."

Les then asked Bill, "Can you get Walter on the telephone, I'd like to talk to him about you."

Bill, looking a little concerned, replied, "I don't know his phone number off the top of my head, if you let me call home, I'm sure that my wife can get it for me."

Les then pushed the phone on his desk toward Bill and said, "Go ahead and get his number." Bill quickly called home and got the phone number from his wife. When Bill hung up with his wife, Les told Bill to call Walter Corsano.

****

The job search for Bill Shields had been a grueling process over the past couple of months. In 1977, the economy was terrible, the new president Jimmy Carter had the country in a tail spin heading for the highest inflation rate, the highest unemployment rate, and the lowest confidence rating of any president in the history of the United States of America. Trying to get a job, with very little experience and even fewer opportunities, was a challenge, to say the least. With a new wife, a small baby, and no future, a miracle needed to happen for Bill Shields to get a break. The excruciating pain of being without a job after working so hard all his life seemed more intense than the pain he felt when he broke his arms. He knew that he had to find something so that he could again be the provider that he had been before he fell and got hurt.

****

Les Marino hung up the phone after talking with Walter Corsano and then looked intently at Bill Shields as he somewhat painfully responded, "You don't have the experience or the background that we are looking for. However, Walter Corsano assured me that you are a good, smart kid and that you're a good worker. I trust Walter's judgment, I'm going to take a chance with you." After a slight pause, Les lets Bill know, "You've got the job as our company safety officer!"

Upon the completion of the interview, Edna Hughes asked Bill to follow her to the reception area. As she closed the door to Les Marino's office, Edna let Bill know that he would start on the day after Labor Day and that the proper employment forms and related new hire information would be collected on that date. With a somewhat curt response, Edna Hughes dismissed Bill Shields and headed back toward her office.

The long and somewhat painful job search had ended for Bill Shields. Feeling a little bewildered, he left the Modern Continental Construction Company office at 905 Main Street in Cambridge, Massachusetts elated that he had finally landed a job, but puzzled and perplexed as to how he was going to successfully execute the duties of the job that he was just awarded. Yes, he knew all about construction safety, having worked for Bethlehem Steel Corporation and American Bridge Company, two of the largest steel erection companies in the country. Both companies were sticklers for job site safety and enforced their corporate safety agenda with an iron fist. It was exactly two weeks before his starting date of 6 September 1977, becoming familiar with what would be needed with regard to information and knowledge would become a priority between now and then for Bill Shields.

Since the existence of Modern Continental Construction Company in 1967, Les Marino and Kenny Anderson had concentrated their efforts on acquiring work and subsequently completing the work that they had secured in an expeditious and profitable manner. That is not to say that they did not comply with safety-related measures that were necessary with regard to performing dangerous construction operations, but understandably, they did not completely understand the consequences associated with the problems that would arise from worker injuries and property damage.

Having a reputation as a 'run and gun' company that threw caution to the wind, Modern Continental Construction Company had recently been recognized as a 'high-risk' company to the entities that were issuing work along with the insurance companies that were providing the indemnity. With four deaths and numerous property damage incidents over the past couple of years, the character and opinion of the company had diminished. They needed to rectify the safety and claims issues that were so prevalent and had become a serious situation. The insurance company, which was onboard as their current carrier insisted that Modern Continental hire a full-time, 'in-house', safety person to help get the safety situation under control, or they would not provide insurance. Although Modern Continental had plenty of work on the books and was growing at a phenomenal rate, safety controls needed to be implemented or the growth of the company would come to a very rapid standstill. Bob Heterich, the bonding agent, concurred with the insurance people as he informed Les Marino that the bonding company providing the surety line of credit for the company was also concerned about the safety problems that had taken place over the past year. Jeopardizing the surety line of credit got the immediate attention of both Les Marino and Kenny Anderson. They both realized that the safety situation that existed in the company needed to be properly addressed.

****

The recent addition of Bruce Repoza, to assist with bidding and to work as a purchasing agent, Bob Wetherbee, the engineering person who was overseeing the administration of the contracts and effectively pursuing any additional extra work order payments that might be necessary, along with Brad Bumpus, the accounting and business development person, to the office staff showed that Modern Continental was serious about developing a structure within the company to alleviate some of the involvement that was originally the sole responsibilities of Les Marino and Kenny Anderson. Although, it was not by choice, the addition of Bill Shields as the safety person was necessary to satisfy the mandates and demands of the insurance and bonding people.

In the fall of 1977, Modern Continental continued to acquire Environmental Protection Agency (EPA) funded projects. Fortunately, under former president Richard Nixon, the funding of the national water pollution and harbor cleanup activity which were the original initiatives of the EPA, had been put in place and the funds for these contracts had already been set aside. With the economy and the country on a severe downhill slide, Modern Continental was able to keep its head above water because of these EPA-funded projects.

Work was taking place in Ellsworth, Maine, Portland, Maine, Bellows Falls, Vermont, and Harrison Avenue in Boston, Massachusetts, Agawam, Massachusetts, New Bedford, Massachusetts, and Hull Massachusetts. There were still some cleanup and punch list items to complete on the Haverhill, Massachusetts, and the New London, Connecticut projects along with closing out a couple of other projects that were finishing up. The workforce performing the construction work was very stable and efficient. The supervisory personnel were also seasoned and proficient.

Kenny Anderson was handling the Ellsworth, Maine project along with the Portland, Maine job. Kenny figured that if he was going to be traveling north so often, it might be worthwhile to learn how to fly so that he could get from place to place a little quicker. In late 1976, Kenny started taking flying lessons at the Beverly, Massachusetts airport. He would take lessons on weekends and on some late afternoons. By 1977, Kenny was able to fly up to Bar Harbor, Maine airport on his own which made the supervision of the Ellsworth, Maine project just a little bit easier. By now, the duties and responsibilities of both Les Marino and Kenny Anderson had been pretty much defined.

Kenny was the 'pusher' the outside guy who made sure that the jobs were up and running and productive. Les Marino was concentrating most of his time and effort on bidding work and putting out fires that would crop up in the office. Les also spent time going over business development opportunities with Brad Bumpus. The city of Boston parking garage contracts were in place as Modern Continental was now managing the four downtown Boston parking facilities. If Kenny could not make some of the jobs that were close to the office, Les would make it a point to get out of the office and visit these jobs. As he had bid the jobs and was very familiar with them, Les knew just how much production was needed on each project to keep them profitable.

****

Les Marino, after spending many years living in Cambridge, Massachusetts, purchased a house in Quincy, Massachusetts for his wife Anna Maria, and his two daughters, Laura, and Lorraine. This house was much larger than the Cambridge location. It had a large dining room which made the Sunday dinner get-togethers a little more inviting. It was not long after the move to Quincy that Les felt it necessary to keep a better handle on exactly who was doing what on a Monday morning. Therefore, Les made it mandatory that all supervisors had to place a call to him on Sunday evening between 7 and 9 p.m. and for them to let him know what they had planned for Monday morning. There was no call waiting, or answering machines at that time, which meant that if you were not fortunate enough to catch Les between calls, you had to keep trying until you were successful. For many supervisors, this meant spending much of Sunday night playing the dialing for Les game. Although the company had grown tremendously, Les still felt the need to keep his finger on the pulse of the company and to be aware of what everyone in the company was doing. Being on top of things and keeping control was paramount for Les.

It did not take long for Bill Shields to be indoctrinated into the company. On his first morning, at the Modern Continental office, in Cambridge, Massachusetts, he began his employment as the newly hired 'company safety officer'. He arrived bright and early and was standing at the front door when Edna Hughes arrived to open the office. Not long after signing employment papers, as he was just settling into familiarizing himself with the surroundings, Les Marino showed up at Bill's desk. Les looked at Bill and gave him no greeting, he just proceeded to rapidly tap his right forefinger on the surface of Bill's desk and then he pointed his index finger at Bill and said, "I don't need you and I don't want you, but the insurance company made me hire you." With that welcoming speech, Les proceeded to turn and walk away. Bill, sitting there among the other three people who had their desks in the room, just sat there a little shocked and downtrodden at what the owner of the company had just said to him. Bill, thankful that he had a job, reminded himself that he better make himself useful and needed, or he would soon be on the outside looking in, again!

Since being hired as the office manager, Edna Hughes has worn many hats in the Modern Continental organization, one of the many hats was human resources officer. At this particular juncture of the company, being the 'HR' person kind of meant, you take the new employee's social security number and accept the W2 form that they completed and then file it in a cabinet. There was no formal employee handbook or guideline booklet explaining company policies, procedures, and benefits. There were a total of eight people working at the 905 Main Street office location, their job functions were all self-explanatory. You either performed your duties and proved to be of benefit to the company or you were replaced, a plain and simple company policy. Knowing that the company had a horrendous safety record and that they did not seem to incorporate any form of safety into the overall activities performed in their construction operations, was clearly evident. However, it did not take the mind of a rocket scientist to figure out that each and every guy working on the jobs got their indirect marching orders from Les Marino and Kenny Anderson. Writing a flawless safety program would be nothing but a waste of time if the owners of the company did not accept and honestly profess its use and application.

Bill Shields knew that his job as the company safety officer was not going to be easy. Putting together a safety program was not a challenge, the major obstacle he recognized was getting the powers-to-be to go along with its implementation. Back in 1977, there was no internet, World Wide Web, or smartphones that you could say, 'Safety program for an excavation contractor' and a plethora of choices would pop up on your screen. Research had to be done the old-fashioned way, well some might say 'archaic' way, by spending time at the local library reading books and researching trade journals along with accessing reams of rules, regulations, and statutes. The process was tedious and time-consuming, most research was performed at night and on weekends as asking for time to do research did not seem like a very good idea at the time.

The mindset, which had been instilled in both Kenny Anderson and Les Marino from just about the beginning of time was that people running machines, shoveling dirt, and installing pipes, were productive and made money for the company. People who pushed a pencil in an office and hit the keys on a typewriter were not productive and cost money for the company. Being useful, productive, and producing profitability for the company was not an easy task for a Modern Continental office employee in 1977. Bruce Rapoza, the guy who helped Les with the bids and purchased the materials needed for the jobs, could justify his existence by saving money on the materials that he purchased. Bob Wetherbee, the engineer, and project coordinator could help with his existence by pursuing extra work orders and getting paid for this work. Brad Bumpus, the business development, and accounting guy could find ways to invest and make money. How could a guy who professed 'work safe' be valuable? That was exactly how Les Marino felt about the new safety guy, no doubt, he was a drain on company resources and assets!

In all fairness to Les Marino, as much as he felt that hiring a safety guy was a waste of company money, he did commit to the experiment, for the immediate time being, and knew that he had to make the most of it. After his initial assessment and reluctant acceptance of the situation, Les approached Bill Shields and informed him, "I'm taking a chance with you. You do not have the experience or background for this job. It would be beneficial to you and the company for you to learn as much as you can. The smarter you are, the more the company will benefit. Take as many courses possible that will help you, the company will pay for them." This was a huge breakthrough, gaining knowledge by taking courses made perfect sense. Learning about things that were directly related to insurance and safety would be very beneficial.

The very first course that Bill Shields signed up for was a program being taught that directly related to workers' compensation and how the scope of activities and rating values were promulgated and determined. This course was being offered by Aetna Insurance Company and was taking place in Concord, Massachusetts. The course involved a series of six Wednesday evening sessions from 6:00 p.m. to 8:00 p.m. The course began in October of 1977 and would finish just before Thanksgiving. Taking this learning session would prove to be the catalyst that would change the concept of a useless office worker to a money-saving employee.

A bona fide safety program was written and put in place that directly related to the activities that Modern Continental was involved with. Visits to the various job sites took place and safety meetings were being conducted on a regular basis. However, there always appeared to be a reluctance to get completely involved, and the issue of safety was being paid 'lip service' to appease who knows who. The insurance company was happy that an effort was being made, but clearly, the superintendents and even the foremen who were working on the jobs did not have their heart in the safety matters that were being presented to them.

The information taught at the course put on by Aetna Insurance Company proved to be of great value in more ways than one. As a result of the information obtained in this course, it was determined how workers' compensation rates were created and how the importance of safety played a major factor in the amount of premiums that were charged. It was explained that each category of work has a code number assigned to it. The primary code that Modern Continental was involved with was code #6217 which relates to excavation activities. What the rating bureau does is take into consideration the number of claims that take place for that specific code, along with the amount of premium that is collected for that particular code, and then they come up with an average, which is considered 1.00.

If your company does better than the average that has been calculated, meaning that if your company incurs fewer claims and injuries, than the average that was calculated, then you can receive a credit. The same holds true for a company that does worse than the average and has more claims that are severe and costly than the average then that company would be charged a debit and be penalized. Using the 1.00 average with a premium being $100,000.00 would mean if you did better than the average and got a credit of 10% that would bring your rating to 0.90 then your company would only pay $90,000.00 rather than the average of 1.00 at $100,000.00. The same holds true for a company that does worse than the average and gets say a debit of 10% bringing them to a 1.10 rating then that company would now pay $110,000.00 for their premium. Showing that the safe company that got the credit would pay less than the unsafe company that got penalized.

Knowing that Modern Continental had a poor safety record, it was determined that as a result of the many accidents and fatalities that had previously taken place, in 1977 Modern Continental was being charged a 91% debit bringing their current rating to 1.91 which was almost twice as much as the average for the industry that they worked in. Armed with this information, Bill Shields approached Les Marino and asked, "How can you competitively compete against your rivals if you are paying almost twice as much for your workers' compensation insurance than the average for the industry?"

Les was needless to say, totally caught off guard with this revelation. He asked Bill Shields, "What exactly do you mean that we are paying twice as much as our competitors for insurance?" Bill went on to explain to Les what he had learned and he let him know that because Modern Continental had blown things up, torn out telephone duct lines, broken natural gas pipes, and underground Edison electric cables in addition to the much higher workers' compensation insurance premiums, they were also paying higher liability insurance, and the company also had to pay big fines for damaging and digging up the underground utilities.

A nerve had been struck and it was struck with impudence when Les Marino realized that he was trying to save nickels and dimes on line items in a bid when he was blowing all sorts of money by paying extremely high insurance premiums. As if a flashbulb went off in Les's head, he realized that if he could save money on insurance premiums it would make the company more competitive. It was finally coming to light that if the company became safer, they could in fact save money. Armed with this new found understanding, Les expressed to Bill Shields, "We have to change this situation right away."

Bill explained to Les, "This kind of situation does not change overnight. This change must be a company philosophy change, this change has to come with your express approval and everyone in the company needs to understand that you, Les Marino, are fully behind the need for the company to perform safely and for everyone to follow all safety rules and regulations." Les understood and agreed to be an advocate of safety.

Starting on the first Monday of January 1978 and continuing every first Monday going forward, a company safety meeting would be held at the Stoughton, Massachusetts Modern Continental maintenance facility. All Superintendents, foremen, and management people had to attend this meeting. There were no excuses for missing the meeting. The law had been laid down, everyone must attend the meeting. At this first meeting, Les Marino took the floor and let everyone know, in no uncertain terms, that the company was now taking on a new philosophy, the company would act and perform in a safe and productive manner, and that Bill Shields would be putting safety rules in place and that they must be followed, without question.

Understanding that safety now equated to saving money, Les Marino became a changed man, he was now an outright advocate of all thing's safety. And so, a philosophical change did take place, in reality, it, just took some understanding of how an effective safety program could benefit the company in more ways than one. Yes, there would eventually be a saving of money, but there would also be a transformation in the thought process of how work and activities were conducted. The change was definitely for the better. A safe place to work will become a more productive place, and productivity increases profit. In a relatively short period of time, the hiring and usefulness of Bill Shields was looked at in a different light. It also helped that he understood that he needed to be involved and make himself useful, or his days would be numbered. Having Les on board with all things safety would make his job a little bit easier.

It was right around this time that 'affirmative action' began to become more involved with compliance situations. Not only did compliance issues with employment begin to evolve but there also became sanctions that required that a certain percentage of work acquired in any federally funded project that a percentage had to be performed by a minority subcontractor. This required that Modern Continental had to appoint a minority business 'compliance officer' to monitor both employment and minority subcontract compliance. Bill Shields was quick to raise his hand and take on this duty. With the increase in work taking place and the need to effectively and productively assign specific pieces of heavy equipment, to designated job sites, the need to have someone coordinate the movement of heavy equipment became a necessity.

Therefore, someone was needed to monitor the movement of the equipment from job to job.

Again, Bill Shields raised his hand for this job as well. Did someone say job security?

It was a hectic time in early 1978 for Modern Continental Construction Company, Kenny Anderson was running around like a chicken with his head cut off as he raced from job to job kicking ass and pushing for more production. Although the Ellsworth, Maine project was occupying much of his time, Kenny also kept an eye on the Agawam, Massachusetts project. Alex Crowers was running the job under Kenny's guidance and supervision. Alex Crowers had been working for the engineering firm of Camp, Dresser & McKee when an opportunity opened up for Modern Continental to hire him as a project superintendent. It was on the Agawam job that Kenny Anderson, kind of lost his cool. The project engineering firm on this job was Tighe & Bond Engineering, the project involved the installation of a concrete sewer pipe which much of it passed through the field of an asparagus farm. The farmer did not take too kindly to having heavy equipment digging up his farm and fields.

Kenny Anderson, while visiting the job, got in an altercation with the farmer, who was trying to deny access to an area that required heavy equipment to mobilize in that location. While this altercation was taking place, the Tighe & Bond engineer on the job made the mistake of getting in Kenny Anderson's way when Kenny was about to leave the site, in a much-aggravated condition, the engineer tried to flag Kenny's car down and was almost run over, as Kenny headed right at the guy. To avoid Kenny's Oldsmobile Tornado the engineer had to jump in a puddle of mud. He got up covered in mud waving his fist at Kenny. Alex Crowers had to let Kenny know that the engineer called the Agawam Police and that Kenny could not come on the job anymore. Kenny, when confronted by the police, sheepishly denied trying to run the guy over.

****

On Monday 6 February 1978, the day started out cold and cloudy. The Modern Continental office in Cambridge was busy and crowded as Les had Dale Flynn come to the office to work with him and Bruce Rapoza on a bid that involved quite a bit of concrete structures. Bob Wetherbee also had a meeting in the office with representatives from the engineering firm of Metcalf & Eddy who were the engineering firm for the New Bedford, Massachusetts project. They were going over disputed quantities and were trying to iron out some squabbles that had arisen on the project. It was just about 10:30 a.m. that the first few snowflakes started to gently fall from a gray, overcast sky in Central Square, Cambridge, Massachusetts. No one gave the snowflakes that were coming down much thought. At about 1:30 p.m., the snow was coming down at a pretty good clip. Little did anyone know that the snowflakes that were falling were about to become history as this was the start of 'the great blizzard of 78'.

At just a little after 3:00 p.m. having listened to the forecast on the radio, and trusting the good judgment of veteran weather forecaster Don Kent on WBZ radio, Les Marino became somewhat concerned at the increased rate that the snow was falling. Les, who was not an employer that believed much in giving time off, came out of his office and made an announcement to everyone that was somewhat out of character for him, as he let everyone know that he was concerned for their safety and that this was going to be a pretty bad storm. He told everyone to leave and head home early. Although it was only a little after 3:00 p.m., the roads were getting crowded with traffic as it was moving quite slowly with the snowfall intensity increasing and the wind beginning to blow harder.

The track of the storm would prove to be pretty accurate as by 8:00 p.m. in the evening, we had a full-blown blizzard striking New England. The brunt of the hurricane-force winds and the heavy snowfall coincided with the high tide cycle as the ferocious winds and abnormally high tides continued for a record 32 hours straight. It was not until the morning of Wednesday, 8 February 1978 that the full scope of damages could begin to be considered.

One of the hardest-hit areas that got walloped by the storm was the South Shore of Massachusetts. Coincidentally, Modern Continental Construction Company was performing a large sanitary sewer project in the Town of Hull, Massachusetts, not far from Nantasket Beach which was extremely hard hit by the blizzard. With front-end loaders, heavy equipment, along with pumps and generators on the job site, The Army Corp of Engineers, who was the primary entity coordinating the disaster relief, called upon Modern Continental for their help. Immediately upon request, men and equipment leaped into action to help the communities on the ravished South Shore of Boston, as snow plowing, water pumping, and erosion situations were addressed by Modern Continental.

Kenny Anderson and Les Marino coordinated the mobilization of men and equipment during this emergency. The company low bed truck driver, Billy Dauphne, who had been a company guy since the early 1970s was called upon to move heavy equipment all over the state, as machines were taken from various job sites and moved to the designated locations to assist with the disaster relief efforts. Billy Dauphne was to be commended for the above-and-beyond effort that he made traveling through horrendous weather to move equipment during this paralyzing storm. Les Marino and Kenny Anderson were offering to The Army Corp of Engineers all available equipment that Modern Continental had within a 100-mile radius. Although he was stuck at home and unable to get to the office, Bill Shields, who was responsible for the inventory and knowing the location of the heavy equipment, generators and pumps worked with Les Marino to get the equipment to the various sites that The Army Corp of Engineers requested.

The disaster efforts went on for over a week as the Greater Boston area was basically shut down. The massive coastal flooding forced 10,000 people to emergency shelters. Over 3,000 automobiles and 500 trucks were stranded on an eight-mile section of Local Route #128 which had recently become part of US Route #95. Twenty-nine Massachusetts residents lost their lives and 11,000 homes were destroyed by the storm.

Modern Continental Construction Company provided much-needed heavy equipment, plows, pumps, and manpower to help with the blizzard of '78' disaster cleanup. When it was all said and done, and the emergency was over, a significant payment was made to Modern Continental by the Army Corp of Engineers for the use of machinery and equipment along with a very big thank you for their cooperation and effort.

The company was growing and it was not long before the office location at 905 Main Street in Cambridge had become overcrowded. Brad Bumpus had found a location at 2277 Massachusetts Avenue also in Cambridge that was a three-level apartment building that could be acquired for a very reasonable price. The building would need to be renovated and redesigned but it was the right size and a good location. By the summer of 1978, the negotiations had been completed and the building was acquired. Les called upon Billy Durkin Senior to spearhead the renovations, carpentry work, and rehabilitation of the soon-to-be new home and office location for Modern Continental.

The company's safety efforts were developing nicely. Les Marino had become a staunch supporter of all things' safety as he supported Bill Shields with his ongoing efforts to make the company a safe and compliant organization. As Modern Continental had such a dismal reputation with the utility companies not only in Massachusetts Avenue but pretty much in all of New England, an effort would be made to try and change the company's image. The newly formed 'Dig Safe' operations were an effort to include all underground utility companies so that it would be required that before a construction company did any form of underground digging, they call 'Dig Safe' so that the utility companies could place brightly colored markings on the pavement of a road or use flagging to identify any underground pipes, conduits, or ductwork. The natural gas companies, along with the electric and telephone companies participated in this marking program. The intent was to eliminate the disruption or damage to any underground utilities. At the outset, when 'Dig Safe' first began, this organization was primarily made up of the big utility companies, Boston Gas, Boston Edison, and New England Telephone. All of these utilities had a vested interest in the success of this venture.

It was with the true spirit of cooperation, understanding, and assistance that Bill Shields scheduled a meeting with the 'Dig Safe' people. The meeting was to be held at the Boston office of New England Telephone Company in Post Office Square in downtown Boston. Bill traveled to the city and with the intent of collaborating with the 'Dig Safe' people so that Modern Continental could be a participant in this coordinated safety effort. Bill was greeted at the reception area and then ushered into a conference room that included a large table with numerous utility executives sitting at the table. The receptionist accompanied Bill into the room and promptly announced his presence to the seated executives. No sooner had the young lady made the announcement, 'this is Bill Shields from Modern Continental Construction Company' than a series of guffaws, belly laughs and outright howls began to come from the demure, dignified executives seated at the conference table. You could see Bill Shields turn bright red with an expression of anguish, torment, and despair across his face. The gentleman sitting at the head of the table looked at Bill Shields and then said to him, "We really never thought that anyone from Modern Continental would actually have the guts to appear at this meeting."

Again, looking somewhat dumbfounded, Bill innocently replied, "Why?"

The next question asked of Bill Shields was, "How long have you been with Modern Continental?"

Bill replied, "One year."

Another executive then added, "You're aware of the trail of damage that your company has left throughout New England?"

Bill answered, "I'm totally aware of the past history regarding damage to underground utilities."

Bill continued, "I've come here in good faith to try to right a wrong, if you're going to laugh at me then I guess I'm wasting my time?"

The people in the room became quiet and then listened to Bill as he explained to them that he was well aware of the name that the utility people had for his company, 'Modern Continental Destruction'. He let them know that he was brought on board to correct the safety problems that had plagued the company for the past few years. He let them know that the company had changed its ways and that he was looking for 'Dig Safe's' help in assisting him with the changes that needed to be made. Bill could see the smiling looks of conceit and smugness leave their faces as he further explained, in sincere terms, that he understood the importance of avoiding the disruption to underground utilities and that digging up electric lines, telephone ducts, and gas mains in addition to being quite costly, could also be very deadly. The group of utility executives sitting at the big wooden conference table were silent.

Then, a soft voice from the end of the table, in an almost inaudible level spoke and said, "How can we help?"

Bill replied, "Dig Safe have a central call system, correct?"

The gentleman replied, "Yes, we do, we log in all calls with times and dates and locations."

Bill went on, "Good, then if I was to call whoever monitors this call center, then they could let me know who from Modern Continental called and used the service and when they called?" All of a sudden, there was a look of interest and genuine attention from the guys sitting at the table.

Bill explained, "It is our intent to keep our guys honest, we have put in a requirement that all job sites must call and request that the utilities be marked and log in when they called and record the time and date, I would like to be able to verify the use of the system by checking with your people to make sure our guys are actually using the system."

Another executive from the opposite end of the conference table blurts out, "You're asking us to squeal on your guys?"

Bill assured him, "Yes, if they are not using the system like they are supposed to, then there will be consequences. We want to put some teeth in this shark and let the guys know that failure to comply will bring repercussions!" The meeting continued in a very positive manner. Suggestions were made and there was a mutual agreement that the 'Dig Safe' people would definitely keep an open mind with regard to the promised transformation of 'Modern Continental Destruction!'

It was during a trip to the Bellows Falls, Vermont job that Bill made with Les as Bill was checking the safety on the job and Les was monitoring the production. During the long ride back to the office, Les, who had a tendency to prophesize explained to Bill, "Here it is 1979, pretty soon everyone in the country is going to have a sewer and the EPA is eventually going to run out of money. That's why you learn two lessons in school, two and two are four and the farmer plants more than one crop. We've only planted one crop; we need to start diversifying or we are going to have to park all of our equipment. We need to plant another crop; we need to get involved in other work than putting in sewer pipes."

****

With the work increasing, so did everyone's responsibilities. Bruce Rapoza, who worked with Les on all the bids and was also purchasing the materials for all the jobs had spread himself kind of thin. Les decided to hire a full-time purchasing agent so that Bruce could concentrate more on bidding. One of the guys on the job got wind of the situation and mentioned to Les when he was visiting the job site that his dad worked as a purchasing agent for a large company and that he was available. Les suggested that his dad call the office and talk to Bruce.

In early November of 1979, Paul Arabakian was hired as the purchasing agent for Modern Continental. Paul was in his mid-50s and in addition to working as a purchasing agent, he also had worked as a realtor. He came from Southern New Hampshire. The office was crowded so Paul could not work in the same office that Bruce was in, so Edna Hughes the office manager moved a desk into the already crowded front area of the reception room kind of next to Roseanne the receptionist. Things moved very fast in the Modern Continental environment, there was very little time for small talk or rest periods. As congenial as he was, Paul the new purchasing agent just did not have what it took to keep up with the demands that were being placed upon him. Not everyone can fit into the system. Being in the spotlight with regard to his desk, it was noted that Paul was kind of floundering a little as the time frame associated with acquiring numbers for bids kept the bidding and purchasing demands very high. It seemed that most days after he came back from lunch, Paul was observed, nodding off at his desk. In the meantime, Bruce was continually badgering him for quotes on materials and supplies, but Paul was not producing. Having taken a chance with him, the decision was made to move on from Paul, he was a nice guy, but did not 'cut the mustard'.

It was Friday afternoon when Kenny Anderson showed up at the office. He knew it was D-Day for Paul. He didn't want to be around when he got the axe. Kenny motioned for Bob Wetherbee, who sat diagonally across from Paul, to take a walk with him as they two hightailed it out of the office. Roseanne, also knew that 'ole Paul' was going. It was just four o'clock when Bruce called

144

Paul into his office and told him that he was not needed anymore. This was not easy for Bruce to do as it was not his nature. Paul listened to Bruce, gave no response, and then got up and went back to his desk.

Kenny Anderson and Bob Wetherbee knew that zero hour for Paul was four o'clock so they picked up a twelve-pack of Budweiser Natural Light at the package store across the street from the office and headed back at 4:30 p.m. Friday afternoons were historically happy hour as the guys in the office would sit around after work and have a beer together. Les, would join in having a beer but would only drink Budweiser Natural Light or nothing at all, so that meant that everyone had to drink it as well. When Kenny and Bob got back to the office, they were startled to see that Paul was still sitting at his desk. Noting this, Kenny and Bob went into Bruces' office to see what was going on. Bruce saw Kenny and Bob come into his office and he let them know that he let Paul go. Kenny, sarcastically notified Bruce, that although he let him go, he was still sitting at his desk. Roseanne was wondering as well as she knew that Bruce told Paul that he was all through yet, he was still working and going through papers at his desk.

While sitting at his desk, Paul turned to Bill Shields who sat at the desk behind him and inquisitively mentioned to Bill that he thought Bruce was acting odd as he asked him to go and Paul said he didn't understand. Bill knew what was going on as well but didn't reply to Paul, he just shrugged his shoulders. At this point, everyone in the office knew that Paul was getting fired but him! Edna, who was consulted when the decision was made came out of her office and saw Paul still sitting there. She said to Paul, "Why are you still here?"

Paul looked puzzled as he said to Edna, "What do you mean why am I still here?"

Edna, who did not pull any punches, clarified the situation in no uncertain terms and told Paul in her southern drawl, "Paul you're fired, now get the hell out of here!" He then got the message!

It was at the beginning of 1980 that the next crop was planted by Modern Continental as they bid and successfully won the contract for building a new tarmac and runway area at Logan Airport for the Massachusetts Port Authority (MassPort). The contract price was $5 million and primarily involved excavation and concrete work. Not long after acquiring the runway job, Modern Continental Construction Company won another bid with MassPort as they were the successful bidders to rehabilitate and build a new pier system at Castle Island South Boston. This contract price was a little shy of $5 million also. The move to somewhat diversify had been acted upon. Although, the majority of work being performed was still EPA and sewer/drain-related work, the transformation to 'other' work had begun.

The new office location at 2277 Massachusetts Avenue across town in Cambridge was rapidly being renovated. The objective was for Modern Continental to occupy the basement area and the first floor of the building and have the upper two floors become apartments that could be rented out for additional income. With the rapid growth, the renovated building would provide the much-needed additional space. The renovations called for the basement area to be completely remodeled as this area would be prime office space. Along with Billy Durkin Senior, the carpentry foreman, Frank Kalendike, one of Dale Flynn's concrete guys was taking care of the concrete portion of the work. The basement had been dug out and the floor lowered so that proper headroom could be established. Therefore, a new concrete floor would now have to be poured into the basement.

It was early on a Thursday morning that Frank Kalendike had ordered a full load of cement from Boston Sand & Gravel Company so that the new basement floor could be poured. Upon the arrival of the cement truck, Frank took into consideration, the narrow ally to the right of the front of the building that was adjacent to the neighboring mixed-use, retail, and apartment complex as being the most logical location to place the cement truck when it made the pour. This neighboring building was a circa late 1800s-built building with a field stone foundation. When the cement truck arrived, Frank directed him down the narrow ally which would allow the cement truck driver to put his cement chute through the basement window opening to make the process a little easier. As the big, fully loaded cement truck crossed the sidewalk and started traveling down the ally, it got about halfway down the lane when all of a sudden, without warning, and looking as if someone had just shot an elephant, the cement truck toppled to its right and fell into the adjacent building. Apparently, the fieldstone foundation of the aged 1800s building could not support the tremendous weight of the cement truck as the stone wall foundation collapsed under the very heavy weight of the cement truck.

With a look of surprise and a bit of terror, Frank Kalendike watched as the truck was leaning into the building on its side. The new safety edicts that had been put in place required that when an accident took place Bill Shields needed to be contacted immediately. Frank Kalendike ran over to the pay phone that was on the corner and in a panic called Modern Continental's office and asked for Bill Shields. Fortunately, Bill was in the office and told Frank to call the police and fire department and that he would be there as soon as possible.

Like Batman leaving the bat Cave, Bill Shields raced to the site and immediately noticed upon observation that there was a hissing sound and a strong odor of natural gas coming from the basement of the building. Assuming that a gas pipe had been ruptured and fearing a gas explosion, Bill frantically began ringing door buzzers in the apartments and then noticed the guy in the window of the laundry located on the street level of the building busily ironing a white dress shirt on an ironing board. Bill motioned for the man to get out of the building, after looking puzzled he finally understood and told the people working with him to vacate the premises. The police and fire departments arrived and took over the evacuation efforts. When Frank Kalendike called the police and fire department, he also had the good sense to call the gas company as well. Not long after the police and fire departments arrived a representative from Boston Gas Company showed up and turned off the gas to the building. A major disaster had been averted. Now the problem was how do you get a fully loaded cement truck out from the side of a building?

The TV camera crews showed up in force and microphones were being shoved in the face of just about anyone who was walking around the job site. A gag order was put in place by Bill Shields and he asked the TV people to please move out from the area so that the emergency response people could do their jobs. A make-shift conduit system was put in place so that the concrete could be taken out of the truck to reduce the weight. The material was emptied into the basement of the Modern Continental building that was being built and once the weight had been reduced, a crane was brought in to lift the truck to get it standing upright again. The process took the better part of the day, but by late in the afternoon, the cement truck was removed and the side of the building boarded up and secured. The fire drill was over!

****

The pier job at Castle Island South Boston was being run by John Malm. A new section of fender cross bracing had to be installed along with driving new piles to create another portion of the pier. This work was the primary segment to be performed in addition to removing the old and installing new concrete abutments. Technically, this job was a 'marine' job that put a different set of rules, regulations, and statutes in place to comply with. The funding for this project was through the United States Department of Transportation. This federally funded project had a provision that required a minority subcontractor to perform 17% of the work. This would amount to $850,000.00 which was a significant amount of work. At the time of the bid, the subcontractor that Modern Continental carried to perform this work was a small contractor that they had used previously on a couple of jobs and hoped that he could adapt to take care of this portion of work. The subcontractor was Metro Boston Contracting which was owned by Dan Fernandez.

Dan Fernandez had previously worked for Franki Pile Corporation as a pile driver. However, transforming his fledgling operation into a bona fide pile-driving company could be a bit of a stretch. After meeting with Danny Fernandez from Metro Boston Contracting, it was established that Dan Fernandez did have the know-how, and expertise to perform the pile-driving work that was assigned to him. The only problem was he didn't have any money to rent a pile-driving machine or to buy the piles that needed to be driven.

After an in-depth meeting and tossing ideas back and forth, it was determined that the only way that Metro Boston Contracting could perform their portion of the work at Castle Island South Boston was to be assisted by Modern Continental. No bank or lending company would lend money to a small minority contractor that had no collateral or experience. The same held true that an equipment rental company would not rent a high-priced specialty pile-driving machine to someone who could not pay for it. The possibility of getting a line of credit with the company that sold the wooden piles was not a practicality as well. In an effort to show good faith and to help a struggling minority contractor get a chance to prove that they could perform work in a proficient and professional manner, Modern Continental Construction Company assisted Metro Boston Contracting with their efforts to become a qualified contracting company.

As the old saying, *no good deed goes unpunished*, the good faith effort made by Modern Continental to help out Metro Boston Contracting was not recognized by the United States Department of Transportation minority business liaison office. Not long after the work was performed by Metro Boston Contracting, Bill Shields, the Modern Continental minority business compliance officer received a call from the US DOT legal department, and a meeting was requested with them to explain why the minority business commitment for this project was $850,000.00 but that Metro Boston Contracting was only paid $450,000.00 the US DOT wanted an explanation and was going to issue a 'cease and desist' order on the job if the problem was not rectified.

The meeting took place at the Federal Building across from City Hall Plaza in Boston. The attorney from the US DOT minority business liaison office demanded an explanation as to why Metro Boston Contracting was short-changed. Bill Shields brought all of the records that related to the Castle Island South Boston Project and explained that Metro Boston Contracting could not afford to rent a machine and did not have the money to buy the piles and materials needed to perform the work. It was explained that without the help of Modern Continental to assist Metro Boston Contracting, they would never have been able to perform the work and would not have received the experience necessary for them to become a viable entity and a seasoned contractor.

Bill further explained that the contract price of $850,000.00 was honored and that $400,000.00 of that amount was the cost of the piles, materials, and the price for renting a pile-driving machine, which Modern Continental paid for on behalf of Metro Boston Contracting. Once the situation was properly explained, the US DOT apologized and actually commended Modern Continental for its positive actions. The new crops were growing for Modern Continental, it just took a little more watering to get them to finally blossom.

Chapter Eleven
And Away We Go!

1980–1983

What is necessary is never a risk—Les Marino

Palmer, Massachusetts
Massachusetts Turnpike-Mile Marker 60.1
West Bound, Exit #8, Local Route #32 Bridge (Main Street)
Monday, 12 May 1980
11:19 a.m.

The flashing blue lights on the Massachusetts State Trooper-1980 Ford Crown Victoria Sedan were clearly evident as you approached the bridge that crosses over Main Street—Route #32 in Palmer, Massachusetts. The flashing yellow arrow boards and the bright orange signs provided ample warning, but the flashing blue lights really caught your attention and slowed you down as you approached the work zone. The laborers were busy with jackhammers as they removed the old concrete on the bridge deck so that new steel reinforcing rods and wire mesh could be installed over the sections of steel beams on the bridge that were originally installed in the late 1950s.

Cliff Simula, the Modern Continental superintendent on the Massachusetts Turnpike bridge deck project was familiar with the area as he lived a couple of towns away in Hubbardston, Massachusetts. Cliff had been with the company since the start of the Bellows Falls, Vermont sewer project in 1976. His sidekick Tommy Padula, who covered as the foreman on the job also lived close by in Belchertown, Massachusetts. Tommy had been working on the Agawam sewer project but because of the influx of new work, he was helping Cliff out with the demolition portion of the bridge decks. The transition to moderate the type of work that Modern Continental was involved with now included sewer, drain, and water pipework along with airport runways, waterfront pier work, and the renovation of aged bridge decks on the Massachusetts Turnpike. This project in Palmer was just one of many that the Massachusetts Turnpike Authority would be putting out to bid in the near future, as the aged bridge decks needed updating.

Cliff was knee-deep in his 'on-the-job training' as this type of work is something new for Modern Continental. He was learning as the job progressed. It's not all that involved, it includes jackhammer work to break up the existing concrete, evaluate the condition of the existing steel reinforcing rods and replace what the state engineer deemed necessary, and sandblasting the salvageable steel rods. Once the new subsurface material is replaced, or rehabilitated, then new concrete is poured to complete the process. The work is somewhat monotonous and labor intensive, but once the process begins it moves along in a repetitious manner. There are a total of four bridge decks to be replaced, two in each direction, westbound and then eastbound. The work is seasonal and must be completed by early October before the snow flies.

****

It's hard to believe that in addition to the Massachusetts Turnpike Bridge deck work that was taking place in early 1980, Modern Continental Construction Company had an additional nine construction projects in progress. The construction company work did not include the operations that Modern Continental Enterprises was involved with. Brad Bumpus had been very busy identifying additional opportunities other than the management of the four City of Boston Parking Garages for the non-construction segment of the firm to get involved. It had been recognized by Brad Bumpus that there was a market associated with the exporting of exotic seafood products to both Europe and many Asia locations.

What most New England fishermen, specifically those located on the east coast, would consider a major nuisance if they were deep sea fishing and caught one, turned out to be somewhat of a delicacy in the British Isles. Dogfish, also known as a mud shark is used as a Cod substitute for fish and chips in the United Kingdom. Mild and slightly sweet when fried, the meat turns white and is quite enjoyable to the taste buds of the English connoisseur. In addition to exporting dogfish, Modern Continental Enterprises also found a market for another type of shark known as 'skate fish'. The wings of this shark are meaty and edible and are known as 'skate wings'. Along with the United Kingdom, many Asian nations also devour this edible treat which tastes like and can be a substitute for sea scallops.

The third type of seafood that Modern Continental Enterprises became involved with was lobsters. Yes, the New England staple that was once in such abundance and so plentiful that they were considered a nuisance and were served exclusively to prisoners as a type of torture and penalty for being incarcerated. Although the cost can be expensive nowadays, fresh New England lobsters in Japan are such a luxury that the seller can pretty much name their price for these tasty crustaceans.

Needless to say, shipping fresh seafood to faraway locations can be risky. Flight delays, mechanical breakdowns, and weather conditions could capsize the effort to cash in on these products. This is what made the process so intriguing to Les Marino. Pulling off, what most other entrepreneurs could not was a challenge that Les would take in a heartbeat!

In order to process the dogfish, skatefish wings, and lobsters, Modern Continental Enterprises opened a fish processing plant in Everett, Massachusetts. Being plentiful, cheap, and easy to catch made the acquisition of these products readily available. Well, the dogfish and skatefish were readily available; the lobsters were a different situation. Two fishing boats based out of Gloucester, Massachusetts, fished exclusively for Modern Continental Enterprises for dogfish and skatefish. Lobster transactions were through a different arrangement. There was quite a bit of legwork involved with the overall undertaking of this exotic seafood operation. However, the initial introduction of the products proved successful and very profitable.

There was one downside to the processing of dogfish and skatefish, sharks, unlike most other ocean-going fish, retain their uric acid, as such, sharks do not 'pee!' Therefore, when you filet a shark, there is an immediate, very strong smell of ammonia. The smell is so pungent that the fish processors needed to wear disposable clothing and face masks. A situation that would eventually become an issue. The people in the Everett neighborhood, where the fish processing plant was located, did not like the lingering smell that the fish processing left in their neighborhood.

Through the efforts of Brad Bumpus, another opportunity also became available. A once elegant residential building located in the Beacon Hill section of Boston, which through a lack of attention and care became somewhat rundown, was available for sale. Charles Gate Manor had become a transient residential building and rooming house that included short-term tenants and those in need of an overnight place to sleep. The building had tremendous potential and was in a very advantageous location. The former 'Charlesgate Hotel' was built in 1901 and was a Romanesque Revival-style building with a conical tower on the northwest corner of the structure. It also had beautiful copper cladding at the bottom of the buildings projecting bay windows.

The intent would be to renovate and upgrade the property with the ultimate goal of selling the building to one of the colleges in the area, either Boston University or Emerson College. It took some time to make a transition from a rooming house to a vacant building and then get the permits in place to improve the quality of the location. Ultimately, after both structural and cosmetic refurbishing that was performed by the Modern Continental Construction Company's artisans and craftsmen, the building was sold to Emerson College and used as student housing.

With the workload constantly increasing, in both Modern Continental Construction and Modern Continental Enterprises, it was necessary to add some key people to the payroll. Looking to find someone young and impressionable with no bad habits, Les Marino had Bill Shields put a call into the Engineering Department at Northeastern University with the hope of connecting with an engineering student that would be looking for a 'work-study' opportunity. The connection was in fact made, as Bob Berry, who was in his junior year at Northeastern came in for an interview with Modern Continental Construction Company. He was a smart and congenial young man who was eager to become involved with the company.

His first assignment was to work on the Fall River, Massachusetts project that involved a unique application, as the original sewer system that was installed at the turn of century was made of brick and was collapsing, and in a deteriorated condition. The replacement of the original sewer system was cost-prohibitive for the city of Fall River. However, an alternative was designed that would allow the original system to stay in place but be updated. The process to be employed relating to the update was called 'slip lining'. The method used, involved high-impact polypropylene pipe that was fused together by 'butt welding' which allowed twenty-foot sections of pipe to be fused together to create a long cylinder of up to 100 feet long that could be installed in the existing brick sewer system. This method was cost-effective and very practical as it provided a strong and updated sewer system for a fraction of what it would cost to completely excavate and replace the existing sewer pipelines. The Modern Continental superintendent on the Fall River job was Al Santos. Bob Berry worked as the office engineer and provided valuable assistance regarding the progress reports and related contract information. Bob Berry would also interact with Kenny Anderson who was the project manager for this particular venture.

Bob Berry would eventually become a most important and intricate part of the future Modern Continental Construction Company. He did indeed become an impressionable and an excellent and influential student that Les Marino would mold into someone who thought and reasoned in the same manner that he did. Bob's contributions with regard to the work that was bid would eventually play a big part in the overall success of the company.

The position of 'purchasing agent' had not been formally filled since the abrupt departure of Paul Arabakian in late 1979. This position was one of great importance to the company as any savings on the purchasing of materials would ultimately equate to profit. There would be no more trial and error hiring of an employee's relative; this time a trusted and knowledgeable candidate was needed to take charge of this essential function. As was somewhat customary for Les Marino, when an important decision had to be made, he would look back on situations that might be influential with regard to past relationships and friendships that he had cultivated over the years. Sure enough, an old name came to mind of someone who had helped him out in the past. The old friend remembered was George Gardner whom Les had hired when he put together survey parties way back when he was associated with Jack Riciardi in the now-defunct Geodetic Engineering Company.

Les got in touch with George Gardner and discussed with him the position of purchasing agent. Again, Les was depending more on loyalty and past performance rather than on expert qualifications. Hiring George Gardner to be the purchasing agent would allow Les to mold George into the person who could perform the duties in the manner that Les would do the job. Les Marino and Kenny Anderson had never deviated from their initial and core beliefs that in order to be successful in business you needed to surround yourself with like-minded and like-thinking people. George Gardner agreed to assume the role of purchasing agent for Modern Continental Construction Company. With the position now filled with someone that Les felt comfortable with, this would allow Les and Bruce Rapoza to work with someone who understood what was needed and knew how to efficiently acquire the materials and properly negotiate with the subcontractors that were approached for pricing relating to jobs that were being bid and would need subcontractors to perform specific work.

It was in the fall of 1980 that what had been suspected by some people working at the 905 Main Street Cambridge location actually came to fruition. The once, somewhat budding romance between the cute receptionist Roseanne and the handsome and ever determined, and ambitious co-owner of Modern Continental, Kenny Anderson, finally became confirmed and firmly established. Kenny and Roseanne had fallen in love! It was in the spring of 1981 that their wedding took place.

It was also in the early spring of 1981, that the transition and move from the somewhat crowded and cramped office at 905 Main Street, to the new and much more spacious office location at 2277 Massachusetts Avenue in Cambridge took place. The move was desperately needed as the conditions at 905 Main Street had become overcrowded. The new office provided the much-needed organizational and departmental alignment that could not be established at the 905 Main Street office. The accounting and payroll people were in the lower level of the building. The first floor provided a reception area with a front corner office for Les Marino. Edna Hughes occupied the first-floor office at the opposite end of the first level. The engineering and purchasing departments also occupied the first level along with a secretarial room which included copying and teletype machines. The second and third levels of the building had been set up as residential apartments but were not occupied as Les Marino wanted to monitor the growth of the company and did not want to commit to any long-term lease situations if the need to expand the office came about in the not-too-distant future. The 905 Main Street space was 700 square feet. The two levels now occupied at 2277 Massachusetts Avenue totaled almost 2,000 square feet with an additional 1,900 square feet of residential space also available between the second and third levels of the new building.

Although there were still many EPA-funded sewer projects being advertised and bid on in the early 1980s, the decision to diversify and expand the scope of work being performed by Modern Continental Construction Company was well underway. By 1981, the mix had become almost a 50/50 split between sanitary sewer projects and non-sewer-related work that was being performed.

The major sewer project that had been underway for going on two years now in the Harrison Avenue area of Boston, involved the Boston Redevelopment Authority (BRA). This organization had specific and somewhat stringent constraints relating to minority participation in any of the projects that they were involved with. There was a 50% Boston resident employee requirement along with a 17% minority and 6% women employee obligation. The key to compliance was that a 'good faith' effort must be made to fulfill these obligations. As Modern Continental Construction was a 'union' company, this meant that the workforce must be union members, and the employee participation that was needed, had to be provided by the various unions that were providing Modern Continental with workers. In the early 1980s, there was a minimal amount of Boston residents, minorities, and especially women who were members of the various unions that were providing workers for the jobs. Therefore, requests were made in writing to each union and documented to show that the 'good faith' effort was being made to comply with the BRA requirements.

Bill Shields, in addition to the safety duties that he was involved with for the company, was also the minority business and employee liaison person who kept track of the compliance situations relating to minority employee and subcontractor activities. Bill would both phone and then follow up in writing with requests for Boston residents, minorities, and women employees from the various unions that were involved in the contract work that was taking place for the BRA. A relationship had also been established with the Contractors Association of Boston (CAB) which was an organization that promoted the use of minority contractors to fulfill obligations necessary to meet compliance requirements of the BRA and other organizations. Bill Shields had developed a very strong relationship with Gerry Cofield who was the director of CAB. Quite a few of the subcontractors that Gerry had recommended were now performing work for Modern Continental.

It was on a Friday morning that Bill Shields received a call from Ronnie Mason, the minority compliance officer for the Boston Redevelopment Authority. Mr. Mason let Bill know, that with no uncertain terms, his presence was requested for a meeting in his office at 2:00 p.m. that afternoon. Bill was not sure exactly what this meeting might pertain to but he had a pretty good idea that it had to do with compliance efforts on the Harrison Avenue project.

Fortunately, with Modern Continental Enterprises managing and operating the city of Boston parking garage facility near Faneuil Hall getting a parking spot was not a problem. Actually, Bill Shields would make this a dual effort as he could check the safety at the parking garage when he parked there. Ronnie Mason's office was in Boston City Hall which was a relatively short walk from Faneuil Hall. Upon arriving at Mr. Mason's office, Bill was escorted into his office. Ronnie Mason got up and went over and shut the door to his office as Bill sat down in the chair that was in front of his desk. Ronnie Mason proceeded to take out a folder and opened it; he looked at the numbers on the page and then with a stern and determined look, he let Bill Shields know that these documents showed that Modern Continental was not meeting the minority participation that was required.

Ronnie Mason was doing his best to make Bill Shields feel uncomfortable. He went on to let Bill know that he had the power to notify the Federal Authorities and let them know if a contractor was not in compliance with regard to minority participation on a federally funded project. If he did contact the Federal Authorities, it would surely jeopardize the contractor's ability to bid on any more federally funded projects. Ronnie let Bill know that Modern Continental's numbers were not up to snuff. He then, put the folder aside and directly looked into the eyes of Bill Shields and said, "I'm about to call the Feds and have them bar your company from ever bidding on any more federally funded work, which would most likely put your company out of business." He then paused and said, "Or you can buy me a new Buick Electra and I won't make the call."

Bill Shields was somewhat mystified and perplexed by this conversation. It took a moment for the facts of the matter to really sink in. Bill tried his best to compose himself but he knew that their numbers, no matter how much documentation he had, did not meet compliance. Trying not to show that he was about to break into a cold sweat and that he was close to throwing up on his desk, he then replied, "Geez Ronnie, I don't have that authority, can you give me a couple of days to get back to you?"

Ronnie Mason then smiled, looked at Bill Shields and said, "Sure, come back here at 2:00 o'clock on Tuesday afternoon and let me know at which dealer I can pick the car up." Bill got up and left the office with his head spinning over what had just taken place.

The Boston traffic on any Friday afternoon is historically brutal as everyone is trying to escape for the weekend. Bill got back to the office in Cambridge as quickly as he could. Upon entering the front door of the building, Bill climbed the four stairs up to the reception area and then looked to his right to see if Les Marino was in his office. Les was there talking to Edna Hughes who was standing in front of his desk. Bill caught Les's attention and asked if he could have a word with him. Les finished up with Edna and then asked Bill what he needed. Bill proceeded to turn and then close the office door. Les looked a little concerned as Bill explained to him what had just taken place at Ronnie Mason's office. Les's face went blank as he absorbed what he was being told. Les then picked up the phone and called the office of Herman Snyder, the company attorney. Mr. Snyder's secretary put Les on hold and then got back on the line and told Les that Mr. Snyder wanted Les and Bill Shields to come to his office right away.

Although the company had done a few 'favors' for a couple of people that the company was associated with and it was no secret that almost every contractor that was doing business with the city of Boston and The Commonwealth of Massachusetts did, on occasion, provide a bottle of liquor as a gesture of gratitude and thanks, being solicited for an outright bribe was a first for the company. This particular situation was not something that Les Marino wanted to be involved with.

The traffic was just as bad going back into Boston as it had been coming out of the city a few minutes ago. Upon arrival at the State Street law office of Snyder, Tepper & Berlin, Les, and Bill were brought directly into Mr. Snyder's office. Upon sitting down Les turned to Bill and said, "Go ahead Bill, tell Mr. Snyder what happened this afternoon." Bill let Mr. Snyder know exactly what took place that afternoon at the office of Ronnie Mason at the Boston Redevelopment Authority (BRA). Mr. Snyder listened with great interest as Bill told the story.

Mr. Snyder was leaning back in his plush leather chair, with the thumb and index finger of his right hand slowly rubbing his chin as he thought about the situation. He then paused for a moment and looked directly at Bill Shields and said, "So, this compliance issue, there are many other contractors doing work for the BRA in the city, right?"

Bill Shields nervously replied, "Yes, there are quite a few contractors that are doing work for the BRA in the same area that we are currently working."

Mr. Snyder continued, "So, how are your compliance numbers compared to theirs?"

Bill sat up and with a look of certainty, proudly announced, "Modern Continental's compliance numbers are the best in the city. I've documented every request to each union regarding the need for them to provide Modern Continental with the city of Boston residents, minority and women union members."

Mr. Snyder then, sat forward in his chair and looked closely at Bill Shields, and said, "Call his bluff!"

Bill, a little cautious, looked over at Les for some direction on the matter, Les was just sitting there taking in what was being discussed and offered no visible response, Bill, then replied to Mr. Snyder, "So, you think I should go back to Ronnie Mason's office at 2:00 o'clock on Tuesday and tell him that we are not going to buy him the Buick Electra?"

Mr. Snyder, somewhat annoyed at Bill's questioning his directive lets him know, "Yes, I figure this guy has probably called in every other contractor doing work for the BRA and has pulled the same thing with them, tell him to call the Feds, we would have no trouble resolving the matter with them, I'm sure of that!"

On Tuesday afternoon, at precisely 2:00 p.m., Bill Shields showed up at Ronnie Mason's office. He was ushered into his office by his secretary and stood in front of his desk. Ronnie Mason, with a smug look on his face, leaned back in his chair and put his hands behind his head as he asked, "So, where and when do I pick up my new Buick Electra?"

Bill Shields moved to the side of his desk and reached for the phone and then he slid it in front of him and told him, "Call the Feds!"

It was observed by numerous sources about a week later, Ronnie Mason was seen driving a brand new shiny red Buick Electra. Mr. Snyder was absolutely correct, Ronnie Mason must have pulled the same act on all the other contractors that were doing work for the BRA; one of them apparently took the bait!

It was in the fall of 1981 that Modern Continental Construction Company made another move in their diversification transition as they were the successful bidders on an MBTA commuter rail rehabilitation project on the

Hamilton-Wenham section of the Newburyport to Boston commuter rail line. The work would include the replacement of rail, railroad ties, and stone ballast from Beverly to Ipswich. This railroad project was a first for Modern Continental Construction Company. Kenny Anderson would oversee the project and interact with the MBTA project manager, Chris Lincoln.

Getting involved with the Massachusetts Bay Transportation Authority (MBTA) was a significant accomplishment for the company that had been exclusively involved with being a 'sewer contractor'. Securing their first railroad job was just the beginning of what would become a lucrative relationship with the MBTA. Performing work for the MBTA had its concerns. The work needed to be performed within a specific time frame. The rail system would remain live throughout the project which meant that one-way track service from Newburyport to Boston had to be maintained which involved delicate communications with the railroad flagging and safety personnel.

The Hamilton-Wenham MBTA railroad project proved to be a beneficial addition to the broadening type of projects that Modern Continental Construction Company was becoming involved with. The aged systems that were in place for the MBTA in addition to the plans for expansion of their operations would open a big door for Modern Continental. However, the inner workings of the MBTA were significantly different from the awarding authorities that Modern Continental had previously been involved with. The payment requisitions and the extra work orders were handled in a manner that included numerous layers of bureaucracy. Even Bob Wetherbee, Modern Continentals engineering whiz-kid, who was quite proficient at expediting payments and appropriations, was running into brick wall roadblocks that he could not navigate. The work was being performed but the payments were difficult to obtain.

Chris Lincoln, the MBTA project manager on the Hamilton-Wenham project was intelligent and quite savvy. He did a good job directing and coordinating the various benchmarks that needed to be accomplished on the job. Les Marino became concerned that the payment requests that were being made to the MBTA did not get processed in the timely manner that he was accustomed to. The project was about 70% completed but Modern Continental had only received about 50% of their payments.

It was in the spring of 1982 when Les Marino took a ride out to the Hamilton-Wenham MBTA project with a distinct objective. He had set up an on-site meeting with the MBTA project manager Chris Lincoln. Upon arrival at the job site, Les went around the job and took a look at what was taking place; he then approached Chris Lincoln and asked him to take a walk with him. Les and Chris took a leisurely stroll along the side of the railroad tracks. The countryside in this Hamilton Massachusetts location was absolutely beautiful. The pink dogwood trees and the bright yellow forsythia plants along the side of the easement were in full bloom, the air was filled with the pleasant fragrance of budding flora as the two leisurely walked and talked.

As Les Marino and Chris Lincoln arrived back at the staging area, Bill Shields had just pulled onto the site to perform a job site safety review. He parked his car and walked over to the area near where Les and Chris were standing, upon his approach, Les motioned to Bill to come over to them. Bill quickly stepped up his pace as he caught up to them. Les, with a smile on his face, let Bill know, "Say hello to the newest member of the Modern Continental staff, Chris Lincoln."

Bill Shields with a quizzical look on his face stuck out his hand to Chris Lincoln and told him, "Welcome to the company."

In an effort to stabilize the new MBTA work division that was being formed and with the hopes of overcoming the difficulties that the company had been having with collecting payments, Les made a bold move by snatching Chris Lincoln out of the clutches of the MBTA and making him 'an offer that he couldn't refuse'. It was a genius move, hiring someone who knew the inside corridors of the MBTA and having a person who could navigate the convoluted process that was involved with acquiring timely payments. It was a two-fold success as Chris Lincoln was a very bright and promising project manager who could assist with any work that was acquired from the MBTA, and he also had the inside track when it came to expediting the collection of progress payments.

Not long after Chris Lincoln came on board, Modern Continental Construction Company picked up another railroad project. However, this particular railroad job was going to be performed for the federal railroad organization known as 'Conrail' in the Newton-Wellesley area. President Ronald Reagan, in an effort to bolster the missile defense system of the United States of America, had spearheaded a movement to ship ballistic missiles around the country by rail. In order to do this, there had to be a clearance of sixteen feet from the top of the rail to the bottom of any overhead structure. Unfortunately, the section of track passing through the Wellesley area only had a fourteen-foot clearance. Therefore, as you could not raise the bridges, you would have to lower the track. The section that was being affected would need to have the track lowered by at least two feet. The rail system needed to remain live and functioning so the task at hand would need to be performed in segments. The area in question had inbound and outbound tracks. During the first phase, the inbound track would be taken out of service and the outbound side would be used for travel in both directions. The Conrail people would coordinate the traffic pattern and the switching operations.

Removal of the existing track and the stone ballast would take place first. After the track and stone were removed, the track bed would be lowered to the proper elevation and then new stone and track would be installed. The new track would be continuous welded rail with no separations which would decrease the 'clanking' noise that was common because of the uneven rail connections.

The project superintendent on the Wellesley Conrail job was an old Suburban Construction guy that Les and Kenny had hired when Suburban Construction closed their doors. Sam Melei, the guy that Les and Kenny had both worked for at Suburban Construction back in their early road-building days. He had become a project superintendent for Modern Continental Construction Company. Les Marino was big into recycling way before it was popular; well, the recycling of old friends and acquaintances that is. He never forgot anyone, especially people who left an impression on him and had helped him along the way. Sam was still a hard driver and taskmaster; he might have aged a few years but he still had that burning fire inside of him.

As is somewhat customary, when an opportunity to make a couple of extra bucks presented itself, most project superintendents would take advantage of the situation. The removal of the old ballast stone presented a chance for Sam Melei to make a few extra dollars. The old ballast stone was being hauled by ten-wheel dump trucks to a designated location that had been negotiated prior to the start of the project. However, a couple of local homeowners approached Sam and asked him if they could buy a few truckloads of stone to fill in sections of their property that were low areas and needed to be raised in elevation for better drainage. Sam figured, what the heck, I'll sell them a few truckloads of old ballast stone and make a few dollars.

It was on the morning of July third in 1982, that the proverbial 'shit hit the fan' on the Wellesley Conrail project. Apparently, the Town of Wellesley got wind of the fact that ballast stone from the Conrail project was being diverted and shipped to local residents in Wellesley and not to the agreed-upon designated dumping site. It also became known that the location of a considerable amount of the stone was being placed in an area that was adjacent to the Town of Wellesley underground well site. The well site provided drinking water to much of the town. A problem was identified because the stone that was being dumped had been tested and confirmed that it was treated with chemicals.

It was determined that the insecticide 'dichlorodiphenyltrichloroethane' (DDT) along with numerous other deadly chemicals along with diesel fuel were identified on the ballast stones that had been tested. The Town of Wellesley was not very pleased with contaminated stone being dumped next to the town well system. An immediate cease and desist was ordered. The project was brought to a standstill until the problem could be rectified. The town wanted an explanation as to how this happened, and how it would be corrected, and they wanted answers right away!

On the evening of 3 July, Kenny Anderson, Bill Shields, and Attorney Chuck Schaub from the law office of Snyder. Tepper & Berlin represented Modern Continental, rather than celebrating the eve of Independence Day with their families eating burgers and weenies, had to appear before the Town of Wellesley Selectmen and numerous other town officials to explain how they would solve this contaminated materials problem.

It was agreed that all contaminated stone that had been delivered to residents in the town would be completely removed and any remedial measures necessary would be taken by a certified hazardous material company to alleviate the situation. This action would be taken immediately and the distribution of materials from the job site would be monitored going forward. It was also agreed that weekly testing of the town water supply would be conducted for the next six months at the expense of Modern Continental. Another fire had been extinguished and Sam Melei's source of extra cash was no more!

****

The addition of Chris Lincoln to the Modern Continental Construction staff opened the door for a couple of other key people from the MBTA to be coerced to join the Modern team as well. Charlie Appley another project manager at the MBTA and Sal Tecci, a business development manager at the MBTA also joined Modern Continental within the next couple of months. As a result of these new additions, the office space that was recently occupied at 2277 Massachusetts Avenue in Cambridge was becoming almost as cramped as the 905 Main Street location. In the fall of 1982, Les Marino determined that it would be necessary for the operations of Modern Continental Construction Company and Modern Continental Enterprises to occupy the entire building at 2277 Massachusetts Avenue. Les moved his office upstairs, and the engineering staff, which now included both Bruce Rapoza and Bob Berry took over the third level of the building. This opened up office space for Chris Lincoln and the other recent additions. The company was growing in leaps and bounds!

It did not take long for the Modern Continental Construction Company to take advantage of the newly added MBTA personnel as the long-anticipated construction of the MBTA Green Line tunnel project from Newton to Boston was being advertised for bid. This work would involve the construction of a 'cut and cover' tunnel project. The tunnel would be constructed in three separate, simultaneous contracts. The tunnel work would include the open excavation of the tunnel and when the proper grade was established, a concrete tunnel would be built and then covered. Modern Continental was the successful bidder on the third tunnel section that was to be built. This was a very large contract and would require a considerable amount of manpower to complete the job.

The engineering department had really sharpened their pencils, as right after winning the MBTA Greenline Tunnel project, they were successful in winning the bid to build a large sewer pipe installation project in Tewksbury, Massachusetts. The job in Tewksbury was a unique project. The section of sewer pipe that Modern Continental would be installing was the final section that tied into the new pumping station that had been built on the banks of the Merrimac River. As the sewer pipe is a gravity system, the final section leading to the pumping station would be excessively deep. The majority of the excavation work would be performed at about fifty feet deep.

The engineer's estimate for the completion of the Tewksbury sewer project was $4.1 million. However, Modern Continental's successful bid was $3.2 million, almost a million dollars lower than the engineers estimated. Word of

Modern Continental leaving almost a million dollars on the table as the low bidder was music to the ears of their competitors. Whispers of Modern's demise quickly spread like wildfire throughout the industry. Was this the blunder that would sink the Modern Continental luxury liner that had been cruising along and growing at an unimaginable rate?

The truth was that with a deep cut of fifty feet, no conventional backhoe could dig that deep. The longest mast and arm backhoe on the market could only dig forty-two feet. That would mean that in order to reach the depth of fifty feet, the cut would need to be benched in two sections. The first cut would be twenty-five feet and then a second excavation of twenty-five feet would be needed to reach the proper depth. A necessary and conventional way to dig the deep hole in two separate sections was how the contractors that bid on the job considered accomplishing the task. Ahh, but that was not how Les Marino looked at the job! The ole 'ace up the sleeve' card shark was one step ahead of the competition. Les had done his research; he had located a backhoe that actually had a fifty-two-foot reach. Northwest Equipment Company had built a limited amount of Model #190 backhoes that were primarily used for excavating in salt mines. By acquiring this backhoe, the excavation could be done in one step rather than two as most contractors had considered. Furthermore, the bottom section of the trench was noted to include a considerable amount of rock which would need to be blasted. The rock section on the lower part of the trench would be advantageous as no shoring would be needed to prevent the sides of the trench from collapsing.

Delivery of the Northwest-190 backhoe to the Tewksbury job site was like the arrival of a circus to town. A total of ten tractor-trailers were necessary to deliver all of the backhoe's components and parts. This big white machine looked like a white elephant as it was being put together. The Town of Tewksbury became almost a tourist destination as many curious contractors paraded by the assembly area as they watched this phenomenon being put together.

The project went off like clockwork as all of the pieces fit together as Modern Continental breezed through the project in record-breaking time. The coordination of digging and blasting was timely as the process progressed and the sewer pipe was installed. Although the many naysayers had predicted doom and gloom for Modern Continental Construction Company on the Tewksbury project, and believed that this would be the end of the company, the bottom line was that when all the digging and blasting was done and the pipe was installed, Modern Continental recognized a solid one-million-dollar profit on the job, and a big sigh of relieve from their bonding company!

****

By 1983, both Modern Continental Construction Company and Modern Continental Enterprises had fully blossomed. The diversification of Modern Continental Construction had been successful as the company was now involved with railroad work, the building of a tunnel, marine work, bridge deck rehabilitation, building site work, and numerous sewer projects. Modern Continental Enterprises was involved with managing parking garages, the renovation of a large hotel complex and they recently purchased two brownstone apartment buildings on Commonwealth Avenue that were being converted into condominiums.

It was in early 1983 that Brad Bumpus began a project that involved the acquisition of a rundown bar room that was located on Massachusetts Avenue not too far up the street from the 2277 Massachusetts Avenue office location. The 'Green Parrot' was known as kind of a biker's bar that did not have the best reputation in the Cambridge Massachusetts community. The thought process was for Modern Continental Enterprises to acquire this location and to buy the liquor license. Obtaining a liquor license in Cambridge Massachusetts was not an easy task. Les Marino had visions of someday knocking down the Green Parrot building and constructing a new complex that eventually would be a high-end gourmet restaurant, lounge, and function facility.

****

The city of Boston, Mayor Kevin White, had done a very good job of developing many areas and bringing major business and retail establishments to the city of Boston during his tenure as mayor which began in 1968. However, there was one section of Boston that had been a continuous eye-sore for the city for many years; the area known as 'the combat zone'. This section of Boston included the 'adult entertainment district' which was home to strip clubs, peep shows, X-rated movies, and a collection of streetwalkers that would provide additional 'adult entertainment'. During the Second World War and into the 1960s, the port of Boston, with a very active Naval Ship Yard, was home port to many of the well-known fighting ships such as the aircraft carriers, the Essex and the Wasp which were repaired and rebuilt at the navy yard, allowed many sailors and marines to spend time in the city. The 'combat zone' was a popular place for America's fighting men to let off a little steam when they were in port!

With the Navy Yard now closed, Mayor Kevin White had visions of transforming this seedy section of Boston into a tourist-friendly location. He introduced his idea to transform the area into two vibrant sections. One would be 'Lafayette Place' which would include a large hotel complex and retail space and the other would be known as 'downtown crossing' which would be a shopper's paradise that contained the Jordan Marsh Store and Filenes Department Store which included the famous Filene's basement. All sorts of enticements were offered, including deferred taxes and adding that the city of Boston would encompass, and pay for the installation of utilities and appurtenances to the buildings that would be built in this area. Not long after introducing his projections to the public, Mayor White acted upon his proposal and put out to bid a contract that included site work and foundation stabilization, and the installation of utilities, including, city water and sewer connections. This was a rather large site work contract that Modern Continental Construction Company was fortunate enough to acquire.

****

The core groups that had been the back bone of the company for many years were still intact. This would include the Valentim family and the Fall River/New Bedford connections, along with Dale Flynn and his group of carpenters. There had also been another stalworth group of Modern Continental employees that came from the Northshore, 'Cape Ann' area, which included Gloucester, Rockport, Manchester-by-the-sea, and Beverly Massachusetts. This group included Brad Carpenter, Joe Ginn, Glenn Parisi, Bobby Wogan, and a young fellow who had recently come on board after his active duty as a member of a reconnaissance unit in the United States Marine Corp. Mike Pivero.

Modern Continental picked up another, site work development project in downtown Boston of which, Dale Flynn would be the project manager and

Mike Pivero would become the foreman on this job site. This project was part of the newly acquired site work project that Modern Continental Construction had successfully negotiated, which included excavation, site work, shoring, and concrete work for the building of the new Four Seasons Hotel in the Park Square section of Boston.

The overall growth of Modern Continental during the period of 1980, through 1983 was phenomenal. The transition from a 'sewer contractor' to a full-fledged general contracting conglomerate had been accomplished. The addition of key personnel to the company, along with having the foresight to understand that change is inevitable and in order to survive you need to adapt. That fact, and having the outright audacity to take chances and calculated risks that most conventional contractors would never take, were many contributing factors to this anomaly, but the driving force would always be Les Marino and Kenny Anderson. Their friendship only got stronger as the company continued to grow. Sunday dinner still took place, Les and Kenny just had more things to chat about when they sat down to eat!

Chapter Twelve
New Kids on the Block

1983–1986

There is but one secret to success—never give up!—Kenny Anderson

Cambridge, Massachusetts
2277 Massachusetts Avenue
Modern Continental Construction Company Office
Friday, 16 September 1983
5:29 p.m.

The four burners on the stove in the third-floor kitchen were all occupied. Pots were bubbling as the fragrant smell of Italian tomato sauce filled the air. A hint of garlic, a smidgen of onion, and a whiff of basil tickled the senses. The Friday night feast was being prepared.

Les Marino was busy putting the finishing touches on what he considered his personal favorite meal, 'spaghetti alla Bolognese'. He had got an apron wrapped around his waist as he added a pinch of salt to the pot of boiling water on the front left burner of the stove.

When Les Marino decided to move his office to the third level of the office building at 2277 Massachusetts Avenue, he knew that the location was originally set up as a residential apartment and that there was a full kitchen included. Being a man of many talents, but not often having the time to accomplish everything that he would like to, he had decided to treat the lingering die-hard guys who spent a few minutes after work enjoying a cocktail or two before heading home to a fabulous meal that he decided to put together. This was not the first time that Les had prepared a meal for the boys on a Friday night; he enjoyed cooking and Friday nights seemed to bring out the chef in him. The past few Fridays had been kind of a guest chef night as last week Bill Shields made a couple of pizzas for the crew and the week before, Sal Tecci treated everyone to chicken and broccoli alfredo. Tonight, Les Marino had taken back the apron and was feverishly chopping and sauteing as he sipped on a Bud Natural Light.

****

The hard work, kick ass and take names later environment that took place every Monday through Friday at Modern Continental eased a little come Friday nights. The third level suite that Les and the engineering/bidding team had secured for their work area had a kitchen and dining area that was set up with a counter that had stools like a bar and a couple of easy chairs and a sofa. On Friday nights, it became the Modern Continental club house. With the five o'clock traffic at a standstill in Cambridge, the guys figured that relaxing and having a cocktail or two and leaving a little later seemed to work as the traffic had eased up and they got home at the same time anyway. It also gave the guys a chance to catch up with each other and find out what was going on with the various jobs that each was involved with.

The old adage of *all work and no play makes Jack a dull boy* is so very true. As an almost cult environment had been created with regard to the work ethic that had been instilled in each and every Modern Continental employee, a little break was needed on occasion. The Friday night feasts and the comradery that was created through this event made for a better work situation.

The tradition started not long after the move from 905 Main Street to the 2277 Massachusetts Avenue location. Les and Kenny fully understood that although the work day ended at five o'clock, the wheels in the brains of the managers, superintendents, and project managers were still turning and they needed a chance to slow down. The refrigerator was always stocked with whatever particular beer or wine a guy might drink. The same held true for the liquor cabinet as it was furnished with most high-end spirits. An added treat was that in the fall of each year, Les made a few barrels of homemade wine at the shop location in Stoughton where he created his own vintage. The wine was aged until spring and then a few bottles were brought to the office. It was right around Easter when the wine was introduced. The white wine Les made was exceptionally good, it was nicknamed, 'white lighting' because it snuck up and gave a quick buzz. A two-glass limit was instilled for safety reasons!

****

The fall of 1983 brought a new crop of employees to Modern Continental Construction Company. As the company had transitioned to be more of a conventional General Contractor rather than just the sewer contractor that they had been, the need had been created to hire and bring in some individuals who had more engineering and project manager experience and background. The new kids on the block were Rory Newbauer, Jim Onegian, Steve Harrington, John McNamara, Ward Eisenhauer, and John Pastore. Of the six new employees, four of them would work in the field and two in the office. And there was plenty to keep them all busy!

John Pastore, joined Les Marino, Bruce Rapoza, and Bob Berry in the estimating and bidding department as he would work on the bids and calculate quantities. John Pastore, like Bob Berry, would become a key figure with regard to the future of the company. John, like Bob Berry, was a Northeastern University Engineering School graduate who was young and eager to learn.

Although there were plenty of new faces, it was a couple of the old faces that came forward to steer the Modern Continental luxury liner in the right direction. Cosmo Pallazola took the helm of the Deere Island Project that Modern Continental secured in late 1983 and Kenny Anderson went back to his core roots as he became the project manager of the almost fifteen-million-dollar road-building job in Uxbridge, Massachusetts.

John McNamara, the new project manager, was in charge of the five-million-dollar sewer project on Nantucket Island that Modern Continental was the successful bidder on. A somewhat difficult job as it had to be performed in the 'off season' meaning that the tremendous amount of work that needed to be completed had to be installed between October and May when the tourists and summer residents where not on the island.

Although, he had been confined to the office for many years, the tremendous number of projects that were taking place required that Bruce Rapoza take a sabbatical from bidding and act as a project manager on a dredging project that was to take place at Logan Airport.

In addition to the large road-building project in Uxbridge, Massachusetts Modern Continental Construction picked up another railroad project. This project was for Amtrack and was located in South Boston. The project included the building of a transportation building which in the old days would have been called a 'round house', although it was not round. This job also included a fair amount of track work and there was utility work involved that included sewer and drain pipe installation. Jim Onegian worked on this project along with Mike Pivero. However, it was Chris Lincoln who was responsible for the coordination and expeditious manner in which the job moved forward. Chris Lincoln's experience with railroad nomenclature and his amiable personality helped this over ten-million-dollar project to be a very successful and profitable one.

It was in early 1984 that opportunity knocked for a couple of the Modern Continental employees who had been very instrumental in the early success of the company. Bob Wetherbee and George Gardner were presented with an opportunity to create their own construction company. The two left Modern and started Garweth Construction Company. They got in on the ground floor of the newly created cell phone industry sensation that was just beginning to take place. George and Bob secured a contract to erect cell phone towers for Cellular One which was part of AT&T.

What has always been a bit of a mystery, the resignation of Brad Bumpus from Modern Continental Enterprises also took place in early 1984. He had pretty much single-handedly spearheaded a fledgling operation and created some extraordinary and profitable business development opportunities. Brad had successfully completed his Master of Business Administration (MBA) and perhaps decided to seek a favorable position in that field. His presence was sorely missed by the company. Brad had a staff that worked under him for which his prodigy Bob Shepherd moved up and successfully took control of the Modern Continental Enterprise operations.

One of the last negotiations that Brad Bumpus was involved with prior to his leaving Modern Continental Enterprises was that he identified a rather large tract of land in North Reading, Massachusetts that was available for an extremely reasonable price. This section of North Reading was zoned as residential land. After proper due diligence, analysis and assessment, Modern Continental Enterprises purchased this piece of property. The land was accessible from the end of a cul-de-sac which opened up to an area that could accommodate numerous single-family homes. After securing the proper permits, rights of way, and funding, work commenced on the building of an exclusive community. This particular development became one of the most desirable places to own a single-family home in the North Reading community.

With the absence of Bob Wetherbee from Modern Continental Construction, a void had developed with regard to extra work orders and changed condition scenarios that were crucial to the success and profitability of many projects. It's one thing to do the work, it's another to make sure that you get paid for everything that you have actually done. Although not a registered professional engineer like Bob Wetherbee was, Chris Lincoln had a keen eye and a thorough understanding of how contract language was worded. With the assistance of the engineering people who were part of the company, Chris Lincoln took charge of just about all of the issues that related to extra work and changed conditions. Chris had a natural instinct for business and money. His intelligence, abilities, and effort made a distinct difference in how contract payments were made.

By the spring of 1984, the Southwest corridor MBTA tunnel project was well underway. The concept of building a 'cut and cover' tunnel meant that you needed to excavate a tremendous amount of material to build the tunnel. The material that was excavated needed to be dumped somewhere. This was a major part of the operation. Finding a place to dump large amounts of dirt in the Boston area was a daunting task. When the project began, the only location that would accept this much material was the Randolph, Massachusetts former landfill. The Town of Randolph was accepting good clean fill to cap the landfill. Modern Continental Construction Company had hired a local minority contractor that was recommended to them through the Contractors Association of Boston to truck the material away from the site. The trucks being used were tractor-trailer end dumps that could hold a considerable amount of material more than a normal ten-wheel dump truck. These trucks were hired by the hour. As the haul from Roxbury to Randolph in traffic was tedious, an average of four round trips in an eight-hour day were being made by each tractor-trailer. When Les Marino saw that the material hauling portion of the project was going so slowly, he knew that at this rate, the contract pricing relating to the removal of dirt would go way over budget.

During his tenure at Modern Continental Construction, Bill Shields had a chance to develop some very important relationships that would benefit the company. One interesting friendship that he had developed was with an organization known as 'The Boston Natural Resource Fund'. This organization was involved with acquiring vacant pieces of land that became available in the city of Boston. Their intent was to keep the vacant land green and free of any buildings or developments. The director of this group was introduced to Bill Shields during a fund-raising event that he had attended. Mr. John Blackburn was the esteemed director and figurehead of this benevolent organization. Mr. Blackburn was a well-to-do, distinguished, and congenial fellow who had a fascination with construction operations. In an effort to maintain a positive connection with him, Bill Shields would invite him for coffee and while they were together Bill would travel by the construction operations that Modern Continental had going on in the area and show them to Mr. Blackburn. Not long after Bill had a discussion with Les Marino relating to the trucking operations at the MBTA tunnel project and how the trip from Roxbury to Randolph was causing concerns, Bill set up a meeting with Mr. Blackburn.

Upon picking Mr. Blackburn up at his residence on Beacon Hill, they proceeded to a coffee shop on Charles Street. While sipping coffee and chatting, Bill mentioned the situation regarding the removal of soil from Roxbury and how it was taken to Randolph. Bill then inquired if Mr. Blackburn knew of any vacant pieces of land in the Roxbury area that might need some good clean fill. Mr. Blackburn let Bill know that he would inquire about the matter and would let him know if there was an interest.

A couple of days after their meeting, Mr. Blackburn placed a call to Bill Shields and let him know that he had an interested party. It appeared that Mr. Blackburn's high school alma mater, the Roxbury Latin School which is located in West Roxbury, owned a parcel of land adjacent to the school that was once part of a quarry. The big depression if filled in would make an excellent playing field for all types of sports. The inquiry, made by the directors of the school was if it would be possible for Modern Continental to fill in the deep pit and make it into a level playing field for the school. The reply was Modern Continental would and could fill in the former quarry and they would make it into a first-class playing field when it was filled in. The deal was made with The Roxbury Latin School.

As a result of the new location to dump the dirt from the Southwest corridor MBTA tunnel project from the Randolph landfill to The Roxbury Latin School in West Roxbury the tractor-trailer dump trucks increased their round-trip loads from four a day to seventeen a day. This turn of events was a major factor in the profitability of this project. The relationship between Bill Shields and John Blackburn proved to be a beneficial friendship. It was a definite plus that Mr. Blackburn's wife was also a newly elected Boston City Counselor.

The transformation of the company continued as in early 1984, Modern Continental Construction was the successful bidder on a bridge project on

Morrisey Boulevard in Boston, Massachusetts. A new bridge was being constructed which would span the existing MBTA Red Line tracks. This bridge would have a rather large span with steel beams measuring close to eighty feet. The building of a bridge involved the construction of the abutments which are concrete, the placement of the steel bridge beams, and then the installation of the bridge deck. The primary component in the bridge equation would be the steel beams. Prior to the job being bid, solicitations from steel fabricating companies were made regarding the cost and availability of the steel beams. Cost was important but having the beams be available in a timely manner was just as important. Wilson Steel Fabricators from Everett, Massachusetts provided the lowest cost and indicated that they could fabricate the large beams and have them available within the time frame noted in the bid documents.

Charlie Appley, the former MBTA Manager was chosen as the project manager on the Morrisey Boulevard bridge project (the bridge would eventually be named the Lech Walesa Bridge). It was part of Charlie's duties to coordinate the various segments of the operations that needed to be exercised. Charlie Appley had a solid background and had once worked for a pile-driving company so he knew that the first portion of work would be to drive piles and footings for the bridge abutments. Charlie also had to man the job which included dealing with the various unions so that he could acquire the proper personnel to perform the labor. One of the unions that Charlie had to deal with was the South Boston Chapter of the Laborers Union. It did not take long for the first hiccup to take place on the job. In an effort to start the project with Modern Continental's existing employees, it was identified that not all of the workers were members of the South Boston laborer's local union. The business agent for the South Boston laborer's Union was Pat Walsh (Uncle of future city of Boston Mayor Marty Walsh). Pat Walsh was a feisty Irishman who was fiercely loyal to his local union members. From basically the first day of the project, Pat Walsh and Charlie Appley would go toe to toe on some issue or another on a regular basis.

Having a working relationship with the various unions was very important. If an adversarial relationship existed between the contractor and the union, it could break the project. As Modern Continental got more diversified the work would include more trades which introduced more unions. Equipment operators, laborers, carpenters, cement finishers, bricklayers, and pile drivers were the primary unions that Modern Continental was involved. However, as the company grew and diversified, the various types of union workers would be increased. Relationships with unions could be adversarial if conflicts with personalities existed. Modern Continental Construction did a pretty good job of maintaining an even keel with the unions that they were involved.

****

At this point in the growth of the company, many balls were being juggled and one that was linger high up in the air was the road job in Uxbridge. Uxbridge, Massachusetts was located almost half way between the State of Rhode Island border and Worcester, Massachusetts. The Route #146 relocation project involved the renovation of what had been a local road to a highway. This portion of the roadway would link the already built highway systems that had been completed near Worcester and a completed section near the Rhode Island border. This was a rather large road-building project with a contract price of almost fifteen million dollars.

Kenny Anderson was a busy boy trying to watch over numerous projects. It was the challenge that he craved. The personal pride of leading men and equipment to success was what Kenny seemed to be born for. His tenacity, coupled with Les Marino's ingenuity proved to be a very winning combination.

Chapter Thirteen
The Times, They Are Changing

1986–1989
*A good manager understands that motivation is
the key to success*—Les Marino

Boston, Massachusetts
26 Summer Street, Modern Continental Construction
Office trailer & equipment yard
Thursday, 3 April 1986
8:25 a.m.

Kenny Anderson sat at the drafting table in the office trailer looking at the blue prints as he hastily made some notes in preparation for the upcoming meeting with the Boston Water & Sewer Commission, and their on-site engineering representatives, Camp, Dresser & McKee. The Federal Reserve pipe job as it was referred to, in Boston, had run into some difficulties. The pipe foreman, Joe Rocha let Kenny Anderson know late yesterday afternoon that his crew had run into some very big boulders and that the 40-H Bucyrus-Erie backhoe could not budge them. This posed a problem, as in the 'old days', Joe Ricci would have just drilled a couple of holes in the boulders and stuck some dynamite in them, and then blasted them out of the hole. Times had changed as performing any form of blasting work in the downtown section of Boston had been banned back when the 'Preacher' blew up a section of Atlantic Avenue. An old sin that came back to haunt Modern Continental Construction Company.

The direction of the 66-inch circumference pipeline that was being installed in the vicinity of the newly constructed Federal Reserve Building at 600 Atlantic Avenue would most likely have to be altered and re-directed. It was merely coincidental that this location on Atlantic Avenue, Boston was close to where the infamous blast by 'the Preacher' took place on 2 February 1973. With this particular section of Atlantic Avenue being so congested and confined, and if you add the fact that excavating a relatively deep and wide trench in this area had been wreaking havoc with the rush hour traffic, this particular location had been causing some major concern for all involved parties.

The most logical way to solve the problem was being worked on by Kenny Anderson and his job site engineer, John Pastore. Although John Pastore had been hired to work with Bob Berry and Les Marino in the Cambridge office on bids, Les thought it prudent that John spend some time working in the field so that he had a better idea of how things worked. Les had done the same thing with Bob Berry when he started, as Les sent Bob Berry to Fall River to work as the job site engineer. Kenny and John were looking at a viable way to get the large sewer pipe from point 'A' to point 'B' without causing too much trouble. As Kenny and John analyzed the situation, the thought came to Kenny that maybe jacking the pipe underground rather than opening up the busy streets might very well be the most logical way to solve the problem.

Now, all that Kenny Anderson needed to do was to convince the powers-to-be that jacking the pipe underground rather than excavating and keeping an open trench in the downtown section of Boston was the way to go. Hopefully, the long-time friend of Kenny Anderson and Les Marino, Don Breeda, the Senior Vice President of the Engineering firm of Camp, Dresser & McKee who was scheduled to show up at the office trailer in a few minutes would help convince the Boston Water & Sewer Commission people that making this change would be the most logical and prudent way to solve the problem. We will soon find out!

****

In early 1986, although Modern Continental Construction had a massive amount of work taking place, there were also some financial issues happening. As is somewhat customary, well maybe not all that customary for all contractors, but customary for Modern Continental when a job would start, the mobilization costs and related start-up expenses were factored into the first estimate or payment. This would be creatively known as 'front-end' loading a job.

Receiving a large payment upfront when a job started would help fund the project.

Unfortunately, the rear end of the job, loaming and seeding, and paving activities, were usually carried with relatively low pricing. The term also used for this type of creative accounting was affectionately referred to as 'riding the wave'. The wave being the excessive flow of cash when a job would start up. Regrettably, when there are not any new jobs starting up and when many of the active jobs move into the final stages of the contract, there comes a situation woefully known as 'the crashing wave' or to be explained in simple terms, 'we got all the money upfront and now do not have any money left to finish the job!' Even with close to one hundred million dollars' worth of work on the books, and with Chris Lincoln also performing his 'Houdini' acts of coercing payments from the MBTA there was still a need for an influx of cash so that business could go on as usual. At the time, Les Marino, made one of his philosophical comments as he pointed out, "Companies don't go broke from lack of work, they go broke when they have too much work!" A comment that would surface again a little further on down the road!

The good fortune that seemed to shine on Les Marino and Kenny Anderson, right from the very beginning when Modern Continental Construction Company started came through again. And yes, with help from a friend, the much-needed injection of 'cash' came in the form of changed conditions on the Federal Reserve pipe line project as Don Breeda, the long-time friend of Les and Kenny, totally agreed with the changes proposed regarding the redirection and jacking of the pipeline at Atlantic Avenue in Boston. The changes endorsed by Camp Dresser & McKee were recommended to their client by the Boston Water & Sewer Commission. The altered route of the pipeline eventually created additional revenue which was generated from this change order resulting in the $10,000,000.00 Federal Reserve Pipeline project subsequently realizing a $4,000,000.00 profit. This small miracle basically bailed the company out at that time as this necessary cash infusion kept the wolves away from the door of Modern Continental.

****

It was in the late spring of 1986 that an opportunity evolved for Modern Continental Construction Company. Coincidentally, the opportunity came in the form of the decision by one of the large, older, and more established general contractors in the New England regions, Framingham-based contractor Perini Corporation, which had historically controlled the building and development market in the fifty-million-dollar range, decided to abandon what they called the 'lower' level of work and decided to only concentrate on projects that were in the one hundred million dollar and above range. This decision by Perini Corporation, and the timely closure of the long-time New England developer and contractor Volpe Construction Company, the company that was owned by former Massachusetts Governor John Volpe, opened up some very good opportunities for the building and development portion of Modern Continental.

Former Harvard University linebacker turned developer, Don Chiofaro decided to change the Boston Skyline by erecting a 45-story office tower at the site of the former Fort Hill Square, city of Boston parking garage. The demolition and implosion of the Fort Hill Square parking garage took place on Super Bowl Sunday, 20 January 1985. The high-profile implosion of the building was performed by the infamous blasting and implosion company Controlled Demolition Incorporated 'CDI', which is owned by the Loizeauxs family and was part of the Super Bowl Sunday hoopla. Don Chiofaro later used the filming of this implosion as a commercial on the local Boston television stations to promote his upcoming development of what would be called 'International Place'.

The managing contractor that developer Don Chiofaro chose to design and oversee the building of International Place was The McCarthy Brothers Enterprises, a Saint Louis, Missouri development company. After numerous meetings and negotiations with the McCarthy Brothers development team, Modern Continental Construction Company was chosen as the primary contractor on this massive building project. The awarding of this contractor to Modern Continental Construction encompassed over forty million dollars' worth of work for them and introduced them to the glamorous world of high-rise construction.

It was also in 1986 that Modern Continental Construction Company became involved with Schiavone Construction Company, Inc. a large, east coast contractor that was based in Secaucus, New Jersey. Schiavone Construction Company was owned in part by Raymond J. Donovan who was the United States Secretary of Labor under President Ronald Reagan, from 1981–1985. Schiavone Construction wanted to get involved in the large contracts being advertised for bids relating to the installation of steel rail and concrete railroad ties on the Southwest Corridor of the MBTA tunnel and South Station access projects. Schiavone Construction was looking for a 'joint venture' partner in the Boston area that had amicable relationships with the local unions. Careful negotiations took place involving Les Marino, Kenny Anderson, and Chris Lincoln who secured a 35% partnership for Modern Continental Construction Company in the joint venture operation that was the successful bidder on this seventy-five-million-dollar project.

An interesting sideline to the negotiations that took place between Modern Continental Construction and Schiavone Construction involving the joint venture partnership was the demand by Schiavone Construction that Modern Continental sign an agreement with the Teamsters Union. Although Modern Continental Construction had signed agreements with just about all of the local trade unions in the Greater Boston area and maintained a good working relationship with them, Les Marino had always been leery of becoming involved with the Teamsters Union. Les felt that this organization was a little too aggressive with regard to the enforcement of their rules and regulations.

In an effort to somewhat coerce Les Marino into accepting to sign an agreement with the Teamsters Union, Schiavone Construction arranged for a meeting between one of the Teamsters Union's high-level executives from Washington, DC, and Les Marino. This high-level Teamsters executive from Washington, DC consented to flying to Boston for the day and meeting with Les Marino in an effort to work out any misconceptions, and to hammer out a mutually agreeable conclusion to Les's concerns about signing an agreement with the Teamsters Union. Chris Lincoln picked up the teamster executive at Logan Airport along with Schiavone's project manager, Ron Tudor (older brother of Major League baseball pitcher John Tudor who had a short stint with the Red Sox at one time) and brought them to Modern Continental's office in Cambridge. Chris Lincoln and Les Marino spent time with the Teamsters Union executive and Ron Tudor from Schiavone Construction, as they toured the Boston job site and then dined at the Top of the Hub restaurant at the Prudential Center in Copley Square in Boston.

During their time together Les and the Teamster Union executive were able to work out most of the 'sticking points' that Les had concerns with. One point in particular was the fact that the Teamsters had a clause in their agreement that required that any truck with a gross vehicle weight of 20,000 pounds or more would require a 'second' driver. This meant that any truck on the job site that was larger than 20,000 GVW would require two full-time Teamsters to operate the vehicle. This was a major irritation point for Les Marino as he felt that this was clearly overkill and double dipping with regard to the Teamsters workforce. Once everything was consented to and all of the 'side bar-gentlemen's agreements' were in place, although the union agreement that Les would sign might show different than what was agreed to. It was accepted by Les, on the power of a handshake, and a promise from this high-level executive, that he would personally see that what they shook hands on was the actual gospel truth and only what the two of them shook hands on actually counted and would be enforced. With the blessing and consent of Ron Tudor from Schiavone Construction Company, Les Marino officially signed a union agreement with the International Teamsters Union, which allowed the joint venture arrangement between Schiavone Construction and Modern Continental Construction Company to be finalized and executed. Chris Lincoln and Les Marino traveled to Logan Airport and said goodbye to both Ron Tudor and the high-level Teamsters Union official. All of the signed agreements were now in place.

Within 48 hours of the meeting that took place between Les Marino and the high-level Teamster's Union executive, it was reported that this middle-aged, somewhat healthy-looking gentleman, died of a massive heart attack. Unfortunately, when he died, so did all of his 'sidebar gentlemen's agreements that were included in the off-the-record handshake with Les!'

The moral of the story, from that day on, Les Marino demanded that everything that he was involved with, especially any agreements that would affect the company must be put in writing, no exceptions, and no more handshakes!

****

The Nantucket Island pipeline project finished up on schedule, well, almost on schedule. There was an agreement in place regarding a vacant piece of land that was leased from a local resident that was used as a staging area and for storage of materials and equipment while the job was in progress. This agreement was for the period 1 September through 1 May. The installation of the pipe was completed but there was still some material and a couple of pieces of equipment in the storage yard as of 1 May. Bright and early on the morning of 2 May, John McNamara the Modern Continental project manager showed up at the storage yard to supervise the removal of the materials. Unfortunately, also there to meet John McNamara was the Town of Nantucket police chief. Without any discussion and with basically no explanation, the police chief and a couple of his police officers approached John McNamara and told him to put his hands behind his back as they placed handcuffs on him and tossed him in the backseat of the police cruiser.

When they got to the police station, it was described to John McNamara by the police chief that Modern Continental Construction Company was illegally trespassing on the property in question and that the resident, a local crony, and friend of the police chief that owned the land demanded that Mr. McNamara be detained until the matter could be resolved.

As he was in custardy and considered a prisoner by the Town of Nantucket, John McNamara requested to make the one phone call that was allowed to him. Although he was totally dumbfounded and shaken by this turn of events, he had the foresight to call the person who had negotiated the agreement on behalf of Modern Continental, the company risk manager, Bill Shields. When Bill Shields received the call from John McNamara and was informed of his incarceration, he immediately reviewed the agreement that was in place between Modern Continental and the land owner. Upon review of the agreement, it was noticed that the actual signed agreement in place was dated 1 September to 15 May, Somehow the dates of the agreement as reported to the police chief were misconstrued and incorrect.

Bill Shields faxed a copy of the agreement to the Nantucket police chief along with a note that explained that the Town of Nantucket would now be sued for wrongful arrest, malfeasance, and blatant wrong doing! The police chief immediately released John McNamara from custody and begged for leniency on the part of Modern Continental. It was agreed that no charges would be filed as long as Mr. McNamara was allowed to complete his activities and leave the island without any further complications. These conditions were agreed upon. Modern Continental immediately removed all material and equipment from the land in question. When the land owner heard of the changed dates, he immediately brought his signed copy to the police chief showing 1 May, not 15 May. Apparently, the fax machine had distorted the numbers in the copy sent to him by Bill Shields.

John McNamara left the island on the last ferry of the day along with his men and equipment. The discrepancy in the agreement dates never seemed to be resolved. The basis of the arrest and detention of Mr. McNamara, and the confiscation of the equipment and materials was something that the land owner believed would be a good way to charge Modern Continental an exorbitant additional price to continue leasing the property, which would be enforced by the local police chief. A no doubt despicable act to coerce additional money from the company that had already paid a hefty cost to lease the property to begin with. As it is often said, *Two can play the same game!*

****

In the summer of 1986, Modern Continental was the successful bidder on the new road project that was about to take place in Quincy, Massachusetts. The Burgin Parkway job was a connecting road from Route #3 to downtown Quincy. A roadway that would alleviate the commuter traffic from the crowded Quincy roadways. The highway was named after the former City of Quincy five-term mayor, and long-time city councilor, Tom Burgin. John McNamara would be the Modern Continental Construction Company project manager on this new road-building project. Fortunately, no land had to be leased for storage on this project!

****

A good example of how Modern Continental Construction Company worked the system to their advantage and how they took the gambles that were necessary to be successful, would be the pipeline project in Springfield, Massachusetts. Bright and early, six o'clock to be exact, on a Sunday morning, Les Marino phoned the home of Bill Shields and informed him that he and Kenny Anderson were going to look at a job in Springfield, MA, and that he wanted Bill to come along as he needed his input. Upon reaching the location, Les told Bill to take a good look at the conditions on the job site as the direction of the proposed pipeline was to hug the curb line on Taylor Street for about 500 yards and then take a forty-five-degree left turn and cut across the road and through an open lot and would end at the railroad tracks. The reason Les wanted Bill to look at the surroundings was that the depth of the excavation called for sheathing (wood shoring) to be used so that the structures adjacent to the trench would not be susceptible to being undermined by the excavated trench.

Les wanted to know that if they did not use sheathing what potential damage might they be exposed to. Bill took a look at the proximity of a two-family dwelling that was about 40 feet from the trench line. A little further down Taylor Street was a one-car, joisted masonry garage that was used to fix flat tires and the guy that owned it also sold some used tires. The next area was the driveway to the 'Adriatic Club' the club building was set far back so the parking area was the only problem there. At the location where the pipeline turned was a one-story, joisted masonry manufacturing building. The proximity to the corner of the building was a concern. After reviewing the exposures, Bill let Les know that if they did not use sheathing and left an open trench with a trench box only, they could possibly lose the front porch of the two-family dwelling, they would probably lose the little flat tire garage building, they would have to repair and pave the parking area at the Adriatic Club, and they might lose the front left corner of the manufacturing building. Upon taking in and processing the feedback that Bill Shields gave to him, Les then asked, "How much will this cost?" Bill let Les know that the estimate would be around $50–60 thousand dollars.

Les stood there and then asked Kenny, "How much did we estimate the left-in-place wood sheathing will cost?"

Kenny quickly replied, "Four hundred thousand dollars."

Les smiled and then said, "Well, we won't use the sheathing and take our chances." Modern Continental won the bid as they did not carry any money for left-in-place wood sheathing like the other contractors that bid the job did. As for damages, they did lose the front porch of the house; Bill Shields negotiated a settlement of $4,000.00. Modern Continental did make the front page of the Sunday edition of the Springfield *Union Newspaper* as there was a horrendous weekend thunderstorm that sent rivulets of water down Taylor Street which allowed the flat tire garage shop to slip into the open trench that was in front of the building when they stopped work on Friday afternoon. Surprisingly, the elderly fellow who owned and operated the tire shop looked at the incident as a gift from God, as Bill Shields showed up on Monday morning and offered him ten thousand dollars to settle the matter, he couldn't sign the release form fast enough!

The parking area for the Adriatic Club did get repaved and the members were thrilled with the new paved parking lot which cost four thousand dollars for Modern Continental to do the work. As for the manufacturing building, well, the corner of the building did in fact become undermined which caused some cracks and fissures in the cement blocks. The final settlement for the repair of the manufacturing building was twenty-two thousand dollars. The total amount spent for damages on the job was forty thousand dollars. The profit made on the Taylor Street Springfield, Massachusetts pipeline project was almost six hundred thousand dollars. This is a very good example of how taking chances and following good, sound risk management guidelines and principles allowed the company to be successful.

The summer of 1986 also included the construction of a massive pipeline project in Barrington, Rhode Island. This particular project included the crossing of the Barrington River which is a tributary emptying into nearby Narraganset Bay. The river crossing included the construction of a 'coffer dam' which requires that an earthen dam be built half way across the river and then excavation from the top of the dam is performed and the pipe is installed. The coffer dam is then removed and built again from the opposite side of the river and the process is repeated. The building of the coffer dam, because it involved ground water, had to have 'well points', which are a series of pipes drilled deep in the soil and attached to a very large pump system that is used to drain the excess water that would penetrate the bottom of the coffer dam. A rather intricate procedure that took an awful lot of earthen material and a considerable amount of ingenuity. Kenny Anderson, having adequately resolved the issues on the Boston Federal Reserve pipeline job, agreed to tackle this new project on the Barrington River.

Having survived the financial issues that caused some concerns when no new jobs were beginning, the situation had now totally turned around, while along with the Burgin Parkway, road job and the Barrington Rhode Island River crossing, a new sewer pipe project began in Methuen, Massachusetts. Cosmo Pallazola would be the Project Manager on the Methuen Massachusetts project. The Methuen, Massachusetts project involved the installation of a large sewer pipe that pretty much went down the middle of Broadway which is Route #28 from the town line in Lawrence, Massachusetts to the town line in Salem, New Hampshire. A disruptive operation that would cause a large amount of traffic delays on this heavily traveled roadway.

The sewer pipe project in Methuen involved the excavation of a fairly deep trench. As the excavation work progressed north on Broadway from the City of Lawrence Town Line, an odd smell began to emit from the bottom of the trench. Not too much thought was initially given to the strange odor as it's not uncommon to come across some decaying underground materials when digging, which can give off a 'funky' smell. The excavated trench was deep, so to alleviate backfilling the trench at the end of the work day, the trench was left open but covered each night by large steel plates to allow traffic to flow when the operations were shut down. On a Monday morning after a weekend of the trench being covered, when the plates were removed the strange odor that had previously been detected was so strong that a couple of the workers began to feel a little nauseous and faint from the smell. As soon as this smell and subsequent nauseous feeling by the workers was identified, Bill Shields, the company safety officer and risk manager was immediately contacted so that he could come out to the job site and look into the problem.

Bill showed up on the job site and he brought with him two detection meters, one that provided oxygen levels and another that identified explosive gases. Sure enough, when the testing took place, explosive gases were in fact identified. It just so happened that at the bottom of this section of the trench, a slight trace of ledge and rock outcropping was exposed. With the identification of explosive gases, all employees were directed to not enter the trench until the source or cause of the problem was identified. It was agreed that the open trench would have the steel plates placed over it until further notice. At this point, the resident engineering firm and the Town of Methuen fire and safety personnel were also observing the testing at this location. When the Bucyrus-Erie, 40-H backhoe operator was directed to cover the open trench, he slid the steel plates along the road surface adjacent to the open trench, as the steel plate was dragged over some rocks, a spark flew from the bottom of the steel plate. Without warning and with a sudden bright flash, the errant spark ignited the explosive gases at the bottom of the excavation and a small explosion took place in the bottom of the trench. No one was injured, but it sure scared the heck out of everyone who was in the vicinity of the flash fire. This situation now appeared to be just a little more severe than originally anticipated. The job was immediately shut down pending further investigation.

The Environmental Protection Agency (EPA) was contacted and they sent a couple of representatives to the job site that afternoon. Investigation of the mysterious smell and explosive gases was now well underway. It did not take long to narrow down the suspects that could possibly be the culprits with regard to contaminating the subsurface soil. About 300 yards down the street from the excavation site was an independent gasoline dealer. Bill Shields and the EPA investigator approached the owner of the gas station who was sitting in a folding beach chair just outside the entrance door to the filling station. With the sun shining and a pleasant breeze blowing, the elderly gentleman who owned the gas station was in his sixties, and a bit rotund just sat there smiling, and was asked to see his 'dip stick' log. Back in the 1980s, every gasoline station had to take a long stick with gradation marks on it and check the level when they shut the gas station down at night and again just before they opened in the morning. The purpose of checking the levels was to see if any gasoline night be leaking from the underground tank. He chuckled and smiled and replied, "With all the commotion going on over there, with the fire trucks and all those yellow lights flashing, I knew it would just be a matter of time before you figured out that the gasoline that has been leaking from my tanks for over a year was the cause of all the problems." He then went on to say, "I haven't done a dip stick check in over six months; I was losing between thirty to fifty gallons a day so I just stopped checking."

The EPA inspector let the gasoline station dealer know that he would immediately be shut down and would be required to make arrangements to test and ultimately replace the leaking tanks with an EPA-approved, up-to-date double-walled remotely monitored system. He also let him know that the costs associated with his irrational behavior and the subsequent fines would be his responsibility. The gas station owner just shrugged his shoulders and with a shit-eating grin replied, "I'm filing chapter eleven today; I don't have the money to fix anything or to pay any fines, I was just waiting until somebody found out. I'm happy that no one caught on until now." The EPA inspector proceeded to light into the gas station owner, letting him know how irresponsible and outright devious he was, and that he had not only caused a catastrophic underground pollution situation, but he also put the lives of innocent people in danger by his thoughtless, careless, and rash behavior. Again, the gas station owner just smiled, grinned, and shrugged his shoulders.

The Environmental Protection Agency brought in a special team to perform testing throughout the area within a one-thousand-yard circumference of the gas station. The extent of the underground pollution was a lot more severe than originally anticipated. The whole area around the gas station was contaminated. Fear of explosions existed if the underground soil was disturbed. This unfortunate situation caused a complete change in the operations that Modern Continental Construction was performing. After a two-week shutdown, remediation measures were put in place and the job proceeded on a time and materials basis. When the work began again on Route #28 and as soon as the backhoe started to dig, sure enough, the ledge that was anticipated was in fact encountered. With rock at the bottom of the trench which would not allow the proper grade to be established, blasting would have to take place.

A no doubt precarious and quite dangerous situation with the presence of gasoline in the area. Paul Ladikakis, the basting foreman, who was fondly known as 'the Greek', did a wonderful job, as he showed a professionalism that impressed the many onlookers who were certain that a mushroom cloud would arise when the detonator button was pushed. What was a marginal job to begin with turned out to be a very profitable one!

At this point in the progress and maturity of Modern Continental Construction Company and Modern Continental Enterprises, a common theme had been established that pretty much identified the management form and company mission statement relevant to the functions that were performed within the structure of the company. Les Marino and Kenny Anderson had accomplished what they had set out to do from the inception of the company, they surrounded themselves with competent and loyal employees. From the very top of the flow chart, right down to the janitorial staff, each and every individual was an over achiever. The honesty and sincerity expressed by Les Marino and Kenny Anderson were clearly evident to everyone in the company. There was no set pecking order, the ability, discretion, and integrity of the company were defined by its leadership and organizational independence. However, Les Marino was still the guy in charge!

It was in late 1986, not long after the company Christmas celebration that took place at the LaGroceria Restaurant that was next door to Modern Continental's old office location on Main Street in Central Square in Cambridge, that the bonding company met with Les Marino, Kenny Anderson, Frank Merlino, the company certified public accountant, and Mr. Herman Snyder the head of the company's law firm. The purpose of this meeting was to review the amount of work that the company was involved with, which was in excess of one hundred and fifty million dollars, along with assessing and evaluating the overall management of the company. The bonding company had concerns regarding the demanding role and work functions that Less Marino had been performing. The bonding company did not feel comfortable that a $150,000,000.00 company was still being run by basically one person. It was no secret that Les Marino was somewhat of a control freak, he most certainly let his managers and administrators control their immediate environment being informed as to what they were doing was something that he felt compelled to be aware of though. He always wanted to know exactly what was going on!

The results of this meeting were not a pleasant situation, as Les understood that he would have to eventually relinquish some of his control, but how this would be accomplished was yet to be determined. The bonding company proposed that before any decisions were made a management study and company evaluation be performed by an independent consulting organization. The company that the bonding people chose to perform the study was named 'Fails Management Company'. This company had an excellent reputation with regard to performing strategic organizational and development techniques that identified operational performance and industry-specific expertise. Early in 1987, a memo was distributed to all of both Modern Continental Construction Company and Modern Continental Enterprises management, clerical, and administrative employees. This memo informed everyone that a confidential study was going to be conducted and that representatives from Fails Management Company would be interviewing employees and asking them to complete a profile and a broad-range questionnaire that related to the duties that they were involved. The interviewing process and the collection of data would take a few weeks until the results could be determined.

Needless to say, there were concerns by just about everyone in the company as the sight of unfamiliar people scurrying around the office and conducting clandestine, behind-door meetings with employees, this action was a bit unsettling. Edna Hughes, the office manager had to walk around the office and let everyone know that they needed to cooperate and continue to perform their duties although there were some distractions. As usual, there was a constant buzz of activities going on in the company, even with the Fails Management Company detractions, business was going forward, roads were being built, skyscrapers were being erected, pipelines were being installed, concrete was being poured, and houses were being constructed. No matter what the situation might be, and even if there were distractions, the show had to go on. The questions that keep getting asked, "Just how did they do it? What was the secret? Did they do something out of the ordinary?" Well yes, they did do things out of the ordinary, they were unconventional with regard to how the company operated and was managed. However, we keep returning to the core beliefs of Les Marino and Kenny Anderson, work hard, be honest, and treat people in a civil and fair manner.

It was in the spring of 1987, that the results of the Fails Management Company analysis and review of the Modern Continental study were presented to the bonding company. It was clearly identified that the company was well organized and performing at an above-level capacity, especially with regard to physical accomplishments in both the field operations and the office environment. However, it was identified that a clear chain of command needed to be defined so that executive decisions that needed to be made by managers could be accomplished without delay. The outcome of this study provided the catalyst for the bonding company to basically demand that Modern Continental move to the next level of competency, and for them to increase Modern Continental's bonding line of credit and allow them to delve into greater-sized projects, Les Marino would have to appoint three vice presidents that would alleviate him from specific duties that the bonding company determined were better resolved by intermediaries rather than involve Les Marino in each and every decision that was made within the company. Well, it was kind of more than a suggestion; it was a demand that the bonding company required in order for Modern Continental's bonding line of credit to be increased and the next level of accomplishment to be established.

The bonding company kind of wanted some input as to whom exactly would be identified as potential vice-presidential candidates. Les Marino would be the president, Kenny Anderson would be the executive director, and the three vice presidents were: Chris Lincoln, the business development guy who was involved with just about every aspect of financial and development activities, Cosmo Pallazola, who was a loyal project manager that had shouldered many responsibilities since he joined that company and was familiar with how all aspects of the field operations were conducted. The third vice president named was Aldo Morelli the company master mechanic and long-time friend and companion of Les Marino. Aldo would have responsibility for the equipment and mechanics, along with taking care of the shop in Stoughton, Massachusetts. The appointments of these three vice presidents were to take effect immediately.

Were there some feathers ruffled, well, when it comes to promotions, there will always be some disappointments, it's just the nature of the human being. Les Marino always professed that one of the hardest jobs he ever had was to be equal and fair to every employee. He would state, "The owner of a company is like the father of a family, the employees are his children, no child wants to see a sibling treated better than they are, it will cause discord and animosity." Les did an enviable job of being fair and honest with each and every employee of the company. In 1987, there were over five hundred employees working for the Modern Continental companies.

An example of Les being honest and fair with his employees would be Bill Shields. He came to work for the company when it was on the ropes in the mid-1970s as Modern had an atrocious safety record and paid exorbitant insurance rates and premiums. Les, at the time Bill Shields was hired, felt that he was a burden upon the company. In an effort to increase his usefulness, Les encouraged Bill Shields to take pertinent courses and to educate himself with regard to the duties that encompassed his position. The initial position of 'safety officer' proved to be beneficial as the company's safety record improved tremendously and substantial savings were identified in a concentrated effort with regard to decreased claims and lower insurance premiums. As additional responsibilities were absorbed by Bill Shields, the 'safety officer' position morphed into the position of 'corporate risk manager'. Bill, over time, had become an intricate part of the company's operations.

The realignment of the management positions and related vice-presidential duties at Modern Continental took effect in the early spring of 1987. It was in May of that year when Bill Shields was presented with an opportunity to make a career move. Thanks to the education that he obtained, along with the hands-on activities that he was involved with during his eleven-year tenure with Modern Continental, this allowed him to hone his proficiency with respect to construction safety and compliance along with the skills that he developed handling the purchasing and administering of the various insurance exposures, this allowed him to evolve into a unique talent. He was approached by the Nobel Insurance Company from Dallas, Texas, and was offered, and subsequently accepted, the position of New England Regional Manager of their operations in the New England six-state region. Bill would be responsible for all aspects of underwriting, risk management, and safety compliance for this insurance company that was primarily involved with insuring high-risk contractors and explosive manufacturers. Bill left Modern Continental in May 1987. He was very thankful for the opportunity that he had to be part of such a first-class organization.

****

In late 1987, Modern Continental Construction Company was the successful bidder on a series of bridge deck surface rehabilitations on the Massachusetts Turnpike in the Auburn, Massachusetts section of the Mass Turnpike. George Banks was the project manager for Modern Continental on this particular project. As the project progressed and the need to complete the project prior to the Thanksgiving Holiday, the activities increased which facilitated the need to have the presence of numerous Massachusetts State Police cruisers, with flashing blue lights, on the roadway. Back in 1987, employee paychecks could not be directly deposited in the bank; the old-fashioned paycheck was issued and the employee had to actually take the check to the bank and get it cashed. It just so happened that a peculiar incident took place on the payday that the two Massachusetts State Police Officers who were hired to perform a safety detail on the bridge deck project in Auburn, Massachusetts.

Both of the state troopers had worked a night shift and stopped by the Charlton, Massachusetts barracks and picked up their paychecks before proceeding to their assignments up the road in Auburn. One trooper suggested to the other that he stop by the bank and cash both of the paychecks, and that he would pick up a cup of coffee for each of them, and that he would be on-site in a short time. Therefore, one state trooper headed to the bank while the other went to the job site. This behavior was quite common and did not, at the time, appear to be a major concern. Showing up a few minutes after the start of a detail shift was not a mortal sin.

When George Banks, the project manager on the Mass Turnpike bridge deck project showed up on the particular section of the turnpike that the two aforementioned troopers were assigned to, he did not perform the courteous act of checking with the state trooper who was present, as to where the other state trooper just might be. George Banks, merely observed that only one state trooper was there and not the two that he had ordered. Again, without checking with the State Trooper who was at the job site and finding out that the other state trooper would be along momentarily, thanks to the new car phone that had recently been installed in his pick-up truck, George proceeded to call the colonel of the state police in the Framingham, Massachusetts headquarters and let him know that he expected to see two state police cruisers and that there was only one there!

The colonel, once he was apprised of the situation, was obliged to respond. George Banks had made the situation appear to be a serious matter. The colonel decided to take a ride to the location and see what was going on. Naturally, by the time the state police colonel arrived in Auburn, Massachusetts the matter had been resolved, as the other trooper showed up within a few minutes of George Banks making the call.

What could have been resolved by a simple inquiry by the Modern Continental project manager to the state trooper that was on the job, turned into a major fiasco. When the state police colonel arrived in Auburn, he was annoyed at what had transpired and he gave both of the State Troopers who were there an earful before he left the scene. This 'dusting' that was received by the two State Troopers from their boss did not sit well with them. A considerable amount of contempt was also directed toward George Banks by them for his careless act of being inconsiderate to the two men.

When Modern Continental Construction was building the new Route #146 roadway in Uxbridge, Massachusetts, Kenny Anderson became friendly with the Massachusetts State police sergeant, Glenn Andersen who coordinated the daily details of the project. Kenny and Glenn Andersen developed a very good friendship. Since the road job in Uxbridge, Glenn Andersen had been promoted to a major in the Massachusetts State Police Department. It was Major Glenn Andersen whom Kenny Anderson placed a call to later on the morning of the little fiasco at the Auburn, Mass Turnpike project. Almost immediately after the incident in question, Kenny Anderson began to receive calls from numerous Modern Continental employees who were driving company vehicles in various parts of Massachusetts. Each call related to the employee being pulled over by what they described as a 'seriously pissed-off state trooper'. One citation issued was for the trailer hitch on the back of the truck obscuring the vehicle number plate. Another violation issued by a Massachusetts State Trooper was for failure to signal while changing lanes. The phone calls Kenny was receiving were coming in left and right. This anomaly regarding Modern Continental company vehicles being pulled over and issued citations for what would be considered very minor infractions seemed to have a purpose. This prompted the call from Kenny to Major Glenn Andersen.

Upon getting through to Major Andersen, after exchanging pleasantries, Kenny Anderson explained to him what was taking place and then asked him what was going on. Glenn Andersen did not hesitate to let Kenny know that as a result of the two State Troopers who were disciplined by their colonel in Auburn on the Mass Turnpike this morning, a lot of their fellow State Troopers have declared open season on all of those very bright yellow Modern Continental trucks that are cruising around the Massachusetts highways. Major Andersen went on to explain to Kenny Anderson that war had been declared and it was a war that Modern Continental would never win. Kenny Anderson explained to Major Andersen that he was not aware of George Banks' actions and that he did not condone them. Kenny went on to inquire as to how this situation might be resolved.

Major Andersen let Kenny Anderson know that the only way that this particular situation could be rectified was for the Modern Continental Construction Company project manager George Banks to be fired, and he had to be fired in front of the two disgraced State Troopers.

After he hung up the phone from his conversation with Massachusetts State Police Major Glenn Andersen, Kenny Anderson explained the situation to Les Marino. Les agreed that George screwed up and should have asked the State Trooper that was at the job when the other one would be showing up, rather than calling the colonel. Kenny Anderson went to Fran Pelrine in the payroll department and picked up George Banks' termination check, and headed for Auburn, Massachusetts. Before he headed to the staging yard just off of the Turnpike, Kenny Anderson motioned for the two State Troopers to follow him to the yard where the ceremony would take place. The war was over and a truce was established; George Banks was gone!

The appointment of the three vice presidents by Les Marino satisfied the bonding company and their concerns regarding the need for delegation of responsibilities. Les Marino was even talked into buying a rubber signature stamp so that he would not have to personally sign the five hundred paychecks that were issued to employees each week. Yes, the company was moving in a positive manner. There were old jobs finishing up and new jobs starting and there were projects that just went on for quite a while and kept earning money, which was the way it should be. Even though the company had grown considerably and was not the struggling sewer contractor that started back in the late 1960s, the small company operation feel still was maintained. Although Bill Shields was no longer with the company. The Wednesday night safety meetings at Saint John's Church still took place on schedule.

Upon the departure of Bill Shields from the company, Les Marino dusted off his old 'Rolodex' and searched for a phone number that he had not called for quite a while. Needing someone to spearhead the safety concerns of the company, and continue to monitor what was taking place in the field, and to continuously instill the importance of 'safety first', Les Marino hired his old friend and the guy that he worked with back in 1959 in the very first survey crew that he was the party chief in, Paul Tibbets. It was a pleasant transition for Paul Tibbets as he had been involved with an engineering company but gladly made the move to Modern Continental when Les Marino called him. Paul had some issues with his kidneys and required dialysis treatment but this did not stand in the way of Les welcoming him with open arms. He knew, full well, that Paul Tibbets was a good man and that he would perform well in the position of 'safety officer'. Les also decided to promote Bill Shields' very capable assistant, Susan Amato to the position of coordinator of insurance activities, as she understood the intricacies related to the insurance policies that were in place; she had been well trained by Bill Shields, and very capable of handling this new position.

It was in the summer of 1988 when a beehive of activities was taking place that tragedy struck the Modern Continental Construction Company. On a recently acquired road-building project in Lowell, Massachusetts, the dear old, close friend, and tenacious road builder that gave both Les Marino and Kenny Anderson a start in the business, the project manager, Sam Melei had a sudden heart attack on the job site and succumbed almost immediately. It was a fitting tribute that a guy who cut his teeth on the building of Route #128 back in the early 1950s should pass away while working on a road-building project. Sam Melei was one of the old bucks that stood by Modern Continental and provided a knowledgeable shoulder for many young guys to lean on as he taught them the tricks of the trade, Sam would be missed by many, as he was cherished by everyone in the company.

Not long after the passing of Sam Melei, another old friend, and very important figure in the Modern Continental family, the recently promoted vice president and company master mechanic, Aldo Morelli also died of a sudden heart attack. The passing of these two prominent figures who were so instrumental in the growth and success of Modern Continental came as a severe blow to both Les Marino and Kenny Anderson. The old guard was suddenly changing as the door was opened for some new talent. It was in late 1988 that the importance of Masimo 'Max' Marino, the young nephew of Les Marino began to surface. Max had joined the company in 1986 and worked as a foreman and had recently become a project manager. He was about to move up the ladder of the company inter-structure as he would soon carve out his own place within the organization, and acquire a much-deserved, 'seat at the grown-up's table!'

Chapter Fourteen
Ruffled Feathers

1989–1992

Whenever they say 'they', remember that we are they—**Kenny Anderson**

Boston, Massachusetts
Nashua Street
The parking area adjacent to the Boston Garden
Thursday, 3 August 1989
7:25 a.m.

It was a hot and humid day that was chosen for the initial meeting between two very powerful contracting companies, Modern Continental Construction Company from Cambridge, Massachusetts, and Obayashi Construction Company with their home office in Osaka, Japan. Although they had spoken numerous times on the phone, it was not until this day that an actual face-to-face meeting would take place. It was a historical meeting that would hopefully lead to a long-lasting relationship. Les Marino, Kenny Anderson, Chris Lincoln, Max Marino and the proposed project manager Rory Neubauer from Modern Continental Construction stood in the open-air parking lot just off Nashua Street in Boston. The rising sun was bright as the Obayashi Construction contingent walked across the open-air parking lot in the direction of the Modern Continental people.

The individuals from both groups smiled, introduced themselves, and shook hands, the Japanese contingent included many bows and smiles as the introductions took place. The purpose of the meeting was to formally meet and assess the conditions of the site that was soon to be the very large, multi-level Boston Garden concrete parking garage that these two construction giants would be bidding on as joint venture partners.

198

After initial introductions, a cursory look at the site took place and after making notes relating to the conditions, the two parties would travel to Modern Continental's office in Cambridge, Massachusetts to further discuss negotiations regarding the proposed joint venture.

****

Obayashi Construction Company was looking to get involved with and participate in the lucrative, Boston construction environment. With the proposed 'Big Dig' on the horizon and the massive amount of related work that would be created as a result of this proposed, enormous construction undertaking, the opportunity to participate was very tempting to this civil engineering and building contractor from Japan. It was Obayashi Construction Company that searched out and ultimately found a willing partner to participate in their first undertaking in the Boston area. The multi-level parking garage at the TD garden location was their first joint venture with Modern Continental Construction Company, but it would not be their last.

Les Marino and Kenny Anderson were flattered when they were first contacted by Obayashi Construction Company. It was somewhat ironic that an established giant in the Japanese building construction industry would seek to partner in the United States with Modern Continental Construction Company. The ironic part is, that for many years, long before any vision of joining forces with a legendary Japanese contractor, Les Marino openly emulated the concept of the Japanese philosophy of 'failure not being an option' and if you did fail, you were obliged to recognize your failure by falling on the sword and performing 'seppuku', which is ritual suicide, also known as 'hara-kiri'.

Early on, when Modern Continental was just beginning to emerge into the competitive world of heavy construction work, in an effort to motivate his people, and to instill in them the importance of success versus failure; at one of the early Monday night safety meetings at the shop in Stoughton, Massachusetts, Les made an impassioned speech to the foremen and supervisors where he alluded to the Japanese ideology of if you fail, you must fall on the sword. How paradoxical that the doctrine of Obayashi's homeland, which was long ago adopted by Les Marino, would actually become a part of Modern Continental's outlook.

1989 was somewhat of a turning point for Modern Continental Construction Company, construction money was flowing like dirty water in the Charles River during the late 1980s and early 1990s in the Greater Boston area. And Modern Continental had its fair share of lucrative contracts and business ventures taking place during this time frame. Although they had made the transition to a full-fledged general contractor from the 'sewer' contractor that put them on the map, they still delved into sewer pipe contracts when they presented themselves. A rather large sanitary sewer pipe contract was taking place in Salisbury, Massachusetts that Cosmo Pallazola would be overseeing.

It was also at this particular time frame that the long-ago Modern Continental Enterprises Brad Bumpus acquisition of the seedy, biker bar, The Green Parrot which was located on Massachusetts Avenue in Cambridge, finally got moved to the front of the batting order on the docket of the Cambridge City Council. After numerous City Council meetings and long-drawn-out orders of conditions and neighborhood 'input' meetings, the liquor license was transferred and a building permit was finally issued so that the long-time vision of Les Marino could finally come to fruition. The building of 'Ristorante Marino' began in early 1990.

Frank Frongillo was a very valuable acquisition from the now-defunct building contractor Volpe Construction Company. Frank was a very capable and component project manager and was a true asset and a valuable addition to the Modern Continental family. Frank Frongillo, along with Steve Harrington, one of the recently hired engineering 'whiz kids' from Tufts Engineering School would team together, as Frank Frongillo along with Steve Harrington began the building of the new restaurant at 2465 Massachusetts Avenue in Cambridge, Massachusetts.

The new restaurant would be a state-of-the-art model of total transparency when it came to food preparation and kitchen cleanliness. A never-before concept would be introduced at this establishment with regard to food preparation. Unlike just about every restaurant that existed, where the kitchen is conveniently tucked away out of sight in the back of the building, at Ristorante Marino the very first thing that you noticed when you entered the building was the actual kitchen. The kitchen was a large, open area that was enclosed in glass. The patrons that frequented the restaurant would be treated to a visual delight as they watched the numerous chefs who were dressed in white prepare their food in an atmosphere that was as clean as a Massachusetts General Hospital operating room.

In early 1990 through the efforts of Bob Shepard, Modern Continental Enterprises made another acquisition that would coincide with Ristorante Marino as they purchased the 180-acre 'Lookout Farm' in Natick, Massachusetts. What would become 'Marino's Lookout' farm would be the provider of fresh, organic fruits and vegetables along with humanely raised and bred, cattle, sheep, chickens, and ostriches that would be used exclusively by Ristorante Marino.

The notion of having fresh, fruits and vegetables, organically grown on your own farm, and providing these pristine products daily to be used in the preparation of patron's meals at your own restaurant, this 'farm to table' concept was unheard of. The fact that each and every entrée on the menu included farm-raised produce and recently butchered meat that was grown and bred exclusively for Ristorante Marino was something that was a totally new conviction for a restaurateur.

****

In the summer of 1990, Modern Continental Construction Company secured a contract with the MBTA that included railroad track rehabilitation that would run from South Station in Boston, all the way to the Rhode Island border. This MBTA contract was in excess of forty million dollars. This project would further establish Modern Continental as one of the premier railroad contractors in the Northeast portion of the United States. It would also be on this MBTA project that went from South Boston to Rhode Island that a relationship would be rekindled. The long-ago Boston & Maine Railroad employee John Scalli, who had recently retired and started his own railroad construction company, would again be involved with his old friends Les and Kenny. John Scalli's new company would have an opportunity to perform work for Modern Continental as a subcontractor. He had worked with Les and Kenny back in the late 1960s on the Woburn, Massachusetts sewer project. His company would perform numerous activities on this railroad project. As pointed out previously, Les and Kenny never forgot their friends. When, and if, they could help or assist a friend, they made every effort to be obliging. This loyalty aspect that both men possessed proved beneficial regarding both friendships and business.

Unfortunately, although Les Marino and Kenny Anderson had developed many friends and good acquaintances during their careers, they also developed their fair share of envious enemies. These were not enemies that would identify themselves as foes or combatants, these were primarily enemies that were jealous and begrudging of the success that Modern Continental Construction Company had experienced in the past few years. The old saying *success breeds contempt* is so very true!

In the early 1990s, although cell phones had become available, albeit expensive but readily available, the use of the now antiquated and no longer existing 'pay phone' was still a very popular way to communicate. In the early 1990s, the cost was still ten cents, or better known as a 'dime' to place a local phone call. The long ago used slang expression of 'drop a dime' meant that someone placed a phone call, and usually that phone call was made anonymously to someone with the sole intent of getting the party that they were calling about in some sort of difficulties or trouble.

The disdain that some develop for the successful, is actually envy and a lack of self-control that a hater has toward a triumphant competitor, or someone or some organization that they would like to see fail or receive negative attention. It was in the early 1990s that a few 'dimes' began to drop on behalf of Modern Continental's prosperity from some very jealous individuals.

Although he was no longer employed by Modern Continental Construction Company and had not been involved with them for almost three years, former employee Bill Shields was contacted by a Special Agent from the Federal Bureau of Investigation (FBI) as well as the inspector general's office from the Commonwealth of Massachusetts. They informed Bill Shields that they were alerted to some inconsistencies that involved minority business participation on some contracts that Modern Continental Construction Company had been involved with and that the name 'William Shields' was signed to the minority business participation portion on the official bid documents. The FBI and the inspector general's office indicated that they requested a voluntary visit from Mr. Shields, or if he decided not to show up voluntarily, then he would be subpoenaed to appear before a grand jury.

Bill Shields did voluntarily visit with the FBI and the Commonwealth of Massachusetts Inspector General's Office as requested. The meeting took place at One Federal Plaza across from Boston City Hall. Upon arrival at the meeting, Bill Shields was shown copies of bid documents that had his signature and was asked if he had signed them. Bill indicated that he was the minority business officer for the company during his employment and that he was obliged to sign the documents that would be part of the competitive bidding process. He also enlightened the FBI and inspector general that at the time of the various bids, it was not fully determined which minority contractor would in fact be used on any particular job and that the last-minute pricing would actually determine participation. Therefore, many blank forms would be signed as the bidding department would make last-minute decisions and chances were good that Bill Shields might not be available at the time of the bid to sign a particular form.

After subsequent visits to the FBI and inspector general's office by both past and present Modern Continental employees, it was eventually established that no wrongdoing took place and that the process used with regard to minority business participation was quite common among contractors. However, it was determined that the anonymous phone call placed to the FBI and the inspector general's office was an effort to discredit and tarnish the reputation of the Modern Continental Construction Company.

When you employ a considerable amount of people and the majority of these people are primarily union trade laborers, misconceptions and misunderstandings can take place, and as a result of a poor work ethic, or malaise, some workers do get dismissed. Modern Continental had very high standards when it came to working on any of their projects. Employees were paid a good decent wage and in return, they were required to provide an honest day's effort. However, it didn't always happen that way, and for whatever reason, complacency and unhappiness might occur with an employee who did not feel that they were treated with complete compassion on the part of their employer. With most employees that were dismissed, it was a mutual understanding and they moved on. Unfortunately, some disgruntled former employees felt that perhaps 'dropping a dime' with OSHA or some other regulatory organization just might rattle the cage of their nemeses.

During the late 1980s and early 1990s, Modern Continental was the most visited contractor by the Federal Occupation Safety and Health Administration

(OSHA) in the Greater Boston area. The majority of the visits from OSHA were related to an 'anonymous' phone call. Fortunately, the stringent safety rules and regulations that were long ago put in place by Modern Continental Construction Company proved to be very beneficial as most of the visits from OSHA did not generate any infractions, fines, or concerns from them.

When you're the biggest kid on the block, someone's going to try and be the bully and take you down; someone always get annoyed or irritated. This was an unfortunate price to pay for being successful. As much as the disgruntled tried, they were never successful as Modern Continental just kept getting bigger and better. The truth of the matter is that both Les Marino and Kenny Anderson, as gruff as they may have seemed at times, genuinely cared about each and every employee who worked for them. Chances were good that if either one of them showed up on a job site, they would greet you by name if they saw you. This trait that both Les and Kenny had was inbred and part of their makeup. They both never forgot where they came from and what it took to get them to be as big and successful as they had become. As shown by the many kind gestures to past friends and business acquaintances, Les Marino and Kenny Anderson did care about the people that were involved in their business, and in their lives.

****

In early 1991, Modern Continental had gone through another growth stage. This growth was clearly visible to many interested parties. One such captivated party was the people who provided surety and bonding to the construction industry. Knowing full well that Modern Continental was an excellent risk and that their financials had been very stable for the past few years, inquiries began to come to the attention of the powers-to-be at Modern Continental. A surety company representative from Connecticut sat down with Modern Continental and discussed the upcoming 'Big Dig' opportunities. He indicated that he could provide Modern Continental with the surety capabilities necessary for them to be the prime contractor on the upcoming projects that would be bid. Although Modern Continental had been loyal to their current bonding company, they knew that in order for them to be positioned in the most advantageous place, they needed to have the proper bonding capacity to achieve their goals.

Although it was something that turned out to be a necessity as the benefits outweighed the problems, it was still a difficult task for Les Marino to change loyalties. However, with the big picture in mind and knowing full well that an increased bonding capacity would allow Modern Continental to secure the work that they desired, a change was made and a new bonding entity took over at Modern Continental. The results were immediately recognized, as Modern Continental became the low bidder on the very first contract that was put out for bid on the 'Big Dig' project. This contract was for the haul road that circumvented the central artery. Modern Continental was also successful with bidding and being awarded the demolition portion of the existing elevated 'Express Way' that ran through downtown Boston. With the 'Big Dig' just getting underway, Modern Continental surged to the front of the pack and rapidly became known as the contractor with the most expertise, both technically and financially to gather their fair share of opportunities with regard to work on the massive 'Big Dig' project.

****

With new financial power due to the profitability of the numerous ventures that Modern Continental Enterprises had become involved with, an opportunity was created that would allow them to become more of a global operation. Although, in the early stages of Modern Continental Enterprises, the exporting of seafood products to England and Asia allowed the company to dip its toe in foreign waters, a new potential venture came into existence that would provide a more substantial global undertaking and awareness.

In late 1991 on the beautiful Island of Saint Lucia, in the sunny Caribbean, a tract of land that encompassed some sixty acres became available and was ultimately purchased by Modern Continental Enterprises. Bob Shepherd, the driving force of the Modern Continental Enterprises operations had done his due diligence and came up with a very lucrative opportunity. This pristine location would eventually become a luxury Caribbean resort that would include opulent amenities and activities for the affluent, as well as the upscale and prudent.

The construction of a large and posh resort in a distant, far-off location would include logistical arrangements that involved both a very detailed critical path method along with an experienced project manager who had knowledge and understanding about working in the Caribbean. The chosen project manager would have to handle the many issues that might arise due to numerous unforeseen circumstances. To begin with, the acquisition of materials and having the proper heavy equipment to perform the site work would be imperative. Dealing with labor and weather issues must also be taken into consideration. Fortunately, a former employee who had the proper credentials and qualifications to perform the duties as the project manager at this Saint Lucia extrapolation did become available.

Bob Cayer, a proud former Marine, Vietnam Veteran, and a previous project manager for Modern Continental Construction Company, had worked in Puerto Rico as a superintendent for a large construction company that performed site work and utility installation. Bob Cayer had recently tried his hand at running a heavy construction company that he and some other investors started. Although the company that he started initially showed success at the beginning stages of operations, issues arose that ultimately doomed the company.

As was somewhat common with Modern Continental Construction Company employees who ventured off for bigger and better opportunities, they eventually realized that the world outside of Modern Continental could be crueler than expected. This was the case with Bob Cayer, as he understood that working with Modern Continental and knowing that Les and Kenny would most likely take him back, allowed for a 'win-win' situation for both Modern Continental and Bob Cayer. His services as a seasoned project manager were in demand and needed. Bob Cayer and Bob Shepherd would team up to develop this luxury resort that will hopefully be an accomplishment and achievement in international growth for Modern Continental Enterprises.

The scenario with Bob Cayer and Modern Continental was relatively familiar. Les Marino and Kenny Anderson seldom burned bridges. They both understood that success was determined by mutual respect and understanding. Although they both had high standards and criteria with regard to people who worked for them, that loyalty aspect was always in the mix. Bob Cayer was just one of many former Modern Continental employees who left and subsequently returned. With Les Marino and Kenny Anderson, that knowledge of both business and human nature always influenced their decisions. It was their constant common interest in ascendancy and attainment that seemed to drive both Les Marino and Kenny Anderson. Having established early on in their relationship that both individuals brought something unique and vital to their association, allowed them to create an environment that encouraged opportunity and a good atmosphere to develop talent and loyalty, which ultimately transgressed to triumph and profit.

****

By 1992, the joint venture project between Modern Continental and Obayashi Construction at the TD Garden parking garage location in the North Station and Nashua Street area of Boston, MA was completed and was a smashing success. Both companies worked well together with the ultimate completion of the joint venture being a positive financial outcome for both organizations. This initial joint venture project led to another opportunity for the two diligent companies. There was a portion of the new proposed almost two-mile Ted Williams tunnel that would be located under Boston Harbor, It would begin at the end of the Massachusetts Turnpike in South Boston and eventually terminate at Logan Airport in East Boston. This contract was soon coming out for bid. The section that would end at Logan Airport was one of the first sections to be bid for this distinctive project. This particular section of the tunnel, and the ensuing roadway, was to be bid was estimated to be in the three hundred and fifty-million-dollar range.

No doubt, a considerable amount of leg work and preparedness would need to be taken into consideration before an estimated cost could be accurately calculated for this uncommon undertaking. The Modern Continental and Obayashi Construction estimating team worked ardently on the many aspects of this project. The fruits of their labor produced a winning bid that was awarded to the joint venture partners in the amount of three hundred and forty-nine million dollars. With a subsequent profit of fifty million dollars for Modern Continental.

Handling difficulties was something that Modern Continental had learned early on in their development. Taking care of problems was what the company was built on. Therefore, on Wednesday morning, 12 December 1992 at 8:23 a.m. when the Amtrak 'night owl' train from Washington, D.C. was approaching the Back Bay Station in Boston, for some unknown reason, this rambling train, jumped the track and plowed into the rear of a stopped MBTA commuter rail train. This untimely collision created an underground inferno of fire, smoke, and twisted metal. It was a miracle that no one was killed. However, 453 people were injured and transported to numerous area hospitals.

The two locomotives that were powering the Amtrak train spilled approximately 1,500 gallons of diesel fuel which ignited and caused the inferno. After the National Transportation and Safety Board had taken their photos, measurements and had done their analysis of the scene, the need to remove the smashed and twisted metal from the area became a high priority. Modern Continental Construction Company was already working in the area as they had an existing MBTA contract at the Bay State Station of which they completed some items related to their contract that had involved the remodeling of the Back Bay Station. Knowing that Modern Continental was already in the immediate vicinity of the crash, it prompted the officials at the MBTA to contact Modern Continental and ask them if they could develop a plan to remove the damaged locomotives and commuter rail cars from the tunnel and clean up the mess.

Rory Neubauer, who was the existing project manager for the Modern Continental on the Back Bay Station project, along with Kenny Anderson, immediately got involved with the cleanup and extraction measures. Around-the-clock efforts were made to remove the twisted steel and metal from the area and to get the station and rail system up and running and back in working condition. Shifting rail traffic to tracks that were not affected along with expediting the removal of debris in a very timely manner brought praise from Amtrak, MBTA, and the Commonwealth of Massachusetts Department of Public Safety. Massachusetts Governor Michael Dukakis made it a point to personally thank Rory Neubauer and Kenny Anderson for their herculean efforts and for expediting the cleanup measures at Back Bay Station. Problem solved!

The workload for Modern Continental Construction and Modern Continental Enterprises in early 1992 included a multitude of projects. In addition to the 'Big Dig' and 'Ted Williams Tunnel' projects, the Saint Lucia development, and the Marino Lookout Farm venture, which were ongoing, work was also taking place on the MBTA railroad project going from South Boston to the Rhode Island border. The large pipeline work that had been going on in Manchester New Hampshire was finishing up. The completion of the Manchester New Hampshire project would now allow Cosmo Pallazola to be freed up and become the project manager of the Deere Island operations for Modern Continental Construction in East Boston.

Additional work was also picked up by Modern Continental Construction Company at the Deere Island Sewerage Treatment plant that was put out to bid by the Massachusetts Water Resources Authority (MWRA). This work coincided with the Boston Harbor four-billion-dollar cleanup project that had begun in the late 1970s. Modern Continental Construction Company was the successful bidder on the Anaerobic Sludge Digestive system, which was a vital part of the overall process involved with transforming raw sewage into a clean water by-product that does not harm or damage the environment or eco-systems in the ocean. The sludge digestive system is an absolutely amazing process that became such an intricate part of the overall Boston Harbor cleanup endeavor. Prior to the separation of storm drains and sewer systems that began in the 1970s untreated sewerage would be dumped in Boston Harbor which would wreak havoc with all aspects of aquatic and marine life. The development of the anaerobic digestive sludge management system should be considered the single biggest attribute of the cleanup of Boston Harbor. This particular sludge digestive project that Modern Continental Construction was the successful bidder on was in the forty-million-dollar range.

One of the final projects to be put out for bid at the MWRA Deere Island sewerage treatment facility project was the multifaceted administrative building. This building would house the administrative offices along with maintenance and logistic operation segments of the Massachusetts Water Resources Authority in East Boston. The engineer's estimate for this building project was forty-six million dollars. Modern Continental was the successful bidder on this project with a bid of just a shade over forty-five million dollars.

Frank Frongillo, the accomplished Modern Continental Construction superintendent who had successfully built the beautiful Ristorante Marino on Massachusetts Avenue in Cambridge would be assigned the task of building the MWRA administration building on Deere Island in East Boston Massachusetts.

The planning and coordination efforts involved with a large building project were somewhat second nature for Frank Frongillo. He came from a long line of construction people. His father was a foreman for Volpe Construction for decades. When Frank Frongillo graduated from college, his dad was instrumental in getting him hired at Volpe Construction where Frank had a very successful career before joining Modern Continental. Frank's uncle, his dad's brother, was also involved with construction and heavy equipment as he was the manager of the town of Winchester Massachusetts landfill operations. Construction was in the Frongillo bloodline.

Between the sludge digestive system project and the building of the new MWRA administration building, Modern Continental Construction Company now had well over two hundred construction employees working out on the Deere Island projects. The overall arrangements and planning involved with transporting so many workers to an island had become a concern for Modern Continental, one that the organization would surely come up with a solution to like they always did. Ingenuity and creative thinking were some of the many strong points that this organization had developed over the years. Solving problems was a way of life for them!

Chapter Fifteen
Sharing the Wealth

1993–1996

If we make more than we anticipated,
*we must share the wealth—***Les Marino**

Cambridge, Massachusetts
Ristorante Marino
2465 Massachusetts Avenue
Wednesday, 3 February 1993
7:25 p.m.

The Wednesday night safety meeting had concluded in the basement of Saint John's Church which was across the street from the Modern Continental offices in Cambridge. The attendance was standing room only. A lively conversation had taken place with one of the subjects being the transportation of workers to the Deere Island job and the newly acquired Nut Island tunnel project. The time factor involved with shift work and getting everyone to the locations on time was becoming a concern for the Modern Continental management team. Therefore, Les Marino scheduled a working dinner meeting at 'Ristorante Marino' for his top-level executives so that they could go over the issues brought up at the just concluded safety meeting.

By seven thirty, dinner was just finishing up. Les took full advantage of the private meeting room he had built when the restaurant building was constructed a couple of years ago. The meeting room was just big enough to take care of the growing Modern Continental management team which consisted of:

Les Marino, Kenny Anderson, Max Marino, Senior Vice President Chris Lincoln, Bob Berry, John Pastore, Bruce Rapoza, Cosmo Pallazola, Kevin Matthews, Bob Shepherd, and Brian McNamara.

With dessert finishing up and the wine and spirits flowing freely, the conversation began to get louder and more animated. Cosmo Pallazola, who was the primary figure involved with the work at Deere Island had become somewhat frustrated as he kept asking, "Why can't we get the people to the work site on time?"

After a heated debate, Kevin Matthews, who had recently joined the management team and had an extensive background in transportation-related matters, suggested that Modern Continental become involved with transportation companies that have boats and buses to move people. Les Marino and Kenny Anderson both thought that this idea had considerable merit. Chris Lincoln indicated that he knew some people at the 'T' (MBTA) that could lead them in the right direction. Chris and Kevin agreed to meet in the morning and pursue the idea.

The next subject that was discussed regarding the 4.8-mile tunnel project that was just getting underway at Nut Island, the Boston Harbor Island that collected sewerage from twenty-one south shore communities. The project involved the construction of a twenty-five thousand-foot long and thirteen-foot circumference tunnel that would allow the Nut Island facility to pump raw sewerage to the Deere Island treatment plant.

****

The Nut Island tunnel job was a very big project that had a price tag of well over sixty million dollars.

Les Marino and Kenny Anderson had worked very closely together on this particular bid. It was Kenny Anderson who got in touch with S. A. Healy Company from Chicago, Illinois who was an expert tunnel contractor who would bring experience and continuity to the job by being involved in this massive tunnel operation. When the bid was completed and subsequently submitted to the Massachusetts Water Resources Authority the anticipated profit margin was ten percent (10%) which equated to approximately six million dollars. Les and Kenny both knew that there was much more than the anticipated ten percent profit in this job. Therefore, thinking it though and agonizing over what both Les and Kenny had talked about numerous times in the past, the subject of 'profit sharing' was again brought up and discussed.

For some time now, as the company grew in size and stature, it had been noted by not only Les Marino and Kenny Anderson but also by the company Project Managers and the Superintendents that a certain amount of waste and pilferage was going on at just about all of the job sites.

Although the majority of the workforce put in a hard and honest day's work, there were still some malingerers and shirkers on the various job sites. It was understood that if you keep waste to a minimum and step up production efforts, it would increase profitability. Understanding this fact, the Modern Continental management people would choose to introduce this uncommon concept to the union and trade people. The idea of profit sharing with union trade workers would be somewhat of an experiment with human nature. How do you motivate someone who already has what they basically need? The answer to motivating just about anyone would have to be by offering more money, and lots of it!

The concept of sharing profit with employees was not a new idea; it has been done for centuries. However, for a privately held company and a heavy construction company that primarily employed union labor, this notion was somewhat unique. The situation with union employees has always been that through the benefits paid by an employer to the union on their behalf, the union member would receive adequate compensation in the form of a pension along with health and welfare assistance. The intent of Modern Continental Construction Company was to provide a reward over and above the benefits that each union member was now receiving.

After detailed discussions, with some against the idea and most in favor, it was finally agreed upon that beginning with this project and including all other projects going forward, all workers who spent more than two weeks working on the job site would share in the profit over and above what the initial anticipated percentage of profit was when the bid was won and the job awarded.

There would be some intricate formulas that needed to be tweaked and worked on but basically, any profit over and above what was anticipated at the time of the bid would be shared by both Modern Continental and all of its employees. The first sixty percent (60%) of the additional profit would be retained by Modern Continental and the remaining forty percent (40%) of the profit would be shared equally among the workers on the job site. Not only were the workers on the job to be compensated with a percentage of the profits but the mechanics, management people, and the administrative staff would also receive a piece of the pie. The gauntlet was laid down and the challenge was in place.

****

The day after the dinner meeting at Ristorante Marino, Chris Lincoln, and Kevin Matthews got together and discussed the transporting of an employee situation. Through some mutual contacts and after numerous phone calls and meetings, a plan to joint venture with the Boston Harbor Cruise Company and the Paul Revere Bus Company was developed. The bus company would move the workers on land and the cruise company would perform the transportation of employees on the water. This joint venture concept proved to be an efficient way to address the situation relating to the transportation of workers to and from the Boston Harbor Islands that Modern Continental was working on. It would also, hopefully, provide some additional revenue. Another problem solved!

****

We get back to the overall discussion of having the right people to get the job done. The individuals that Les Marino and Kenny Anderson worked with were people that they could trust and depend on. Most likely, just about every company that is in business will say that they have honest and dependable employees working for them. However, the major difference with people who worked at Modern Continental was that not only were they trustworthy, dependable, and honest but they had something that is hard to explain, they had a fierce loyalty, faithfulness, and a determination that became instilled in them that gave them that competitive desire to succeed and to win. The situation was almost 'cult-like' with an allegiance and devotion to the leaders of the company that is seldom heard of in the business world. The fact that Modern Continental historically paid higher salaries to their management and clerical people would also have to be factored into the overall loyalty equation.

Although Les Marino was a task master and expected a strong work ethic from his people, he also extremely understood. An example of how Les Marino would get the most out of the people that he worked with was that when he

214

needed someone to get something done, he would call them in, explain the situation to them in detail, and then he would say, "Do you know what 'we' have to do?" He never sat you down and said, "You have to do this!" He would bring you into his confidence by including himself in any task that needed to be accomplished. A management function that would go a long way in today's work environment. Les let you know that he had your back and that he understood exactly what needed to be accomplished relating to the task at hand.

The success of any company comes through the example and direction that the company leaders profess to their workforce. At Modern Continental, with Les Marino and Kenny Anderson, there were no false pretenses, no games were played and no corporate ladder climbing was encouraged. You just did your job and did it well; this was enough to prove to them that you belonged. Les Marino and Kenny Anderson were not greedy people. This was another reason for their success.

In addition to transporting workers, the Boston Harbor Cruise Company had a presence in the Long Wharf area in downtown Boston as they operated seasonal sunset harbor cruises. When Modern Continental got involved with Boston Harbor Cruise Company, they suggested that in addition to the sunset harbor cruises, Friday and Saturday night party dance cruises should be offered to the public. This suggestion was accepted and soon after, on most weekends, Long Wharf was full of anxious would-be cruisers that proved the idea to be most advantageous, beneficial, and profitable.

Kevin Matthews was the point person for Modern Continental with regard to their involvement with both the Boston Harbor Cruise Company and the Paul Revere Bus Company. Getting involved with transportation in Boston was somewhat of a natural progression of fate for Modern Continental as they had such a strong presence in the city of Boston.

****

Max Marino was a busy guy. The Big Dig work kept him hopping. His primary job, in addition to being the overall Project Manager on the Big Dig work for Modern Continental Construction Company, was to oversee and supervise the slurry wall work that was taking place. The slurry wall system was an efficient way to build walls and not disturb the general area. Normally, if you were to build a tunnel, you would excavate the earth and then build two walls and a roof. However, if you were trying to build this tunnel in an area that was as congested as downtown Boston, you would not have the luxury to bring in these huge excavators and dig up the existing roads. Therefore, in order to build the tunnel walls with a minimal amount of disruption, the slurry wall process was adopted.

The first step of slurry wall construction is the excavation of a 'template' which in this case would be reinforced concrete walled trenches approximately three feet deep and three feet wide at the top of the would-be slurry wall. These trenches will be spaced the distance of the wall so that the clamshell bucket used by the crane to excavate the trench material will have a steady guide to go by. The clamshell bucket that is attached to the crane will use the guides to excavate spoils. As the excavation takes place, a material known as 'slurry' which is a mixture of a chemical known as 'bentonite' and water. This material has the consistency of pancake batter. Once the excavation takes place, the slurry material is pumped into the cavity. The slurry material prevents the collapse of the surrounding soil by creating outward pressure on the excavated walls. Once the excavation is completed and the proper depth is acquired, in the case of the primary walls constructed for the Big Dig tunnel walls, which was one hundred and forty feet deep (140) the slurry material remains in the open trench even when the installation of the reinforced steel rod structural cage is put in place.

The reinforced steel cages that were placed in the excavated cavity of the Big Dig tunnel walls were constructed above ground by Modern Continental Construction Company Local Union #7 Ironworkers. Once the steel cage walls were completed, they were picked up by the crane and expertly lowered into the excavated trench. The slurry material has remained in the trench and as the slurry material is light in weight when the concrete is poured into the trench to build the walls, the slurry material is pumped out and put in holding tanks to be used in another slurry wall process on a different section of the job.

The slurry material maintains its 'pancake batter' consistency, but will, over a period of time, congeal and become more like soft clay, which can then be used as fill material in places that need to be backfilled on the project.

Max Marino had become a very good student as he learned well from His Uncle Les and also from Kenny Anderson. Max was a bit headstrong at times and capable of letting a slew of profanities out that would be aimed at the people he needed to motivate. Fortunately, the swears he screamed were primarily in the Italian language! Max Marino along with John McNamara and Rory Neubauer had become the primary field Supervisors for Modern Continental Construction Company. Their diligent work ethic and intelligent decisions relating to the progression of work that these young overseers were involved with allowed Les Marino and Kenny Anderson to concentrate on moving Modern Continental forward in numerous and profitable directions.

****

During the summer of 1993, a major renovation and upgrading of the facility and irrigation systems took place at the 'Marino Outlook Farm' in Natick, Massachusetts. Kenny Anderson supervised the planting of an Apple tree orchard which included numerous species of apple trees that encompassed, Macoun, Macintosh, Gala, Rome, Red Delicious, Golden Delicious, Empire, and a somewhat new and popular strain of apple, the Honey Crisp. This effort to add to what apple trees that were already there would help to round out the selections and increase the overall capacity of what has long been a very favorite fall pastime, apple picking. The expansion of the farm and the addition of an efficient irrigation system only enhanced the value of this piece of horticultural paradise that was an oasis of abundance in a suburban setting.

Although they both led very hectic lives and worked unbearable hours, Les Marino and Kenny Anderson would both find solace and gratitude when they spent time at the farm. Getting lost in an early morning stroll through the fragrant hillsides and magnificent farmland, listening to the Robins chirp and sing along with the other melodious birds such as the black-capped chickadees, American Goldfinches and if they were lucky, they might hear the symphonic sound of a rarely sighted Eastern Bluebird. This solitary time spent strolling the rolling fields and pastures at Marino Lookout Farm enjoying the flora and fauna would provide a short, but most needed respite from their frenzied lives.

Marino's Lookout Farm was a pet project for Les Marino. It was a place that always brought great satisfaction to him. He had been keenly interested in the tilling and farming of the soil long before the purchase of the farm took place. At his former home in Quincy, Massachusetts there was a vacant piece of land adjacent to his residence that was used to plant and grow an abundant crop of the most tasty and succulent vine-ripened tomatoes in the area. Big, bright, and red tomatoes that had the sweetest and most flavorful mouth-watering goodness. Les would experiment with various varieties and types of tomatoes which included Beefsteak, Roma, and Early Girl. He also would experiment with heirloom tomatoes and although to be a true San Marzano tomato it needs to grow in the fertile soil of that particular region of Italy; however, Les Marino would acquire the seeds and grow his own tasty version of the San Marzano tomato.

Kenny Anderson would spend time keeping both the mechanical and irrigation workings of the farm functioning in a positive and productive manner. Although it was a farm, the operations were addressed and handled as any other project that Modern Continental was involved with. Meaning that it had proper attention and follow-through so that it would remain prosperous and profitable.

It was in the fall of 1993 when Les Marino's brother Luciano came to America from Italy to spend some time with his younger brother Les and his son Max and their family. It was during an early morning walk through the colorful fields of the farm that Luciano shared with his brother Les the unpleasant news that the family business, the construction company that was started long ago by their father, the very company that Luciano managed when Les graduated college and became briefly involved with, was failing and in serious trouble. It was a long-standing contractor's plague that many times would cripple the best and the strongest companies that had inflicted its wrath on Luciano's company. The dreaded combination of a poor economy and lack of work was the primary culprit associated with this dilemma. It was very difficult for Luciano to confide in his brother and to let him know that he had problems. Being proud has always been an important part of the Marino brothers' makeup, but Luciano knew that he must swallow his pride and humble himself in an effort to revitalize his failing construction company.

In addition to cultivating many different varieties of plants and greenery in his lifetime, Les Marino had also cultivated many relationships, acquaintances, and friendships. One such friendship was an influential governmental figure who was of Italian descent but resided in the South American country of Brazil. This friend of both Les Marino and Kenny Anderson was acutely aware of the overall construction climate in this very warm and steamy country of Brazil.

In the mid-1990s, there was an acronym that was floating around the financial investment world that was known as 'BRIC'. The letters of this acronym stood for 'Brazil, Russia, India and China'. As a result of the astounding outcome associated with the Presidency of Ronald Reagan and his direct involvement with the recent breakup of the Soviet Union, the reformed Soviet Society and the 'glasnost and perestroika' era that was introduced to them by Russian leader Mikhail Gorbachev, made Russia a very advantageous place to invest. Wall Street and Corporate America found that the growth of the United States and the global economy that was developing created the need to increase profits and develop low labor costs. Therefore, as a result of the massive size and population of these countries, China and India immediately became major players in the manufacturing aspect of the world, which increased their fundamental investment outlook. However, the shining jewel in this quartet of countries was surely Brazil. Their strong economic growth, steady job creation, low inflation, rising productivity, economic boom, and a surging stock market, combined with a developing technological environment and sound central monetary policy made this country a worldwide haven for investment and development.

With an urgency to help his brother Luciano bring his construction company back from the depths of the abyss, Les Marino, 'taking a page from the Godfather trilogy, he used all of his powers' and reached out to their friend in Brazil which proved to be a timely connection for all involved. As Luciano Marino's company had primarily been involved with the building of apartment and condominium developments in Italy, the need for qualified and competent contractors of this type in Brazil was clearly evident as work building housing-related projects was very abundant in this country.

In early 1994, an agreement was made and a joint venture was created that would marry the Marino brothers in a business deal that would allow Luciano to now spearhead the 'International' arm of Modern Continental. A contract was put in place that involved the building of a large apartment complex in the Capitol City of Brasilia. Not long after the construction began on this apartment complex in Brasilia, another construction development project became available in Sao Paulo, Brazil. An agreement was put in place which involved the building of a multi-level condominium complex in Sao Paulo that helped strengthen the international division of Modern Continental.

The working circumstances and the general environment associated with construction and development work in the country of Brazil were highly compatible for Luciano Marino. It was this rewarding and rejuvenating experience that ultimately allowed the joint venture of the two Marino brother's construction companies to create and build the Brazilian version of 'Six Flags'. A large two hundred-acre tract of land was acquired near Sao Paulo, Brazil where a state-of-the-art amusement park was developed and built by the joint venture partners

****

By the spring of 1994, the Nut Island Massachusetts Water Resources Authority tunnel project was going full bore. The combined efforts of Modern Continental Construction Company and S. A. Healy Company were making tremendous progress on this monumental tunnel project. The tunnel excavation was taking place two hundred feet under the seabed with a conveyor system that would move the rock and glacial till to a shaft that brought the spoils to the surface.

It was in the afternoon on Wednesday 15 June 1994 that a fire broke out in the underground Nut Island to Deere Island tunnel system. The alarm was sounded which allowed the tunnel workers, affectionately referred to as 'sandhogs' to immediately put on the breathing equipment that they carry for just such emergencies. Although clouds of thick, black, acrid smoke blanketed the atmosphere in the tunnel, the safety training that had been put in place by Modern Continental and S.A. Healy kicked into play within seconds of the incident. The lighting and safety markers directed the workers to an emergency escape tunnel. The workers had to travel almost a mile to reach the escape route from the main tunnel shaft. The escape tunnel exited to Long Island on the Quincy side of Boston Harbor.

Kenny Anderson was visiting the Modern Continental Construction, Massachusetts Avenue bridge project. This concrete bridge structure that dates back to the early nineteen hundreds was being completely renovated and reinforced in a major rehabilitation project. This celebrated bridge connects the Charles Street section just below Beacon Hill in Boston, over the Charles River to the Kendall Square section of Cambridge. Kenny was on the Cambridge side of the bridge when he received a call on his cellular phone letting him know of the fire and the emergency circumstances that were taking place on the tunnel project. Upon receiving the call regarding this precarious situation, a look of pain and anguish immediately came across the face of Kenny Anderson. The Massachusetts State Police Trooper, who was standing next to Kenny

Anderson performing detail duty, noticed the expression on his face and then, in a questioning manner, he asked Kenny if everything was okay. Kenny Anderson looked at the State Police Trooper and simply stated 'no'. Then Kenny explained to the trooper what was happening and that he needed to get to the escape tunnel as soon as possible.

The reason for such panic was that Kenny Anderson knew that the opening of the escape tunnel might be fouled with debris and if it was not clear and unencumbered, it may hinder the rescue operations. The problem was that Kenny would have to drive from Cambridge to Quincy in rush hour traffic and with all of the construction work and detours that were set up around the city, it might take hours. The Massachusetts State Police Trooper looked at Kenny Anderson and said, "Hold on a minute, I might be able to help." The trooper then made a phone call. Upon completion of his phone call, he turned to Kenny Anderson and said, "The state police helicopter is on its way and will pick you up at the Museum of Science in ten minutes."

The state police helicopter picked up Kenny Anderson, he was able to avoid the traffic and congestion, it got him to Long Island in Quincy, Massachusetts in record-breaking time. When Kenny got to the escape tunnel opening, he noticed that there was some debris that indeed had to be removed so that the escape tunnel would be free of any obstructions. Kenny Anderson commandeered a piece of heavy equipment and proceeded to make the escape tunnel open wide enough for the escaping tunnel workers.

A total of forty-seven tunnel workers escaped the underground fire. There were no serious injuries reported to the workers in the tunnel at the time of the fire. One Quincy fireman suffered a gash on his face during the rescue operations. Thanks to proper preparations and safety training, the incident was not a catastrophe or even a serious impediment to the tunnel construction operations. Subsequent investigation of the matter identified that some errant sparks from a welder caught the rubber from the conveyor system on fire. As a result of his heroic efforts relating to the tunnel fire, Kenny Anderson received a citation and acknowledgment for his actions.

****

With enthusiastic encouragement from Modern Continental's surety and bonding entities, by late 1994 the bonding company had pretty much given

Modern Continental 'carte blanche' with regard to limits and capacity for bidding projects. As a result of this free hand-to-bid work, some very adept calculations by the infamous estimators and bidding team secured some very big contracts for Modern Continental Construction Company. This successful bidding work would relate to another major expansion of operations for the ever-growing company.

The acquisition of the one hundred-million-dollar Long Island Expressway project in New York in 1994 would precipitate the opening of a satellite office in Hauppauge, New York. The Long Island Expressway, which is actually Route I-495 or better known by the people that travel it as the 'LIE' is almost sixty-seven miles long and runs through three New York Counties, Queens, Nassau, and Suffolk. This piece of highway is known to be one of the busiest and most traveled roads in the United States. John McNamara, the project manager who had taken on some of the tougher projects for Modern Continental was promoted to vice president and general manager of the New York operations.

The work involved with this enormous undertaking in New York would encompass the widening of both the north and south sides of the roadway. In addition to the widening of the roadway, the expansion and reconstruction of the numerous bridges that intersected with the highway would also take place. The project including the road widening and the bridge work was scheduled with an estimated three-year timetable.

Along with the triumphant acquisition of the Long Island Expressway project, Modern Continental was the successful low bidder on two major bridge reconstruction projects in the State of California. The first successful winning bid in California was for the San Francisco-Oakland Bay Bridge. This particular bridge is made up of two bridge segments: a skyway structure/single anchor suspension bridge between Oakland and Yerba Buena Island, and a suspension span from Yerba Buena Island to San Francisco. The second fortunate winning bid in California was for the reconstruction of the San Diego-Coronado Bridge. This bridge is better known as The San Diego Bridge which has a curved appearance and box and girder architecture. This bridge connects San Diego with Coronado Island.

As a result of the work that was acquired in California, the promotion of Modern Continental's competent and very capable project manager, Rory Neubauer took place which allowed him to become the vice president and general manager of the California operations. An office and shop location was opened in San Bernadino, California which was halfway between both locations With the doors wide open to pursue and bid work in California, by the spring of 1995, Modern Continental Construction Company had acquired and was the successful low bidder on a major sewer pipeline in San Francisco, California and the reconstruction and widening of Highway #101 in San Luis Obispo, California. Early on into the construction of the San Francisco sewer project Modern Continental encountered a 'déjà vu' moment as the presence of gasoline was found to have permeated the subsurface ground conditions, eerily similar to what took place many years before on the Methuen Massachusetts sewer project. Again, the United States Environmental Protection Agency was brought in to sort out the situation and to identify the culprits, and to coordinate the remediation efforts. The San Francisco sewer project, which had started out as a somewhat 'tight' bid, would ultimately become a 'time and material' project that produced an unforeseen profitable situation for the company.

By 1995, Modern Continental Construction and Enterprises, along with the ongoing joint venture endeavors with Obayashi Construction and Luciano Marino's company that included international work, this phenomenon had placed the operations that 'Modern' was involved with in a rare stratosphere in the realm of the construction world. With work taking place on the 'Big Dig' in Boston, the 'Long Island Expressway' in New York, and the numerous projects that were acquired in the State of California, the overall accomplishments that had materialized, especially over just the past couple of years, would have to be recognized as a feat with a magnitude that could not have been considered by just about anyone a few short years ago. However, if in 1967 when Les Marino and Kenny Anderson had the gumption and audacity to start this fledgling company that barely made it through their first sidewalk contract in Peabody, Massachusetts if they thought that they would have the success that they have had, and reach the pinnacle of achievement, chances would be very good that back in 1967, both of them would have said, "Of course!"

The ulterior objective of this narrative about Les Marino and Kenny Anderson, has been from the very beginning, "How did these two, unsuspecting and completely different individuals that would in a 'normal world' most likely have never been compatible, create such a vibrant and successful relationship which brought about this flourishing company?" The answer as to how Les Marino and Kenny Anderson's lives became entwined and interwoven is as elusive as the 'unicorn'! Sometimes, fate gets involved and a treasure that escapes many is recognized by those who have the foresight to look beyond the obvious and uncover the imperceptible. Needless to say, Les and Kenny had that perception!

The subject of 'profit sharing' along with benevolence on the part of Modern Continental goes much deeper than the ability of the company to give to charitable organizations and to support humanitarian endeavors. Never was a worthy cause or a chance to provide philanthropic support to an individual or group denied by Modern Continental. This generous and liberal benevolence was quite common as just about every politician, no matter what their party affiliation may have been was also given contributions. However, the true spirit of giving by both Les Marino and Kenny Anderson might have to be compared to what was taught to us in our Sunday School or Bible studies, especially in the New Testament of the Bible, in the Gospel according to the Apostle Matthew in Chapter Six, when Jesus spoke in the Sermon on the Mount regarding 'teaching about Almsgiving' (being charitable).

Take care not to perform righteous deeds in order that people may see them; otherwise, you will have no recompense from your heavenly father. When you give alms, do not blow a trumpet before you, as the hypocrites do in the synagogues and on the streets to win the praise of others. Amen, I say to you, they have received their reward. But when you give Alms, do not let your left hand know what your right hand is doing, so that your Almsgiving may be secret. And your Father in heaven who sees in secret will repay you.

The personal kind-heartedness and genuine compassion that both Les Marino and Kenny Anderson provided to the many people that they worked with or to those 'down on their luck' people that approached them, cannot be calculated in dollars and cents. Also, the true amount of the many that were helped, or taken care of, may never be properly accounted for. It was just their nature to help. They could never be considered a 'soft touch' or an 'easy mark' when it came to giving or helping, far from it, but they both were well known for having goodness within them. The help provided would fall in the category of selling a company vehicle, for a fraction of what it was worth to an employee who had a kid going off to college and needed a second ride that they could not really afford.

How often did an employee approach either Les or Kenny and ask if they could perhaps get a load of loam, or fill delivered to their house as they had a landscaping project taking place? How many employee driveways were paved or a load of concrete given to them for a retaining wall project for the footing or foundation of an upcoming addition to their home? How many one-hundred-dollar bills were slipped to an employee when Les or Kenny might have known that it was one of an employee's kids' birthday, or how many times did Les or Kenny pick up the tab for a medical procedure that had to be performed for an employee or one of their dependents that was not covered by insurance? Once an employee was going to adopt a child and had to pay for the cost of the flight from Asia to the United States, that cost was picked up personally by Les Marino. No one ever knew about it.

Not that it was required, but more often than not, Les or Kenny, would pay for lunch or dinner when they were with just about anyone. No one ever knew about these acts of random kindness, the left hand never knew what the right hand was doing when it came to charity and 'Almsgiving' for Les Marino and Kenny Anderson. They both fully understood the teachings of Jesus when it came to 'Almsgiving' and these two kind souls never looked for anything in return for their goodwill and charitable efforts. It would be somewhat difficult to go into detail, just how philanthropic and genuinely generous both of these guys really were. The truth would be that Les and Kenny understood the meaning of the beautiful prayer by Saint Francis of Assisi in which he states: "O divine Master, grant that I may not so much seek to be consoled as to console, to be understood as to understand, to be loved as to love. For it is in giving that we receive, it is in pardoning that we are pardoned, and it is in dying that we are born to eternal life."

With the coming of 1996 on the horizon, bigger and better rewards and accomplishments were also just beyond the range of view, but it was destined to be a Happy and Prosperous New Year for the growing workforce at Modern Continental!

Chapter Sixteen
Things Are Going South

1996–1999

The company you keep will determine
the trouble you meet—**Kenny Anderson**

Makati Metro Manila, Philippines
The Peninsula Manila Hotel
1226 Makati Avenue
Monday, 29 January 1996
8:25 a.m.

Kenny Anderson and Bruce Rapoza had just finished breakfast and were seated in the Peninsula Manila hotel lobby waiting for their guide to pick them up and bring them to the Philippine government's equivalent of the United States Army Corp of Engineers office. Although they spent Sunday trying to recover from the twenty-two-hour flight from Boston, Massachusetts to Manila in the Philippines which included a stop in London; it was a grueling flight that they were both still a little groggy from. Knowing that they would have to provide answers, they had done their homework and were ready to sit down with the government officials to help them solve a problem. The reason Kenny Anderson and Bruce Rapoza traveled to the Philippines, is because Modern Continental Construction Company had been contacted and asked to help the Philippine government to come up with a way to properly deal with a lingering issue that was not going away.

****

On Saturday, 15 June 1991 after gurgling and coughing since April of 1991, Mount Pinatubo, in the Philippines Luzon Volcanic Arc became the second largest volcanic eruption of the twentieth century, behind only the huge eruption of Novarupta Volcano in Alaska in 1912. This massive eruption extruded bursts of gas-charged magma exploding into umbrella ash clouds, hot flows of gas and ash descended the volcano's slopes with huge pyroclastic flows of lava as they roared down the flanks filling once-deep valleys with fresh volcanic deposits. The eruption moved so much magma and rock from beneath the volcano that the summit of the mountain actually collapsed.

The fine ash from the eruption fell as far away as the Indian Ocean over three thousand miles away. With the ash fall came darkness and the sound of numerous 'lahars' (a flow of lava, sediment, and debris) rumbling down nearby river valleys. Several smaller 'lahars' washed through the United States Clark Air Base, flowing across the base in enormously powerful sheets, slamming buildings and scattering and damaging vehicles and equipment. The United States government, as a result of the damage caused by the volcano, would eventually abandon the air base. Every bridge within a twenty-mile radius of Mount Pinatubo was destroyed.

In the Luzon region alone, more than 840 people were killed just from the collapse of roofs under heavy wet ash with several more injured. Rain continued to create severe hazards over the next several years, as the volcanic deposits continued to remobilize into secondary mudflows. The fallen ash was in such abundance in the Luzon region of the Philippines that damage to bridges, irrigation-canal systems, roads, cropland, and urban areas was occurring in the wake of each new rainfall over the past few years.

The problem of fallen and accumulated ash was not going away and it needed a solution.

Through diplomatic channels, the name of Modern Continental Construction Company had been mentioned to the Philippine government officials. The fact that Modern Continental could move materials was well known by many influential people and this certainty was enough to entice the people in Luzon to seek their help. Moving rain-soaked ash was not quite the same as digging earth. The weight and density of the volcanic ash were a bit more substantial than common earthen spoils.

However, the concepts were the same when it came to digging, moving, and disposing of materials. Moving materials and lots of it was a staple of Modern Continental, so was solving problems!

After meeting with the various officials who were involved with the disposal of the volcanic ash materials, Bruce Rapoza and Kenny Anderson were given a detailed tour of the region that was most affected by the existence of the years-old ash material. Much of the area was remote and with the presence of the ash material, the ability to access the area was difficult and limited. It was one of those 'can't see the forest for the trees' situations, as the Philippine government officials had seemed to have been focusing on more detail than addressing the big and simplistic picture of just starting to move materials out of the area. Bruce and Kenny looked at the situation with a different approach. They both understood that they would have to locate some very big earth-moving equipment and get it on-site so that the disposal process could begin. Bulldozers, front-end loaders, and a bunch of 'Terex Titan' end dump type trucks would need to be brought to the region. Moving material was not the major issue, where to dispose of the materials was the primary problem that needed to be solved.

The Philippines is an archipelago, or string of over 7,100 islands, in southeastern Asia between the South China Sea and the Pacific Ocean. Many of the islands in this archipelago are simply mounds of earth and rock and are not inhabited. As a matter of fact, there are almost two thousand islands in the area that are not inhabited.

Back at the Peninsula Manila hotel while Kenny Anderson and Bruce Rapoza were having dinner, they discussed the situations and the locations that they had visited. Kenny was looking out the big picture window of the hotel's restaurant and just kind of contemplating things. All of a sudden, Kenny looked at Bruce and said, "We hire a bunch of barges and take the rained soak volcanic ash and dump it on one of those islands out there," as he pointed out the restaurant window to a group of islands in the distance.

Bruce put down his knife and fork and then, after swallowing a big piece of 'tomahawk steak', he nodded and replied, "That's a great idea!"

Bright and early the next day, Bruce Rapoza contacted the person who was assigned to work with him and Kenny and requested a tour of the islands in the area so that they could determine which one, or two, islands might be the best candidates to receive a gift of volcanic ash. Sure enough, a couple of candidates were identified that could handle the massive number of barges loaded with materials. The need to have a docking area and terrain that could be navigated by equipment was included in the deliberations.

Although the problem associated with moving the volcanic ash out of the Luzon area had been studied for a couple of years by the Philippine government, it took two outsiders to finally bring the picture into focus. Bruce and Kenny stayed in Luzon for a couple of months until the systems were all in place and working efficiently. Modern Continental was compensated handsomely for their ingenious efforts relating to solving the big problem of moving and disposing of the volcanic ash that was deposited by one of the worst natural disasters that Planet Earth has ever encountered.

****

By 1996, the conditions associated with the continued growth of Modern Continental had become a concern as the accommodations at the 2277 Massachusetts Avenue office locations had again become quite cramped and crowded. The need to expand the office accommodations had become clearly evident. At the direction of Les Marino, Bob Shepherd began to inquire about locations in the Cambridge, Massachusetts area that might be available and could house the many clerical and management people who currently worked for the company.

It had always been one of Les Marino's many visions and dreams to own a handsome and distinguished office building complex in Cambridge, Massachusetts. Since he first rented a humble apartment in Cambridge when he came over from Cheiti, Italy in quest of the 'American Dream', Les always had a loyal and dedicated allegiance to the City of Cambridge, Massachusetts. This devotion to the City of Cambridge would continue as Bob Shepherd was able to identify a six-story, eighty-five-thousand square feet, very prominent office building that was located on Memorial Drive, on the banks of the Charles River in Cambridge, Massachusetts.

600 Memorial Drive, Cambridge, Massachusetts would become the new home of Modern Continental Construction Company and Modern Continental Enterprises. There were some renovations and betterments that would need to be performed to the office building before the transfer from 2277 Massachusetts Avenue could take place. The basement location was excavated so that the area could have the proper clearance and height associated with the proposed use of the space. Being the 'neat and organized' person that Les Marino was, it would require that both the interior and exterior of the building

be updated, modernized, and refurbished so that the building could adequately portray the image of the company that he was so proud of. This building was an impressive, architectural accomplishment. It was built in the early 1920s, with a reinforced concrete frame. The double bay entrance is marked by the original copper canopy trimmed with anthemia. The colors are characteristic of the late-twentieth-century style—namely lime and strawberry punctuated by spandrels of red brick.

The transfer of operations to the 600 Memorial Drive location was completed by mid-1996. The accommodations at this new building were spacious compared to the cramped quarters at 2277 Massachusetts Avenue. However, there will always be fond memories of the 2277 Massachusetts Avenue location. The company was just developing its 'sea legs' when it moved into the 2277 Mass Ave location. It was a special part of the Modern Continental story, that's for sure. One of the fondest memories would be of the very local environment that this location had. Verna's Coffee Shop and Frank's Steakhouse on Massachusetts Avenue were popular places that were frequented very often by the Modern Continental troops. Also, the 2277 Mass Ave location in North Cambridge made the building a part of Speaker of the House Congressman Thomas Phillip 'Tip' O'Neill's congressional district. It was quite common a couple of times a year, that Congressman O'Neill would walk the streets of North Cambridge and visit with his constituents.

The man was like a 'savant' as he had a memory like that of an elephant. He had the uncanny ability to remember the names and faces of everyone he met. He would walk in the door and address everyone by the name 'first and last' and inquire as to how the health and welfare were of their husbands, wives, and children whom he also recited the names of. Mr. Speaker 'Tip' would stop at every business and spend time chatting with the people. The local Veterans of Foreign Wars (VFW) Post was located just outside of Porter Square on Massachusetts Avenue. Mr. O'Neill would make it a point to stop into the VFW Post and thank the many members for their military service as he sat at the bar and shared a beer with them. The North Cambridge, 2277 Mass Ave location will always be fondly remembered!

****

The move to 600 Memorial Drive felicitated some enhancements to the company's growth and sophistication. Although the certified public accounting firm of Darmondy & Merlino was still the accounting people that handled the reconciliations and oversaw the tax filings and profit and loss statements for the company, the need for an 'in-house' certified public accountant (CPA) became apparent to Les Marino. With the blessings and approval of his good friend, Frank Merlino, the accountant who had been with Modern Continental since the early 1970s, Les was able to coerce one of the Darmondy & Merlino rising stars to join Modern Continental and accept the position of 'chief financial officer' (CFO). The young and very bright candidate who accepted this position was Peter Grela. Peter took over this financial position and immediately implemented some conspicuous cost-saving measures along with alleviating Chris Lincoln from some of the financial duties that he had been involved with. Chris Lincoln had been juggling many balls and was a crucial part of Modern Continental's growth and success. But he was getting spread kind of thin and feared that some of the balls he was juggling just might escape his grip. Chris was actively involved in the decision to bring Peter Grela on board.

After the move to 600 Memorial Drive in Cambridge, the bonding company, more specifically, the agent that represented the bonding company had a series of meetings with Les Marino regarding the growth and direction that the company was taking.

Up until the present time of late 1996, the decisions made with regard to hiring employees and bidding work, along with taking on various development and non-construction activities were done on a 'committee' basis. Les would confide in Kenny Anderson his partner of thirty years and he would also involve Chris Lincoln and the Modern Continental management team. Les would present his thoughts and ideas, and then listen to their feedback, comments, and remarks and ultimately decide which direction to take. Although, back in 1987, when it was established that Les Marino, could not run the company by making every decision and that vice presidents had to be appointed to alleviate his day-to-day involvement and allow a chain of command to take place, the bonding company agent for Modern Continental, now indicated that Les needed to make decisions himself and not depend on others to influence him. This recommendation by the bonding agent, went directly against and conflicted with what the bonding company had determined when they brought in 'Fails Management Company' to evaluate the Modern Continental operations ten years prior.

The bonding company, in 1997 had continued to ride the 'tsunami' that was taking place with Modern Continental and encouraged the company to pursue work in whatever location, environment, or genre, that they determined might be profitable. The per-job bonding limit was non-existent as Modern Continental could bid whatever job they wanted to bid at whatever the cost may be. At this point in the company's burgeoning development, they encompassed many types of work and numerous investments. In 1997, the efforts of both Modern Continental Construction Company and Modern Continental Enterprises had combined annual earnings of over one billion dollars. However, the growth and expansion of the company was still taking place. Numerous construction projects, in New York, California, and Brazil along with the massive amount of construction work that was taking place in Massachusetts, including the 'Big Dig' contracts, made the company one of the largest and most diverse operations in the world. However, the bonding agent felt that perhaps some changes might need to be made internally at the upper levels of management that might enhance the bottom line even more.

****

Although, by 1997, the Modern Continental companies had developed into a smooth, well-oiled, and high-performance money-making machine, it did not change the work ethic of both company owners. Les Marino still arrived at the office before anyone else. He would sometimes, sit for a moment and enjoy the beautiful 600 Memorial Drive building that the company now occupied, he truly enjoyed the fact that the little two-man operation that started in 1967 owned their own office building. No matter how successful the company had become, his rigorous self-discipline did not allow him to deviate from his normal daily activities. He spent a full day working on bids, visiting jobs, and checking the farm and restaurant on a regular basis. Kenny Anderson, who had become the company 'fixer', was out of the house very early in the morning, checking jobs or traveling to far-off locations that might need his attention and expertise. Kenny, like Les, gave his all daily, knowing full well that pushing yourself and not taking anything for granted had become a way of life. Both individuals still; 'brought it every day'.

With a focus on continuing to maintain a prominent presence in the city of Boston and taking full advantage of the thriving real estate market associated with office space in downtown Boston in the late 1990s, Modern Continental Enterprises, purchased a ten-story, one-hundred and fifty-five thousand square foot office building, located at 745 Atlantic Avenue Boston, in the area that was once known as the 'leather district'. Frank Frongillo, the successful and extremely competent project manager who had successfully built the Ristorante Marino in Cambridge and the MWRA administration building at Deere Island, East Boston for Modern Continental Construction, would take on this new project.

The existing building at 745 Atlantic Avenue had a total of ten stories. Les Marino looked at the building and envisioned an additional 'penthouse' located at the top of the building that would allow for spectacular views of Boston Harbor. This added segment of the building would greatly increase per square foot lease revenue. Therefore, architectural drawings were completed and the addition of another story on top of the building became part of the overall renovations and rehabilitation of this office building. The addition of this penthouse level would increase the square footage to over one hundred and seventy-five thousand square feet.

Like just about every other Modern Continental Construction project that had ever taken place, the 745 Atlantic Avenue Boston building project was given top priority and direct marching orders to complete the work in an expeditious manner. The subcontractors were all lined up and materials were delivered to the job site. The work was performed in a controlled and organized fashion. The various trades working on the job site were carefully coordinated and correlated to maximize the production efforts in order to achieve and accelerate the completion of the renovations and the addition of the extra floor to the top of the building. The work being performed was taking place as anticipated.

However, there was one little problem, the work that was taking place, specifically, the addition of the penthouse level and the related appurtenances had not been approved by the City of Boston Building Department. Although, all the renovations and additions were up to grade, code, and compliance, the simple fact that the process of working without an approved permit, kind of frustrated, perturbed, and upset the City of Boston Building Department. The City of Boston Building Department did not process permits in a timely manner that was acceptable to Les Marino. Unfortunately, although the work that was completed was approved and acceptable by all building codes and standards, the mere fact that a little technicality of acquiring an approved permit would ultimately cost the company a couple of dollars in fines and left them with a bit of egg on their face!

****

The 'Big Dig' operations: slurry walls, tunnels, utilities, and infrastructure work were ongoing in 1997. Max Marino was the point person who coordinated the work being performed, which included the supervision of numerous subcontractors who were working on the project for Modern Continental. The actual name of the 'Big Dig' job was the Central Artery/Tunnel Project (CAT).

The company that was the overall program manager of the 'CAT' project was Bechtel and their joint venture partners, Parsons & Brinkerhoff. This joint venture group, Bechtel, Parsons & Brinkerhoff would be responsible for the engineering and design of what would become one of the largest, most complex, and most technically challenging highway projects in American history.

Bechtel Company was founded in 1898 and has become a well-known global engineering, construction, and project management company. The company works on projects that range from civil infrastructure to power, telecommunications, and government services. The company has experienced five generations of family leadership and will forever be remembered for its role in the building of the Hoover Dam and the 31.5-mile Channel Tunnel which goes from Folkestone England under the English Channel to Calais France. Affectionately called 'The Chunnel'.

Needless to say, Modern Continental had a considerable amount of interaction with the Bechtel, Parsons & Brinkerhoff people as Modern Continental was the primary contractor on the over fourteen-billion-dollar 'CAT' project. However, there was one individual that Les Marino had become rather friendly with. Al Benson was one of the many participants who were involved with the overseeing and management of the tunnel work for Bechtel, Parsons & Brinkerhoff. For some strange reason, Les Marino found this person to be very intelligent and savvy when it came to engineering and construction-related activities; he had become somewhat enamored with the guy. Les would spend a considerable amount of time reviewing and discussing with Al Benson the various aspects of the project that were taking place on the Big Dig. It was during one of their extended conversations that Al Benson mentioned to Les Marino that he was considering getting involved in running a construction management company somewhere in the southern United States when he was through with his involvement in the Central Artery project. Al mentioned that he came from the south and would love to go back there and try his hand at developing a business.

This conversation that Les had with Al Benson got Les thinking, perhaps it was time for Modern Continental to venture into the south and open an office there. Not long after this initial conversation about opportunities in the southern part of the United States took place, Les alluded to Al Benson if he might really be serious about business development in the southern part of the country and if an opportunity presented itself would he be interested? Al paused for a moment when Les presented this question to him; then after a bit of contemplation, he looked Les Marino straight in the eyes, and with a bit of anxiousness replied, "I'd be very interested!"

The wheels and gears were turning in the head of Les Marino like the inner workings of a Swiss-made Rolex watch. There was something about Al Benson that intrigued Les Marino and he really felt that this fascination with the man had to be acted upon. There was this feeling of expectancy and excitement about the aspect of being associated with him and actually hiring Al Benson. Les envisioned him as the southern arm of Modern Continental. When Les got back to the office at 600 Memorial Drive, he called an impromptu meeting with Kenny Anderson and the Modern Continental management team.

The powers-to-be of Modern Continental were soon assembled in the conference room. The managers waited as Les was momentarily tied up in his office on a phone call. The collected group waited and started to mumble and whisper as to why they were brought together in such a hurry. All anyone knew was that Les was excited about something. As a matter of fact, Les was acting completely out of context and character as very seldom did he portray himself as being outwardly excited about anything. When he entered the conference room, Les stood at the head of the big, oblong-shaped maple conference table and began his recitation, "The vast progress that we have made thus far is only a symbol of the progress that is possible by constantly striving toward new horizons." He went on to explain that he had a few meetings and discussions with Al Benson, which he assumed everyone, knew. He went on to let them know that he had great confidence in the ability, discretion, and integrity of this man and that he has been considering hiring him and setting up what would be considered as a new horizon; 'Modern Continental South' a company of which he would make Al Benson the president, general manager, and business development person.

It took a couple of moments for the words that Les had just spoken to sink into everyone who was seated at the conference table. No sound was uttered and no comments were made; just silence. After an awkward pause, it was Kenny Anderson who made the first comment, "Les, we really don't know this guy. We understand that you've had interaction with him and that you have mentioned that you think he's a pretty sharp guy, but is that enough for you to hand him the keys to the kingdom of the south?"

Another slight pause took place and then it was Chris Lincoln who chimed in, "Let me get this straight, you're going to hire this guy and just let him do as he pleases in a region that we have not been involved in."

Les was frowning and his face was starting to become a slight tint of rose as the veins in his neck started to pulse just a bit as he listened, then he stated, "We've been planning on expanding to the south for quite some time, a new horizon, I've just been waiting for the right person to come along, believe me, this guy is good and he will do the job and make the company money." Everyone could see that Les was getting frustrated and a little upset as he was not getting the responses that he anticipated. It was then that Les looked out at the group and said, "Let's put this to a vote, I want to see hands raised that agree with me in hiring this guy." The room again went quiet as Les looked around the room and saw that not one of his people raised their hand and supported his decision to hire Al Benson. Les, then turned around and with a look of anger and disgust on his face, he abruptly left the conference room.

It was this meeting that involved the discussion about hiring Al Benson that could be construed as a tipping point in the future decision-making process in the Modern Continental organization. Les Marino, despite the negative response by his management group, in fact, hired Al Benson, and within a month or so, a new 'Modern Continental South' (MCS) was formed and in business. Al Benson left his position at Bechtel, Parsons & Brinkerhoff and headed to Greenville, South Carolina. He opened an office and began to solicit business in the area. Al Benson was familiar with this section of the country; this was an area that was prosperous and filled with paper mills and furniture manufacturers, a target-rich environment.

It was an interesting concept that would provide the catalyst for developing MCS's first business venture. Modern Continental South was a wholly owned subsidiary of Modern Continental Construction Company. Therefore, the insurance that MCS acquired had the same rates as the parent company. As a result of a long and dedicated effort, Modern Continental had maintained an excellent safety record and the workers' compensation rates were very low for the parent company which was now extended to Modern Continental South. On the contrary, the paper mills and the manufacturing facilities in the Greenville, SC area had been perpetually plagued with numerous accidents and claims which drove their workers' compensation rate to be extremely high.

The operations that are performed at paper mills and furniture manufacturing facilities involve semiskilled labor. The work that takes place is labor intensive. Therefore, there are numerous workers on the payroll of these companies. Most of the paper mills and furniture companies again, as a result of accidents and claims, had very high insurance rates which adversely affected their profitability and their bottom line. The very first business venture that Al Benson and MCS got involved with was a negotiated agreement to provide the labor needed to conduct the daily activities at a group of paper mills in the Greenville, South Carolina region. The actual laborers and managers would be Modern Continental South employees and would do the work at the paper mills. Modern Continental South became a staffing agency, a middleman between the employers, in this case, the paper mills, and the workers, who were qualified candidates that performed the paper mill duties but they were employed by Modern Continental South. The markup, or profitability for MCS was in the twenty-five percent (25%) range. This concept and business transaction proved to be a promising start for Al Benson and Modern Continental South.

It was late in 1997, when the situation that had been simmering for quite some time, finally came to a rolling boil. The suggestions, innuendos, references, and hints that had been made by the bonding company representatives to Les Marino for the past few months regarding decision-making and control of the company finally prompted Les to act upon this matter. After consulting with all of the involved parties, legal and financial, Les had a sit-down meeting with his partner of over thirty years, Kenny Anderson. Ever since the 'Al Benson-Modern Continental South' meeting, there had been a bit of friction between these two strong-willed, resolute, and somewhat stubborn individuals. It was time to clear the air and to resolve the matter. Kenny Anderson, knew that something was going on as he had been busy doing his duties chasing after problems and resolving disputes on the various job sites, but he had not had any interaction with Les for quite some time. Furthermore, the Sunday dinner get-togethers had not taken place for a couple of weeks, which was a concern. Throughout the years, no matter what the circumstances may have been, and there were some pretty serious disagreements, Les and Kenny always called a truce on Sunday.

When Kenny was summoned to the office for a meeting with Les, he had this feeling that there may be some issues that might not be reconcilable, but he did not really know exactly what they may be. Kenny now sat in the leather Queen Anne chair that was in front of the polished mahogany desk that Les sat behind. It was only the two of them in Les's office. Kenny noticed that Les was just a bit apprehensive as he started to talk. Les, first of all, expressed his undying dedication and devotion to his long-time friend and business partner. Les went on to explain to Kenny Anderson that he thought that in the best interest of the company and with the guidance and direction of the bonding company and the corporate attorney an agreement and understanding needed to be reached between them both.

Les came right to the point, he let Kenny know that he will always value his opinion and ideas, however, going forward, "I will be making all decisions relating to the work that we are involved with, where we decide to do work and who will be working for the company. You will maintain your position in the company and your twenty-five percent ownership and you will not be reduced in any fashion. But please understand that I alone will be making the decisions going forward. I'll still listen to you, but I don't have to agree with what your thoughts or opinions are. I've also directed Peter Grela to provide additional compensation to you on an annual basis as an understanding that you will no longer be involved with decision-making." Les then pulled out a folder from the top drawer of his desk and then pulled a paper from the folder and handed it to Kenny Anderson. Les let Kenny know, "This is the agreement that the lawyers drew up to confirm what we just talked about. Please take a look at it and then if you want your lawyer to look at it, go right ahead."

When Les was finished, Kenny simply asked, "Are you buying me out?"

Les quickly replied to Kenny's question, "No, please look at the agreement, you are not being bought out, you are being placed in a position that will no longer allow you to share in the company decision-making process." Les then added, "Our friendship will never be jeopardized, we have something that can't be broken, I hope you understand that?"

Kenny kind of nodded and replied, "I understand but that doesn't mean that I have to be happy with your decision."

Les kind of looked down and then softly answered, "It has to be this way."

****

The Ted William Tunnel that travels under Boston Harbor from the Expressway to Logan Airport was opened in late 1995. However, there were still many connecting tunnels that were also being built and had not been completed as of early 1998. One of the last tunnel projects to be bid was the 'Fort Point Channel Tunnel'. This tunnel was part of the Massachusetts Turnpike connecting system. The Massachusetts Turnpike is part of the three-thousand-twenty-mile (3,020) U.S. Route #90 highway system that begins at Logan Airport (the Ted William Tunnel is the beginning of this roadway) and ends in Seattle, Washington. The Fort Point Channel Tunnel would be the last tunnel to be completed and was the final tunnel project that Modern Continental Construction Company would be involved with on the 'Big Dig' Central Artery project. The decision to name the third tunnel to run under Boston Harbor. The 'Ted Williams' tunnel was made by Massachusetts Governor William Weld. A tremendous honor for Boston's greatest Red Sox slugger!

The successful foray by 'Modern Continental South' into the heart of the Southern part of the United States prompted the newly appointed president of the southern division, Al Benson, to expand their operations. The first construction project to be acquired in 1998 was the installation of a sanitary sewer system. Not long after being awarded the sanitary sewer project, MCS was invited to bid on a 'design-build' bridge project that was part of 'CSX' railroad systems that operate in the southern part of the United States. Modern

Continental South was the low bidder on this railroad bridge project. The design and location of the railroad bridge would be the responsibility of the MCS engineering department.

The next project that MCS acquired was in the vicinity of Palm Beach, Florida. They would be involved with another substantial bridge design-build project. This design-build project involved the realignment of Dixie Highway from South of Hillsboro Boulevard in Broward County to North of Hillsboro Canal in Palm Beach County and was approximately three-quarters of a mile long. This project included the realignment of Dixie Highway, a four-lane divided urban arterial that bridges the Hillsboro Canal, Northeast 2nd Avenue, Florida East Coast Railway, and Northeast 1st and 2nd Avenues. In addition to the fourteen-hundred-foot curved steel tub girder mainline structure, a pedestrian walkway structure and an off-ramp structure from Dixie Highway to Northeast 2nd Avenue were also constructed. The cost associated with this project was in excess of thirty-two million dollars.

It appeared that although there had been some opposition to the hiring of Al Benson and his being given complete control of this newly formed southern entity, it seemed as though MCS was finding its way and proving to be another 'ace pulled out from up the sleeve of Les Marino'. The proof would be in the overall profitability of the southern venture. The jury was still out for most of the Modern Continental management team.

****

It wasn't all work and no play for the Modern Continental employees. What had started in the early 1990s as a last-minute, spur-of-the-moment idea, had become by 1998 a 'something to look forward to the annual event' for the Modern Continental people. As there was a very good, long-term, working relationship between the New England Laborers Union and Modern Continental Construction Company, the use of the New England Laborers one-hundred-and forty-acre Laborers Training Academy facility located in Hopkinton, Massachusetts was provided to Modern Continental annually for a late summer August get-together. This annual event was a family-friendly gathering that allowed the Modern Continental employees, their significant others, and their children to attend an old-fashioned 'cook-out' that included lots of events that encompassed games, prizes, and fun for everyone who attended.

It was always a fun day when the hardworking men and women that made up the workforce at Modern Continental put aside their daily tasks and got together for a day of food, fun, games, and lighthearted frivolity. There was never a lack of excitement or enjoyment at this event.

Modern Continental's core principles had been founded on hard work and family values. Although this was a very large company with thousands of employees, the fundamental family-friendly environment and philosophy had never changed. It was a special day that allowed the various segments of the company to congregate and enjoy each other's company. Les Marino and Kenny Anderson both looked forward to this annual event, it was a time to just relax and count their many blessings!

Chapter Seventeen
Days of Decisions

1999–2001

***There is no going back; we either sink or swim*—Les Marino**

West Palm Beach, Florida
Gun Club Road
Monday, 2 August 1999
7:25 a.m.

The warden marched the men two by two down the middle of Gun Club Road as if it were a Fourth of July Parade. But a parade it was not. The inmates at the Palm Beach County Detention Center were actually marching to their first day of work for Modern Continental South (MCS). The labor market in the Southeast part of Florida in the late nineteen nineties was severely taxed. Manpower was at a premium. Modern Continental South was in the middle of building the 'Dixie Highway' bridge. The primary portion of the bridge would be built with pre-cast concrete structures which Modern Continental South was constructing on their own. A metal building was thrown up and several concrete casts were built at the Gun Club Road yard facility that Modern Continental South had recently acquired. However, having the manpower to sufficiently mix the concrete and pour the cement into the prefabricated casts was difficult to achieve.

****

When Kenny Anderson had recently visited the job site, he discussed with Al Benson the need to acquire workers to build the concrete sections that would be needed to construct the bridge. Al Benson threw up his hands in frustration and asked Kenny Anderson, "What do you want me to do, I can't just snap my

242

fingers and workers will appear?" Kenny understood that procuring competent labor to build the pre-cast structures was not going to be easy. Labor was limited and it seemed that no one wanted to get involved with hard, physical labor that required working in the summer sun in Southern Florida.

Kenny was driving from the yard on Gun Club Road to the 'Dixie Highway' bridge job site when he drove past the Palm Beach County Detention Center which is located at the north end of Gun Club Road, about two hundred yards from the MCS concrete pre-cast yard. While he was driving by the prison, Kenny got an idea. He looked at the fenced-in facility that had razor wire strung all around the fence and thought, *this place is full of able-bodied guys who are doing nothing all day*. Kenny pulled his car over and looked up the phone number to the prison. It did not take long for Kenny to get through to the warden of the prison. The discussion that the two men had, Kenny and the warden, proved to be most beneficial to both Palm Beach County Detention Center and to Modern Continental South. A deal was struck that would allow the prisoners who were considered 'non-violent' with a good behavior record to work at the pre-cast concrete yard for Modern Continental South.

The deal struck between Kenny Anderson and the Warden of Palm Beach County Detention Center would include the prison providing a minimum of twenty inmates each day to work at the pre-cast concrete yard and in return, a fair and equitable wage would be paid to the workers with sixty percent of the wage being retained by the inmate and the remaining forty percent of the wage would go to the State of Florida. As the construction of the pre-cast concrete structures was a separate and unrelated operation that was taking place the wages paid to the prison inmates did not fall within the prevailing wage categories. A true 'win-win' for all involved.

****

A problem had been solved with regard to the West Palm Beach 'Dixie Highway' bridge project in Florida, but another problem of a much larger scale was taking place on the design-build 'CSX' railroad bridge project in South Carolina. The term 'design-build' means just that you design the bridge and then after the design is submitted and approved you proceed with the building of the bridge. The illustrious engineers that were employed by Modern Continental South did a fine job designing the bridge in question. The structural integrity and the load-bearing portion of the bridge that was designed met, and exceeded, the specification set forth by the 'CSX Railroad'. However, there was one problem; the construction of the bridge was found to be in the wrong place! The existing railroad tracks and the new bridge did not line up properly. This job was bid rather tight to begin with, with very little wiggle room for additional costs. The portions of the bridge that had already been built would now need to be demolished and removed and the bridge would have to be built again. This time, hopefully in the right place!

It was in the fall of nineteen ninety-nine when this catastrophic 'built the bridge in the wrong place' mistake came to light. This blunder by the Modern Continental South division would prove to be the beginning of a turn of events for the Modern Continental juggernaut that had been rolling along with minimal difficulties. Like any other situation when you suffer a defeat, the immediate reaction is to rebound and come back stronger so that you can offset the loss. Modern Continental South did just that, as they were a successful low bidder on the design-build of the Washington, DC-Fairfax, Virginia sewerage treatment plant that had a bid price of one hundred and thirty million dollars ($130,000,000.00).

In late 1999, MCS was also the successful low bidder on a major sewer pipe construction project in Daytona Beach, Florida. The Modern Continental South division was picking up work but they were not profitable. A premonition by the Modern Continental management team when they voted against the hiring of Al Benson was, unfortunately, coming true. Al Benson would need to pull off a win and show some profit if he was to be the savior that Les Marino had made him out to be. The clock was ticking for the struggling Modern Continental South division. The 'Dixie Highway' bridge project, the 'misplaced' CSX Railroad Bridge job along with the Washington, DC sewerage treatment plant and the Daytona Beach, Florida sewer pipe projects provided MCS the work they needed. Turning a profit would be another story.

****

Although there were some anxious moments and a few fluttering hearts, Modern Continental made it through Y2K without any computer systems crashing or networks catching the 'Millennium Bug'. The coding of the

Modern Continental computers was not affected when 31 December 1999 moved forward to 1 January 2000. The panic, fear, and hype that had been talked about for the past year were unfounded. Modern Continental had just closed a year that showed the largest amount of work that the company had ever performed in one calendar year, $1.1 Billion. Unfortunately, it was not a profitable year for the company. In fact, it was a rather poor year with regard to the overall profitability of the combined Modern Continental Construction Company, Modern Continental Enterprises and its subsidiaries, Modern Continental New York, Modern Continental California, Modern Continental South, and the South American Brazilian operations. There was an awful lot of work going on, but nothing to show for it.

The New Year 2000 started out with a much-needed influx of local work as Modern Continental Construction Company was the successful low bidder on the long-anticipated widening of Route #3 from Burlington, Massachusetts to the Nashua, New Hampshire border. This project which would eventually cost the Massachusetts taxpayer almost four hundred million dollars ($400,000,000.00) was another 'design-build' job that would create many opportunities for the engineering people at Modern Continental to show their expertise with regard to creating and building a major highway. Cosmo Palazzola would be the project manager along with John Foster who would be the project superintendent on this high-profile road-building project.

The original Route #3 was built back in the early 1950s. The road consisted of a two-lane road going north and south with two lanes on each side from Route #128 now Route #95 in Burlington, Massachusetts to the Nashua, New Hampshire border. The New Hampshire side of Route #3 was widened in the early 1990s. You now had three New Hampshire lanes on each side, north and south pouring into two Massachusetts lanes. This was creating a major bottleneck and a horrible commute for the many Massachusetts people who had left the state to move to New Hampshire but still worked in Massachusetts. The decision to finally widen the roadway on the Massachusetts side was sorely needed and a long time to come to fruition.

The work taking place in the State of New York was expanding as Modern Continental Construction picked up a large portion of marine work in Statin Island New York which prompted Modern Continental Construction Company to purchase an existing marine contractor by the name of Spearin, Preston & Burrows. This specialty contractor had been primarily involved with pile-driving, and seismic retrofitting services which included stripping concrete and drilling holes for the installation of tension rods and anchors which are essentially used in tunnel-building operations. This new division would fall under the Modern Continental New York division that was operated by Senior Vice President John McNamara.

It was also in early 2000 that the Modern Continental New York division was the successful low bidder on the one-hundred and forty-two-million-dollar ($142,000,000.00) Fountain Avenue Landfill Reclamation Project. This job was probably the most unusual piece of work that Modern Continental had ever picked up.

The job site was in Brooklyn, New York but the site was so remote that even Brooklyn natives that had lived there all their lives didn't know where it was. The location of the job was in the Fresh Creek area on the Brooklyn, Queens border on the shores of Jamaica Bay. This low-lying shoreline area was one of the City of New York's primary solid waste landfills from the 1960s through the late 1980s before being closed for environmental reasons. The specifications for the job would require that two hundred and eighty-five (285) acres of land be capped and covered. The majority of the clay landfill covering would be brought by barge from New Jersey to the job site. Once the landfill is capped, then the crushed stone and loam topsoil that will come from the Albany New York area would have to be barged down the Hudson River and brought to the site. A total of fourteen giant Terex forty-ton end dump trucks would be on-site along with six D-6 Caterpillar Bull Dozers moving massive amounts of materials.

The New York division of Modern Continental through the Project Manager Barry Longenecker was responsible for the placement of 250,000 cubic yards of crushed stone that will act as a cushion between the plastic liner that covers the landfill and will allow drainage of rainwater into Jamaica Bay. Upon completion of the project, the area was turned over as open space and a refuge for many types of wildlife which greatly improved the environment in the Jamaica Bay New York City area.

It wasn't just the Modern Continental Construction portion of the operations that were chasing new work and expanding their footprint; in 2000, Modern Continental Enterprises began acquiring land in both Raleigh, North Carolina, and Atlanta Georgia locations and began to build single-family home developments in both of these states. The housing developments were similar to the North Reading, Massachusetts complex as the land acquired was located in suburban settings and would allow for mid-range and high-end single-family dwellings to be constructed.

Bob Shepherd, the ambitious and energetic director of Modern Continental Enterprises, established a strong presence in both the Raleigh, North Carolina, and Atlanta, Georgia regions and made a valiant effort to produce a profitable undertaking in the Southern area that was not overly familiar to this northern company. However, Modern Continental Enterprises had a considerable amount of experience with not only building single-family homes but they also were quite capable of performing the related road-building and utility installations including water, sewer, and drain lines that are part of a large housing development.

The templates for the homes that were being built in Raleigh and Atlanta pretty much followed the guidelines and architectural design of the North Reading, Massachusetts project. The North Reading, Massachusetts location had been an ongoing development since the late 1980s and had just been completed in the late 1990s. Well, over two hundred and fifty single-family homes would be the final tally with regard to the number of single-family homes that were built in North Reading, Massachusetts by Modern Continental Enterprises.

Les Marino, who had lived in Quincy, Massachusetts for many years after leaving the humble Cambridge, Massachusetts apartment that Les and his wife Anna Maria started out in when they first came to the United States, decided that the North Reading, Massachusetts location that his company was developing might be a good place to live. Les's daughter Laura also moved into one of the beautiful homes that were built in North Reading. Having his family, which included his beloved grandchildren, close by and living in a suburban setting seemed to please the Marino family.

Modern Continental Enterprises, in conjunction with their acquisition of the Boston Harbor Cruise Company, purchased two full-functioning boat and yacht marinas. One was in Boston Harbor and the other marina was located in Scituate, Massachusetts. Bruce Rapoza, the loyal, long-term employee who was initially involved with bidding and purchasing and was one of the first people hired by Les Marino, took over control of the marinas and the related activities that went along with the operations. The combined Modern Continental operations, which included both the construction division and the enterprise functions, had become very involved with marine activities. A number of various kinds of boats and barges were included in the overall ocean and marine inventory that the 'Modern Continental' conglomerate owned.

****

Marino's Lookout Farm, which was located in Natick, Massachusetts, was by far one of the greatest places to visit with your family. This farm dated back to 1680 and had remained a working farm ever since. There were numerous activities for both children and adults. There were many exotic animals, including bison, lamas, horses, and ostriches along with little lambs and goats that children could pet. There were chickens, ducks, geese, and swans that were all an intricate part of the rustic setting. The farm had purchased three old-time stage coaches that were 1800s vintage and operational as they provided scenic rides around the farmlands. In addition to rides and walks down old red brick paths, there was a snack shack and a restaurant that served items that were grown exclusively on the farm. However, the most celebrated segment of the farm activities was the 'pick your own' which included many different types and varieties of apples along with the opportunity to pick out your own big orange pumpkin and bring it home to carve and decorate as a family.

The farm was a pet project of both Les Marino and Kenny Anderson, in addition to providing an enormous amount of joy and satisfaction for the many visitors and customers, the farm also provided fresh, organically grown vegetables and fruits that were used at the Cambridge, Massachusetts 'Ristorante Marino'. The fresh produce and the healthy animals that were raised on the farm and ultimately consumed at the restaurant provided a much-needed source of wholesome commodities.

Although Marino's Lookout Farm was a major success with regard to the beauty and aesthetics of the breathtaking landscape and surroundings, the truth was that the farm was losing money. The upgrades, animals, and new plantings along with the cost associated with maintaining such large and involved operations had become a drain on the finances for Modern Continental. By the summer of 2000, it had become clearly evident that pouring more money into 'Marino's Lookout Farm' was not a healthy or frugal idea for a company that was experiencing financial difficulties.

Along with having the farm as one of his extracurricular activities, the very health-minded and fitness enthusiast, Les Marino decided to move forward with an idea he had for more than a few years. Les Marino treated his body like a temple. He did not smoke, he drank an occasional glass of wine or a Budweiser Natural Light beer and he worked out every day. This healthy lifestyle had treated Les well. At close to seventy years old, Les still lifted weights, worked out, and ate healthily every day of his life. Therefore, passing along the concept of eating well and living a vigorous and active life was something that Les Marino wanted to pass along to the many people that he believed would benefit from this approach to a long and healthy life.

Les also realized that as someone ages, there are limitations that seem to encroach upon them. One of those limitations was the libido and the ability to perform the satisfying activities that one took for granted in their youth. Therefore, the 'Marino Health Center', which was located on Massachusetts Avenue in Cambridge, Massachusetts not far from Ristorante Marino was formed and began functioning as a holistic medical clinic that offered acupuncture, chiropractic services along with cardiovascular disease and the treatment of issues relating to men. The farm and the clinic were reflections of Les Marino as they provided a source of comfort to him, as he felt that he was providing a public service to the many individuals who appreciated these activities, services and health options.

****

11 September 2001, like Pearl Harbor, would be a day that will live in infamy. The atrocities and the upheaval that was inflicted on our great nation that day would be unforgivable. The foreign terrorists that unleashed this turmoil on our country, were no doubt, sick and deranged individuals who did not understand that although we may have received a severe blow to our nation, we would rally and defend our great United States of America and rebuild it to be stronger than ever. The tragic 'twin towers' attack and ultimate collapse in New York City would be an opportunity for Modern Continental to show its loyalty to our country and to display the patriotic nature of the company. Many of the Modern Continental New York operations would be put on hold so that tugboats, barges, equipment, and manpower could assist in the massive cleanup efforts that took place after the tragic demise of the 'twin towers'. This

was more than a gracious charitable gesture; it was more about American Pride and Patriotic responsibilities. The people who were working for Modern Continental at the time of the '911' tragedy were determined to help our country and the City of New York, along with Washington, DC which took a major hit at the Pentagon, and the good people of Somerset County, Pennsylvania, where one of the terrorist commandeered planes 'flight #93' would ultimately crash.

The general admission by everyone who witnessed the abomination that took place on Tuesday, 11 September 2001 was that our nation, although weakened would rally, and with the help of the many loyal, and devoted people of our wonderful United States of America would survive this treacherous and evil act. The New York division of Modern Continental Construction Company provided much-needed manpower, marine equipment, tugboats, and heavy construction pieces of machinery to the efforts that took place in the aftermath of the 11 September 2001 catastrophe. It was a true patriotic effort that came from the heart of each and every Modern Continental worker who lent their sweat, toil, and expertise to the cleanup efforts at the site of the toppled 'twin towers'.

****

With the 'Big Dig' activities winding down in late 2001, Max Marino was handling the completion of the numerous contracts that were still ongoing. However, in an effort to assist with the numerous projects that Modern Continental had underway in the Boston area, Max Marino also became the Project Manager of the Old Colony Railroad restoration project which was also known as the 'Braintree Yard' contract. This project was a Massachusetts Bay Transportation Authority (MBTA) railroad project that was part of the rehabilitation of the Southern Massachusetts rail beds that the MBTA planned on using as future commuter rail lines. The vast experience that Modern Continental had acquired in the field of railroad construction allowed them to acquire this large contract and to undertake related MBTA projects that involved their railroad expertise.

During the duration of the Braintree Yard MBTA railroad project, Max Marino became involved with the MBTA resident engineer on the project. The daily communication and interaction associated with the development of the various phases of work that were taking place would precipitate a close working relationship between Max Marino and the MBTA resident engineer. Unfortunately, the relationship between these two individuals became somewhat convoluted and a little complex as the MBTA resident engineer began to allude to the need for Max Marino to assist him with some projects he had going on at his home. At first, Max Marino did not comprehend exactly what the resident engineer was talking about. However, it began to sink in that the help the resident engineer was looking for would involve a situation that might not be something that Max should get involved with. His inner voice kept whispering to him to be careful!

Reluctance by Max Marino to participate in the MBTA resident engineers scheme was causing the development of a somewhat contemptuous relationship between the two. It appeared that the resident engineer wanted Max Marino to provide some materials from the job site and have them delivered to the home of the resident engineer. In addition to the materials that he wanted, there was also the removal of a couple of structures from the property that the resident engineer owned that he wanted Modern Continental to take care of. Knowing full well that there were many 'eyes' watching what was going on at the job site, Max was reluctant to oblige. Max Marino, to a degree, began to develop a little bit of a 'slow blinker' personality when he spoke with the resident engineer making it appear that he did not understand exactly what he was asking him to do.

With no uncertain terms, the resident engineer explained, in detail, to Max Marino that he wanted him to deliver a specific amount of materials to his home residence and that he wanted two small buildings at the property demolished and removed from the site by Modern Continental. With a fear that this job might very well become a problem if he did not comply with the wishes of the resident engineer, and knowing full well that the resident engineer held the 'purse strings' and that he provided the monthly payments, Max, reluctantly agreed to take care of what the resident engineer wanted him to do.

The fear of causing a rift between the guy who paid the bills was too much for Max Marino to ignore. The job needed to show a profit so if performing some questionable tasks for the guy that submitted the monthly pay requisitions was required; it was something he would just have to deal with.

Just as Max Marino had feared, there were many eyes watching and numerous ears listening to what was going on at this job site. Not long after performing the work and delivering the materials to the home of the resident engineer, Max and the resident engineer were brought up on charges relating to conspiracy, collusion, and bribery. Max did attempt to explain the pressure that he was put under by the resident engineer, which eventually allowed the prosecution to suspend the sentence and require that Modern Continental Construction Company pay a fine and admit to the act. Max was caught in a no win situation which the prosecution recognized.

****

The financial burden that was placed upon Modern Continental with the 'CSX' railroads bridge in South Carolina being built in the wrong place had become compounded as the water treatment plant job that Modern Continental South (MCS) was working on in Washington, DC was an utter failure. The calculations on the bid for the job left out a considerable number of materials and the quantities were not properly determined. As a result of these unfortunate errors, the cost of the project showed an estimated loss of close to one hundred million dollars ($100,000,000.00). This news was devastating to Les Marino. Al Benson, the one-time thought of savoir of the company had proven to be incompetent and irresponsible. Further investigation into the operations that were being conducted by the Modern Continental South division indicated that the figures being provided by the MCS accounting people were suspect to say the least. Decisions and changes would prompt the restructuring of the Modern Continental South division and the ultimate closure of the office.

With the company on the ropes, and in need of an infusion of cash, the bonding agent, who appeared to be the only one making money on the Modern Continental operations, coerced and influenced Les Marino to continue to bid work so that the 'wave' could continue and the start-up money from a new job would provide the much-needed cash and prevent the wave from crashing. In spite of the fact that Modern Continental was bleeding and close to life support, the bonding company let them continue to bid work. The financial matters had become a serious problem, one that the bonding company seemed to not take as seriously as it clearly was. Perhaps the bonding agent was masking the situation and covering up some of the 'sins' and not painting a complete picture of how things were really going at Modern Continental and was pulling the wool over the bonding companies eyes?

With a low bid of one hundred and ten million dollars ($110,000,000.00) in late 2001, Modern Continental Construction successfully acquired a new tunnel project with the Massachusetts Water Resources Authority (MWRA). This tunnel was a trunk sewer conduit that would run from Weymouth, Massachusetts to Nut Island conveying sewerage to this facility.

The start-up money from the new MWRA tunnel project would indeed provide much-needed cash to Modern Continental, but the amount of cash that was contributed to the company might be comparable to putting a Band-Aid on a ten-inch gash! By this point in time, Peter Grela, the overworked accountant and chief financial operations person at Modern Continental who was shouldering the heavy load regarding financial stability for the company, was now quite concerned for the future.

The Bob Shepherd, Modern Continental Enterprise operations had been contributing cash with their housing operations in North Carolina and Georgia but the profit being made on the housing development work was soon offset by the fact that the development on the Caribbean Island of Saint Lucia had run into trouble, The once smooth flowing operations had run into some problems with materials and equipment issues. The budget associated with this Caribbean paradise had suddenly gone askew and was costing a considerable amount of money the projections for condominium sales had fallen off sharply which curtailed the flow of cash associated with pre-sale operations. Inevitably, the Saint Lucia project would need to be abbreviated as the money just was not there for the project to continue in the manner initially anticipated.

The problems at Modern Continental were mounting on a daily basis. How could a company that knew exactly how to acquire work and be profitable, as they had all of the proverbial bases covered with regard to experience and know-how let these problems be created? The issues relating to the creation of the Modern Continental South Division sure did unravel this once tight and closely-knit company.

The fiscal year was quickly coming to a close as the end of 2001 was fast approaching. The need to take an in-depth and thorough accounting of all operations that were taking place and to make the crucial decisions necessary to survive this financial nightmare was about to take place. The fear was that it just might be getting too late in the game to pull out a win. It was becoming 'sink or swim' time.

It was hard to believe but the once invincible combination of Les Marino and Kenny Anderson, the two guys who could solve just about any problem, were now faced with something that they had to deal with and they both were now beginning to understand the true meaning of the adage:

'Companies don't go broke from lack of work; they go broke from having too much work!'

Chapter Eighteen
The Domino Effect

2002–2003

Faith is what keeps our hopes alive—Kenny Anderson

Tyngsboro, Massachusetts
Southbound Staging Area-Route #3 Project—Adjacent to highway
Sunday, 10 February 2002
11:25 a.m.

Although the job was not working on this Sunday morning, Les Marino thought it prudent to take a ride to the site and spend a few minutes to try and figure out just how things got so complicated and bewildering. It was a warm day for this time of year as the temperature was flirting with 50 degrees; a good day to walk the site and contemplate. As he pulled his 2001 Cadillac Eldorado off the southbound breakdown lane and into the staging area, he noticed that one of the subcontractors was working on fixing a bucket truck in the staging yard. The ground had just a trace of melting snow that was left over from the previous week's little dusting.

Les got out of his car and instinctively put on his hard hat as he began to walk around the construction yard that was full of material and equipment. Thus far, it had not been a bad winter, but the progress on the job was not what it should be. This project was different from the road jobs that had been previously put out for bid by the Commonwealth of Massachusetts. Most projects of this type would include a specific set of drawings with details relating to the quantities and materials, along with benchmarks and elevation references. However, this project, the widening of the Route #3 roadway from Burlington, Massachusetts to Nashua, New Hampshire was a 'design-build' project, which basically means that the contractor that is the low bidder and is awarded the job would be responsible for all aspects of the project. This seems to be where the problems may have come from.

As Les walked he began to think and wonder, *did we leave out some aspects that would require additional costs? Were the quantities correct? Did we factor in enough for inflation? Did we carry enough for all of the subcontractors that are working on the project?* The more he walked and thought, the more he became frustrated and annoyed. He had not been feeling well lately, he did not have much of an appetite and he got tired really fast, His stamina was not what it used to be. He refused to accept the fact that he was aging, heck he had felt like a teenager for most of his life, he couldn't figure out exactly why he was so rundown? Was it the strain and worry, of falling into a financial abyss? Could he salvage things by picking up some new work that would be profitable and help offset the massive losses that Modern Continental South continued to incur? Only time would tell; and the sound of the clock ticking had become maddening!

****

Peter Grela, the company's bean counter had been working with Chris Lincoln, the company magician, to see if they could come up with a way to get an infusion of cash into the company. It was no secret that without acquiring a good-sized chunk of cash, there would inevitably be consequences that might be too numerous and hard for the company to overcome. They both had spent countless hours trying to conceive a way to get some cash. After numerous hours of rumination and scrutiny, it was determined the most logical way to get an influx of cash would be to put up a great many pieces of construction equipment that the company owned as collateral for a loan from the bank.

Peter Grela and Chris Lincoln met with the bank and explained the situation. After putting on a somewhat successful 'dog and pony' show for the bank, it was agreed that the bank would acquire the services of an equipment liquidation company and have them view the equipment and come up with a working figure that would represent an estimated value, which would be the basis for the loan.

It took a little bit of time, but by early May 2002, after the equipment was viewed and assessed, a working figure was established, the resolute duo of Peter Grela and Chris Lincoln were successful in acquiring a loan in the amount of seventy-five million dollars ($75,000,000.00). Would this be enough to ward off the wolves? For the time being, the wolves would be held at bay, but not only were the wolves circling but there was now the smell of blood in the water which brought the attention of the Great White Sharks that had been swimming in the vicinity of the Charles River just across from 600 Memorial Drive in Cambridge, Massachusetts.

With over a billion dollars' worth of work on the books and the company going as strong as ever, there was still a series of menacing cumulonimbus clouds hovering over Modern Continental. The sound of thunder could be heard in the distance and the lightning strikes were getting closer.

The management group, the guys that made up the think tank, better known as Modern Continental's 'dream team' were meeting more often. It seemed to be one crisis after another. The need to decipher and disseminate the factors that had led to the situation that was taking place required that everyone pitch in and roll up their sleeves and come up with ways to get this wayward locomotive back on track. It was always a firm belief of Les Marino to come up with ways to stop the bleeding. That might have worked when the company was local and involved with just sewer construction, but now, the company was a global conglomerate that had way too many irons in the fire and way too many blazes taking place. The bleeding had now become a hemorrhage!

The most logical first step would be to cease and desist with operations that were losing money. The Marino Lookout Farm in Natick, Massachusetts, although functioning and producing cash, the overhead and operating costs offset any profit. However, Les Marino did not want to close or sell this entity. He believed that the farm would begin to show a profit.

The Ristorante Marino, the glory of North Cambridge, Massachusetts, the once eclectic favorite of the culinary elite crowd, had fallen out of favor. The cost to provide organically grown vegetables and fruit along with the raising of the animals that were slaughtered and served at this fine establishment had become cost-prohibitive. The cost to grow and prepare the food at the restaurant far exceeded the prices that were being charged. The concept was phenomenal, but the truth was that although the food, wine and service were excellent, the cost to dine at the Ristorante Marino was very expensive, which limited the clientele. Again, although the restaurant operations were losing money, Les Marino would not close or sell the operations.

It became increasingly difficult for the Modern Continental management team that consistently made the suggestions to cut back on losing operations to be effective as the recommendations that they made seemed to fall upon deaf ears. The blunders that had taken place with the Modern Continental South (MCS) operations had been addressed and acted upon, but the simple fact was that the work acquired by MCS had to be completed by contract so the damage had already been done and would most likely get worse.

The Washington, DC, actually, the Fairfax Virginia wastewater treatment plant that MCS had acquired was ongoing which meant that the losses were also ongoing as well. The Dixie Highway Bridge project in Palm Beach County Florida although initially successful as the inmate labor for the pre-cast concrete structures was beneficial turned sour and was losing money. Even though the MCS division was no longer bidding work and for all intent and purposes had been absorbed back into the Modern Continental Construction parent operations, they had already done their damage and had delivered a very crippling, and severe blow to the company. Modern was on the ropes, dazed and somewhat confused at this point in time.

One of the contributing factors to the issues with cash flow was the failure of Bechtel, Parsons & Brinkerhoff to adequately and in a timely manner process the extra work orders and overruns that were owed to Modern Continental Construction Company for the work performed on the 'Big Dig' Central Artery projects. Millions of dollars were owed to Modern Continental that were being disputed and were not being processed or paid. It was very difficult for a company to buy materials and pay workers if they were not being paid by the entity that they were performing the work. The work was done but not paid for, which also took its toll.

It was a one-blade sword that was used when it came to performing work on the 'Big Dig'. Modern Continental Construction Company, by contract, which included liquidated damages clauses for failure to perform the work and complete it in the time frame noted, had to continue working and buying materials but there were no consequences if the work that was being performed was disputed and not paid for. This one-way action was crippling the company as they continued to pay for labor and materials but were not being properly compensated for the work that they had performed. It was important for Modern to get a handle on the situation as the company was reeling from the lack of payment. The massive amount of slurry wall construction that took place on the 'Big Dig' that was installed by Modern Continental had continuously been disputed with a major portion of what had been constructed not paid for.

By the summer of 2002, with an abundance of work taking place, the scramble to collect money and pay bills was becoming increasingly difficult. Chris Lincoln, better known as the 'David Copperfield' of accounts payable, had his hands full on a daily basis as his phone never seemed to stop ringing. It was one disgruntled subcontractor or supplier after another that was calling him looking for some sort of idea as to when they might receive payment. The seventy-five million dollars that Peter Grela acquired from the bank as a loan on the equipment was very helpful, but it only went so far.

It was in September 2002 that the Modern Continental management team again assembled to review the situation. The conference room was quiet as Les Marino came through the conference room door; it had been a couple of weeks since the team had sat down to go over the dire financial circumstances. Les had not been around much, as he had been doing whatever he could to get a handle on the problems and spending lots of time on the job sites. When he did enter the room, it was clearly evident that he was not himself. He looked gaunt and although he had some color from the sun, as the summer was coming to an end, he looked kind of pale and uncomfortable. Everyone knew what a toll these financial setbacks had been having on him, but it was not until they laid eyes on him this afternoon that they understood just how much these troubles had left their mark on this man. He just didn't look good.

The meeting was brief, as overanalyzing the matter just seemed to have the same effect that rubbing salt in an open wound might have. A summary of the situation took place which basically amounted to the listing of jobs and activities that were losing money and draining the company:

1. The money owed from the extra work orders on the Big Dig-Central Artery project continued to be a concern as the money owed was quite substantial.
2. The Modern Continental South (MCS) division was the primary culprit in this losing money scenario. Each and every project that MCS had been associated with, except the initial 'manpower' operations that they had been involved with at the paper mills were losing activities. It did not help that the accounting figures being provided by

MCS were filled with smoke and mirrors and after proper vetting were found to be 'suspect' at best.

3. The Route #3 Burlington to Nashua, NH design-build road project, although still ongoing was losing money and had little chance of being turned around. The quantities and the sheer magnitude of the project had not been properly addressed or calculated.

4. The Weymouth-Nut Island tunnel project with Massachusetts Water Resources Authority, the job that was bid to acquire some start-up cash flow, was now at the stage that all of the 'juice' had basically been sucked out of it, which would mean that the remainder of the project would now cost the company money, lots of money, it appeared.

5. The once profitable and successful Modern Continental Enterprises operation had now taken a turn for the worse, as the Saint Lucia development project along with the Marino Lookout Farm and the Ristorante Marino operations were all losing substantial money and needed to cease operations, in the very near future.

The meeting ended with no clear path to 'black ink' in the accounting department. Bright Red would be the prevailing color with regard to the future of Modern Continental.

****

In the fall of 2002, as the company was going through this period of difficulty, the long-standing friendship and comradery that had once existed so strongly between Les Marino and Kenny Anderson, but had recently been troubled, was immediately rekindled and was now stronger than ever. Les needed Kenny to share his feelings about the direction that the company was going in and about life in general. Kenny had always been a good listener and a positive sounding board for Les. It was Kenny Anderson that Les confided his deep concern about his recent health issues. Les, who always knew exactly how his body should feel in certain situations, now found that his body was failing him and he understood, full well, that something was wrong.

Les let Kenny know that he was always tired and rundown. He knew that something was wrong. Kenny, who had been through his own share of health issues, explained to Les that he should immediately go to the hospital for tests so that it could be determined exactly what was going on with his body. Les further explained to Kenny that he thought right along that the pressures associated with the problems that had been created by the failure of the Modern Continental South entity and the ongoing issues with the Route #3 Burlington to Nashua, New Hampshire project had been the culprit associated with his feeling rundown and tired. But he finally acknowledged that it just might not be the recent events with the company that have been taking place that were causing his concerns. Les, was now in a position that was unfamiliar to him, as he chatted with Kenny and listened to him pass along his thoughts, Les realized that we take advice in drops but we often give it out in buckets.

After their conversation, Les made arrangements to go through a battery of tests at Mount Auburn Hospital which was on the campus of Harvard University, to help determine what just might be wrong. Kenny agreed to accompany Les when we went to Mount Auburn for his testing. The testing took a good part of the day before they were completed. Les was being checked for every conceivable ailment that might be related to the way he had been feeling. At this point, Les did not want anyone, other than Kenny, to know what was going on. Les and Kenny had a chance to spend some quality, one-on-one time together and to just talk like they used to. The two of them had a chance to reminisce and chat about the old days. When life was just a tad simpler than it was now.

Kenny Anderson acted as Les's eyes and ears when it came to what the doctors were talking about. It is not uncommon for someone that is going through health issues to have a tendency to dwell in their own mind about the feelings that they have, and this being the case there is a chance that the patient just might miss some of the information and feedback that the doctors are explaining when it comes to the test results and what their designated plan of action just might be. This was the case when it came to the test results for all of the different procedures that Les had gone through.

After considerable examination, and careful scrutiny of the test result that the doctors and laboratory technicians at Mount Auburn Hospital had received and reviewed, it was Kenny Anderson who had to let Les know what the test results revealed. It was not easy for Kenny to explain to Les that he had cancer in his system. The type of cancer that Les had was lymphoma. The doctors further explained to Les, exactly what lymphoma was and went on to go over the terms that they were using and helped him understand what exactly lymphoma was.

Les was diagnosed with Hodgkin's Lymphoma, previously known as Hodgkin's disease, it is a type of cancer that affects the lymphatic system. The lymphatic system is a complex system of lymph nodes, vessels, organs, and tissues that carry lymph, a clear fluid. This system is a vital part of the immune system. In Hodgkin's Lymphoma, cells in the lymphatic system grow abnormally and may spread beyond the lymphatic system. Les's immune system had been compromised, that was the primary reason that he seemed to feel rundown and tired all the time.

This news of this cancer diagnosis was devastating to both Les Marino and Kenny Anderson. It took a while for the reality of this diagnosis to actually sink in. Being practical adults and understanding that you can't shoot the messenger, the next step was to find out from the doctors how this condition could be corrected and what would be the course of action with regard to treatment. It was explained that normal treatment would include chemotherapy, radiation and once they knew to what extent the condition was a stem cell transplant might be considered. The oncologist who was brought in to handle the matter did his best to assure Les that this condition could be treated and hopefully put in remission or better yet, cured.

It was Kenny Anderson who gave Les Marino the pep talk that he so desperately needed. This counseling session and very frank conversation was important so that Les could put this situation in proper perspective. A perspective so that he could develop a plan of attack as he had done for just about every other severe and serious problem that he had to confront over the many years that he had been around.

Les Marino was a fighter, a knockdown, drag-out, go-for-the-juggler scrapper who would never think of quitting. As he slowly absorbed the facts and the reality of the battle that he was about to fight, he knew that this confrontation would require great courage, bravery, and a decent amount of fortitude on his part if he was going to defeat this diabolical cancerous foe. However, Les also understood that he had to do his best to fight the good fight with cancer and to maintain the ongoing battle that was raging with regard to his beloved Modern Continental surviving the financial difficulties that the company was experiencing. He accepted the fact that he could not hate what was going on in his life because he knew, if you hate, you have been defeated.

He was not about to go down without a battle royale and he was not about to be defeated!

With his hands properly taped and the gloves put on, Les was eager to begin the fight! His immediate game plan was that once the bell was rung, he would come out swinging and land as many 'haymakers' as he possibly could on this tough and elusive opponent. Les knew that this encounter would not be over in the first round. Les was prepared for a long and drawn-out confrontation. One that would require stamina and unwavering determination.

Les, accompanied by his 'corner man' Kenny Anderson showed up for the first round of chemotherapy. The bell had been rung, the fight was on, and the action was initially fast and furious as this difficult contest had begun!

****

With the year 2002 rapidly coming to a close, the fate of both Modern Continental and its illustrious leader was in jeopardy. There were numerous battles being waged on Memorial Drive in Cambridge, Massachusetts, but all of the struggles seemed to have the same consequences and possible outcomes.

Les Marino and Kenny Anderson spent New Year's Eve 2002 together. They had not spent a New Year's Eve together for a couple of years. The evening was a somber one, to say the least, but they made the most of it as they made a toast to the New Year 2003 with the hope that it would prove to be just a little bit kinder than 2002 had been!

Chapter Nineteen
The Last Harrah

2003–2004

Happiness is beneficial for the body, but it is grief
that develops the mind—Les Marino

Cambridge, Massachusetts
600 Memorial Drive, 6th floor
Kenny Anderson's office
Monday, 10 March 2003
4:25 p.m.

Kenny Anderson was sitting at his desk, feverishly working on an estimate, and taxing his brain to come up with as many quantities for each line item so that he could increase the amount of payment that the company would receive. It was like looking at the ground in the parking lot of a Seven-Eleven Store for a couple of pennies that might have fallen from someone's pants pocket. Kenny, lost in thought, looked up and saw the company CFO Peter Grela, standing in the doorway of his office with a bottle of Jack Daniel's and two eight-ounce glasses in his hands. The look on Peter's face pretty much told the story. Kenny, with an almost poetic gesture, directed Peter to come and sit down. After Peter took a seat in front of Kenny, he then put the glasses on the desk and began to pour a generous amount of Jack Daniel's into each glass. Kenny looked at Peter and with an ever-so-soft whisper, asked Peter, "I take it this is not a celebratory drink?"

Peter took a big slug of Jack Daniel's; he then took his right index finger and slowly rubbed his hand across his lips as he looked deeply into Kenny's blue eyes and stated, "The bank has called in the seventy-five-million-dollar loan."

Kenny then picked up his glass of Jack Daniel's and proceeded to drain the amber liquid in one swallow, he then looked at Peter and said, "It's been a hell of a good run!"

Kenny, a bit befuddled, could not understand why this sudden and drastic action by the bank was taking place. Peter went on to explain to Kenny what exactly took place that prompted the bank to call in their loan. It appeared that although there was still a significant amount of cash being generated and flowing into the company with regard to the various projects and business operations that were being conducted. The payroll and the money that was owed to vendors and subcontractors were still much greater than the amount coming in.

It was not long after Kenny and Peter had commiserated and consoled one another about the action taken by the bank that Chris Lincoln and the rest of the brain trust at Modern Continental had become aware of what was going on. The mood in the Modern Continental office was akin to what it was like on the deck of the Titanic on the evening of 14 April 1912. The only difference was that there was no band playing 'Nearer My God to Thee'!

****

Les Marino had been fighting a valiant battle with cancer. However, the frequent rounds of chemotherapy were taking their toll on him, both physically and mentally. Les was not one to ever complain about misfortune or circumstances that related to his health, but his silent anguish was something that he found very hard to hide. His good friend Kenny Anderson, along with his daughter Lorraine would accompany him to Mount Auburn Hospital when it was time for a consultation with the oncology doctors. Although he was fighting a courageous battle, and knowing full well that he needed to overcome this malady so that he could continue steering the ship, the seas were becoming rougher as the turbulent waves were beginning to break and crash over the bow of the 'SS Modern Continental'.

Although he was in constant discomfort, continuously feeling weak and nauseous, Les Marino knew that he had to take control of the situation relating to the bank calling in their loan. Needless to say, payment could not be made to the bank as Modern Continental was struggling to pay bills and make payroll. Understanding that the wolves needed to be held at bay, this situation prompted an immediate call to the Modern Continental legal representatives. It was the response of the Modern Continental legal people that brought about the need to have a get-together with the Modern Continental corporate officers and division managers.

An emergency meeting was called at the Modern Continental headquarters at 600 Memorial Drive in Cambridge, Massachusetts. It did not take long for the conference room to be filled with dejected, disappointed, and despondent company diehards. The mood was glum, as nary a whisper was spoken in the room. Les stood at the front of the conference room; he was trying his best not to show his anguish and contempt. It seemed like his world was spinning out of control. This was not something that Les Marino, the consummate leader and commander was used to experiencing. He had been through his share of harrowing experiences in the past, but nothing compared to this dilemma.

The room was silent except for one unassuming manager who was apparently lost in his own thoughts as he sat there clicking his ballpoint pen click, click, click, click, click, after the fifth consecutive click of his ballpoint pen, Les, who was wrapped very tight, to begin with, and had been designated an 'A' personality decades ago, could not contain his aggravation with the clicking ballpoint pen. With a bright red face and the ever-present bulging veins in his neck, Les, with a controlled gasp blurted out, "Please stop clicking your pen!"

The meeting was counterproductive as the torment in the room was clearly evident. It seemed as if a downward spiral began to unfurl as finger-pointing and accusations began to be tossed around the room like donuts at a police convention. Les did his best to control the meeting, which he eventually did. The consensus was that the bonding company needed to be contacted and brought into the matter sooner rather than later. As the meeting concluded, a phone call was made to the bonding company informing them of the situation relating to the bank calling in their seventy-five-million-dollar loan and the financial hardship that this development has brought upon the company.

It was not long after the phone call and notification to the bonding company that there was a visit from what the bonding company called a 'fact-finding team'. This 'team' which was being coordinated by two lead figures, one a male and the other a female, came to the Modern Continental offices on Memorial Drive in Cambridge. No sooner had they arrived than their team began to conduct meetings with the various people who were involved with the different Modern Continental operations.

This intrusion by the bonding company was not a pleasant experience for the people at Modern Continental. For the employees that had been with the company back in the late 1980s, it was a 'déjà vu' as the bonding company sent in a group back then to reorganize the upper-level management and conducted similar meetings and interviews. Was there a bit of apprehension and perhaps some animosity, at what was taking place, of course, there was, but this was to be expected.

There were no instantaneous changes, nor any radical disruptions of the Modern Continental Construction operations. The bonding company understood that if the work that was taking place was hindered and not completed then it would only increase their monetary exposure. The objectives of the bonding company's ' fact-finding teams' were to continue with 'business as usual' as best they could. This would not be an easy fix. In addition to trying not to alienate the management people at Modern Continental, the bonding company also had to factor in the ego, self-respect, and importance of the construction supervisory people who were dealing with the construction issues on the numerous job sites.

The bonding company was making every effort to continue with the Modern Continental mission statement that allowed them to achieve the success that they had experienced over the past three-plus decades. Although the company had financial issues, this poor economic aspect did not reflect upon the fact that Modern Continental had a stellar track record with respect to the quality of work that it continuously produced. It was important that quality, safety, and excellence relating to the work being performed would not change.

The first order of business was to sit down with Les Marino and Bob Berry, the two primary individuals who were involved with acquiring work, and inform them that they could no longer bid on any more jobs. This did not come as a surprise. However, the bonding agent, who had a certain amount of culpability with regard to the financial situation that the company had gotten itself in, expressed a desire to have Modern Continental continue to bid and acquire work as the profit from the new work would offset the losses that had been incurred. The bonding company frowned upon this suggestion and did not construe the request of the bonding agent as a wise option.

The process involved getting a grip on what transpired and the situations that allowed the wheels to fall off of the Modern Continental wagon would not be discovered overnight. It would take lots of diligent leg work and investigation to totally understand how the company got to this state of affairs.

****

Business at Modern Continental did go on as usual, well as best it could. Nevertheless, there was that constant, gnawing feeling, always present, in all characteristics of the daily activities that were being performed that would continuously undermine the efforts being made. It was as if an anvil was hanging over each and everyone's head and the anvil was hanging from the thinnest thread imaginable. Now that the bonding company, under the terms and conditions of the legal agreements that were put in place to mutually protect each entity, had somewhat assumed command of the operations, well not the command per se, Les Marino was still in control, but that control was limited to specific duties; the bonding company people did let everyone know that they were making the major decisions now.

Les, his body weakened and wracked by cancer, and his ego devastated by the crumbling of the empire that he had built, would often head over to his one place of solace, his happy place, the Marino Lookout Farm in Natick. He would silently walk and wander through the fragrant fields of the farm and let the beauty of the environment try to heal his many ailments and to lighten his mental load.

As he strolled the verdant pastures, Les, who was a man of faith, would silently whisper to himself, "Lord, teach me to be kind and gentle in all events in my life, let me understand the disappointments that have come my way and to accept the thoughtlessness of others, along with their insincerity and the unfaithfulness on those I depended so much upon. Let me hide my pain and heartaches so that I am the only one suffering from them. Slow me down, ease the pounding of my heart by the quieting of my mind. Please, give me, amid the confusion of the day, calmness as I walk among these beautiful rolling hills."

The farm and the restaurant were the two places that seemed to give Les any kind of comfort at this stage of his life. He spent a considerable amount of time at both locations during the summer and fall of 2003. Les was not a quitter and he knew that he had to try and endure and do his best to work through the problems that had been placed before him. He was making an effort to do his best to keep his chin up and to keep the ball rolling, but this task would be easier said than done!

****

The bonding company's 'fact-finding teams' did come up with numerous facts and certainties that helped identify some of the circumstances relating to the financial calamity that had befallen the company. It was no secret that there were three primary culprits relating to this financial predicament, the Modern Continental South Division, the Mass DOT Route #3 Burlington to Nashua NH design-build road project, and the Big Dig, Central Artery (CAT) project. The estimated losses were calculated to be in the two-hundred-million-dollar range. However, it would take a considerable amount of time to come up with an accurate figure. Peter Grela and his accounting staff were working diligently to satisfy the many demands that the bonding company's 'fact-finding teams' were making upon his people.

The surety aspect of bonding a construction company generally relates to the financial stability of the company and its ability to complete the work that was bonded. The pieces were in place with regard to Modern Continental having the ability to complete the work that was currently taking place. The predominant problem was that there was just not enough money for them to actually buy the materials and pay the numerous subcontractors that were involved in the various projects that were as yet uncompleted. This meant that the bonding company would ultimately have to pay any additional costs that would relate to the successful completion of the outstanding work. The bonding company would now expend its own resources to comply with the contractual obligations that were currently in place, as the bonding company guaranteed the various entities that the work would be completed. Therefore, in order to limit their losses, the bonding company could choose to bring in another company to manage and take over the uncompleted work.

Before any decision was made about bringing in another contracting company to coordinate the unfinished work, the bonding people decided that it might be fruitful to get some input from Kenny Anderson, the primary guy who was involved with the Modern Continental fieldwork that was currently taking place. A time and date were scheduled with Kenny to meet and discuss this somewhat 'touchy' subject. This meeting would not be a pleasant one. Probably the biggest issue that was involved with the ultimate demise of Modern Continental was the tremendous hurt and pain that was being incurred by both Les Marino and Kenny Anderson, the founding fathers of this organization. To say what was taking place was a 'humbling experience' would be an enormous understatement. Both of these guys were devastated and a little shell-shocked that their lifelong dream was coming to an end, an end that no one had imagined would ever take place.

****

Although the bonding company people did pay Kenny Anderson the respect that he deserved, as they sat with him and went through a long and drawn-out meeting regarding what contracting companies had the experience to perform and complete the work that Modern Continental was involved with which company might be a good fit to bring in and get involved with managing and completing the outstanding work. The bonding company people listened, but they ultimately did not take any of Kenny's recommendations as they made their own choice and brought in the contractor that they had an established relationship with.

Jay Cashman, Inc. from Quincy, Massachusetts was the contractor that the bonding company chose to manage and complete the outstanding work that was still on the books at Modern Continental Construction Company. This was the first of what would be a series of management decisions that would be made by the bonding company to try and limit their loss exposure and to eventually phase out the Modern Continental operations. It would take quite a long time to accomplish the phasing out and completion of operations, but the process had begun.

The Cashman Companies, which was what the Jay Cashman, Inc. company would eventually become, was an established contracting company from the Boston area that started out as a marine construction company and evolved into a general contracting operation. It was kind of ironic as back in the late 1970s when Modern Continental Construction Company started doing marine work; it was Jay Cashman, Inc. that would lease their barges to Modern Continental.

****

It was in early 2004 before any half-decent news would enter the life of Les Marino. As a result of an aggressive form of cancer treatment and the cutting-edge medical attention that Les had been receiving for his lymphoma; he was informed that his cancer was in remission. Battered and worn, Les, the consummate fighter, did his best to become totally involved with what was taking place with his company and the involvement of the bonding company and Jay Cashman. Les did his best to cooperate and he directed his employees to work with the bonding people as they continued their due diligence relating to the completion of work and the disposition of the Modern Continental encumbrances.

Actually, the work and business operations that both Modern Continental Construction and Modern Continental Enterprises were involved with had somewhat stabilized. They were still losing money and bleeding terribly, but the shock factor had faded somewhat. The bonding company and Jay Cashman, Inc. did their best to keep a cohesive work unit and environment for the employees who were involved with the day-to-day operations. After numerous meetings and fact-finding tactics, it had been determined that there were approximately three to four years of work still on the books that Modern Continental was involved with. A quick disposition and liquidation of the Modern Continental operations was not going to happen. Modern Continental was just too big and involved to just shut things down.

The bonding company had to take in every aspect of the daily operations and closely monitor the business activities of the company and more so with the managers and the key personnel. The first manager to flee the sinking Modern Continental ship was Chris Lincoln. Chris had done an excellent job during his almost twenty-year tenure at Modern Continental. He was a major part of the growth and success of the organization. His efforts were synonymous with the lofty achievements made by the company during his proprietorship. However, he did not feel that it was in his best interest to continue as his input had now been curtailed. Chris still had a lot to offer and he decided to make his move now rather than later.

The next, key figure and influential person that had also contributed extensively over his twenty-plus year career and was greatly responsible for the growth and success of Modern Continental, was Bob Berry. With the bonding company shutting down all bidding and the acquisition of any future work, this basically put Bob Berry in an awkward position. Bob was not the kind of guy who could just sit back and watch things happen and not be involved. Bob Berry was no doubt, a very well-seasoned and accomplished construction estimator. Therefore, it was no surprise that one of Modern Continental's key competitors over the years, The J.F. White Construction Company, sought to acquire the services of the guy that had them baffled and 'sucking hind tit' for the past twenty years!

It was no surprise that the key people at Modern Continental, the directors, managers, and influential employees were in great demand by their competitors. The bonding company could not do much to stem the flow of defectors. Even Jay Cashman had his eyes on some of the go-getters who worked for Modern Continental.

The bonding company, although they had in their possession, documents, and personal guarantees that both Les Marino and Kenny Anderson had signed relating to their obligations to monetarily indemnify and hold harmless the bonding company from any financial losses relating to the failure of the company, the bonding company also knew that these two guys could leave the operations that they had built and in no time at all start another successful company. This fact caused great concern to the bonding company. Therefore, in the summer of 2004, a meeting took place with the bonding company, Les Marino and Kenny Anderson. This meeting was a key factor involved in the successful disposition of the now financially unstable Modern Continental companies.

The bonding company, in return for the unabated services of both Les Marino and Kenny Anderson, and their promise to continue with their employment at Modern Continental and for a period of no less than five years would agree to the non-compete and not start another construction company. Basically if they remained bound to this non-compete agreement, they would be released of their financial obligations to the bonding company and would be given a one-time monetary bonus if they agreed to keep their loyalty and continued support to the bonding companies activities relating to the dissolving of the Modern Continental companies.

There had never been a demise of this proportion or magnitude in the history of the surety industry relating to a construction company of this size failing and the bonding company having to take on the financial burden created by this failure. The rules and conditions that had previously been in place relating to a construction company defaulting on a bond would be thrown out the window; as Modern Continental Construction Company had single-handedly re-created and re-wrote the surety industry guidelines. Things would never be the same in the bonding business thanks to Modern Continental Construction Company!

****

In the summer of 2004, Les Marino again, had some health issues as he began to experience fatigue and this time, there was a shortness of breath associated with this fatigue. His oncologist suggested that Les immediately come into the hospital for some testing. The initial oncology tests showed that the lymphoma cancer was still in remission. Therefore, Les was directed to Massachusetts General Hospital to meet with a cardiologist as it was determined that his fatigue and shortness of breath may very well be related to the condition of his heart.

Upon initial diagnosis by the cardiologist at Massachusetts General Hospital, he suggested that a battery of test be conducted to further determine what was going on with the heart. He also ordered an angioplasty procedure take place that involves a dye being injected into the blood stream through an artery in the groin which showed any abnormal features relating to the function of the heart. It was during this angioplasty procedure that a defective heart valve was identified. In addition to the faulty heart valve, there was also some atherosclerosis disease recognized. It was determined that a malfunctioning heart valve along with two of Les's arteries were blocked and therefore, a coronary artery bypass graft would need to be performed in addition to the replacement of the malfunctioning heart valve.

The heart condition that Les now had to deal with was, needless to say, another setback for him. He was a fighter, and a brawler, and not afraid to go at it again, but it seemed as if he had just finished a fifteen-round bout with Mickey Ward and now, he had to get back in the ring and face Arturo Gatti!

Les was again, accompanied by Kenny Anderson and his daughter Lorraine when it came time for a consultation. The cardiologist sat down with them and explained the circumstances and then discussed the options with regard to the replacement of the faulty aortic heart valve. In the procedure relating to the removal of the defective aortic heart valve, the surgeon explained that he will remove the damaged valve and replace it with either a mechanical valve or valve made from a cow or a pig tissue. As the damaged aortic valve was interfering with the blood flow to and from the heart, it makes the heart work much harder to send blood through the body.

It was determined that for the application and circumstances related to the damaged heart valve, a pig valve would be the best choice to rectify the problem. As for arteriosclerosis, it was established by the angioplasty procedure that the blockage to the arteries indicated that they needed to replace the arteries rather than to have a coronary balloon passed through the affected area.

In August of 2004, Les Marino underwent open-heart surgery to fix the problems with his heart. Fortunately, the Massachusetts General Hospital is renowned and had been established as the premier hospital for treating heart ailments and for performing open-heart surgery. Les came through the open-heart procedure, battered and worn but he survived the battle. He was again, on the road to recovery.

Les spent the end of the summer and the fall of 2004 primarily at the Marino Lookout Farm in Natick, Massachusetts. He did get into the office at 600 Memorial Drive in Cambridge on occasion but the majority of his time was spent at the farm. It was during this period of time that Les became closer to the many patrons that frequented the Lookout Farm along with his interacting closely with the many employees that worked there as well. Les was responsible for the addition of the railroad train that took people on tours of the farm. He also was instrumental with acquiring the stage coaches that provided tours as well. The environment and his overall participation with the activities at the Marino Lookout Farm seemed to be providing a positive and healing experience for Les Marino. His heart seemed stable and his overall health seemed to be improving.

The atmosphere at the Lookout Farm was therapeutic for Les. Harvest time at the farm was the busiest time of year. Watching the children play and how they genuinely showed their happiness when they visited the farm made Les very thankful that he had maintained his position regarding the farm and that he held fast to his beliefs regarding the benefits of owning such a magical place.

Les had again, begun to slowly get back to his regiment and regime regarding his fitness and exercise program. The doctors had told him to take it easy and not tax the body or push himself beyond the effective limits of his, still-recovering body.

On Thursday morning, 11 November 2004 although it was a holiday, Veteran's Day, which is a union holiday, the job sites were not working, Les still got up at his usual 6:00 a.m. and felt inclined to go through his normal exercise routine, he headed off to the room in his house that he had turned into his personal home gymnasium.

Anna Maria Marino, the dedicated and loving wife of Les Marino for some forty-seven years, upon getting out of bed, decided to check on Les and to see if he wanted her to fix him something for breakfast, or if he needed anything. Upon entering the exercise room, she saw Les, lying face down on the floor. She gasped as she ran to his side only to find him lifeless and not breathing. She immediately called 911. The town of North Reading first responders and EMT's arrived in a very short period of time, but it was to no avail. Lelio (Les) Marino had passed away.

****

The drums are very loud in the construction world. It did not take long for the contractors that had either bid against Modern Continental or had performed work for them, to start a dialogue about the infamous 'giant' of the construction industry and how there will never be another like him. Kenny Anderson, Les's business partner and best friend since 1959 was devastated when he heard the news about Les passing away. Kenny and his wife Roseanne immediately went to the North Reading home of Les so that they could be with his family and to console and comfort them as best they could at this very trying time. We are all taught in Sunday school, that death is part of life. The hardest thing we must accept in life is God's Will. Whether death comes suddenly, comes unexpectedly, or takes place over a period of time, experiencing the death of someone you love is never easy. Grieving hurts!

Although he had his share of medical issues over the past couple of years, no one expected this guy who treated his body as a temple and led a very healthy lifestyle would ever die before his seventieth birthday. There were immediate rumors that he took the easy way out, but those nasty untruths were quickly debunked as anyone who ever knew Les Marino understood that dying was the farthest thought from his mind and that life was precious to him. Were there mitigating circumstances, perhaps, but then again, if you ever spent time with the man, you knew that he could take anything that came his way in stride and that he had the uncanny ability to turn failure into success.

The accolades and tributes began to roll in almost immediately after it was announced that Les Marino had passed away. This humble man who had the ability that few others ever had or ever will have had touched a tremendous amount of people during his brief life.

The funeral arrangements were made by the Cota Funeral Home in North Reading, Massachusetts. The wake for Les Marino had visiting hours from 4:00 p.m. to 8:00 p.m. The crowd that came to pay their respects to a man who had influenced so many of their lives was an unending stream of shocked, sad, and dejected people. It's hard to put in words the feelings that were being emitted at this sorrowful event.

On Monday, 15 November 2004, there was a Requiem Mass held at Saint Theresa's Catholic Church in North Reading, Massachusetts. Following the funeral service, Les Marino was put to rest at The Holy Cross Cemetery in Malden, Massachusetts. The man was gone, but he would never be forgotten!

Chapter Twenty
You Cannot Win if You Don't Try

2005–2008

Only those who dare to fail greatly can ever
achieve greatly—**Kenny Anderson**

Malden, Massachusetts
175 Broadway
The Holy Cross Cemetery
Society of Saint Bridget, Burial Section
Friday, 11 November 2005
8:29 a.m.

Kenny Anderson stood in front of Les Marino's grave with a sorrowful look on his face as he silently talked to his best friend. It had been exactly one year since that fateful day that marked the end of a friendship that probably never should have even been established. Kenny thought about that day way back in August 1959, when he first met Lelio Marino. He kind of chuckled when he recalled the conversation that led to their fellowship. If it had not been for that rude and conniving junior rod man, Morris Casey, who tried to put one over on the new survey party crew chief by telling him that you go to lunch at 11:30 a.m. and come back at 1:00 p.m. And then, Kenny Anderson comes to Les's defense, by letting him know that what Morris said was not true; they may have never bonded as well as they did.

Fate is very fickle; paths cross and pleasantries are exchanged but seldom do random meetings or chance contacts develop into lifelong friendships. Again, Kenny smiled as he remembered how when they were both young and anxious to make their mark in the world, the many conversations that he and Les had about work and starting a construction company. They were dreams and deep inner thoughts that these two loyal friends both shared with one another.

It was a seasonable cold day with temperatures in the low 40s and an overcast sky as Kenny Anderson stood at the gravesite and struggled to maintain his composure as the many thoughts raced through his head about what he and Les had accomplished together. A touch of bitterness and indignation also raced through his mind as well as Kenny came back to reality and understood how their dreams had become disillusions and were now in the process of being tarnished and stained. Kenny collected himself as he smiled and said out loud, "I'll be back soon, Les!"

****

The final nails were being driven into the Modern Continental coffin as the bonding company continued to work with the Jay Cashman Company about completing the projects that were still ongoing and sorting out the problems that seemed to surface on a daily basis. In spite of the somewhat hostile takeover by the bonding people, there was still some of that Modern Continental loyalty in the people who worked for the company. They had been trained to work hard and to give their all. These were valuable lessons that stayed with each and every one of them and would continue to be with them for the rest of their lives.

Modern Continental would continue to function as a viable entity until such time that the uncompleted work on hand was finished and the assets liquidated, the bonding company chose to restructure the upper-level management positions in the company. With the passing of Les Marino, the bonding people decided that Max Marino would be named the Chairman of the Modern Continental Construction Company and John Pastore would be named President of the company.

The bonding company chose to keep Kenny Anderson on as a consultant as Kenny would spearhead the sale and eradication of the majority of the company-owned heavy equipment.

The legal situation, regarding the outstanding loan of seventy-five million dollars from the bank, that basically prompted and triggered the chain of events leading up to the bonding company getting involved, was resolved by the bonding company with the bank. This now put the ownership of the construction equipment owned by Modern Continental Construction Company in the hands of the bonding company. The equipment in question would now be sold and liquidated.

The bonding company made it very clear right from their initial involvement that they were not in the construction business, equipment business, development business, farm business or restaurant business. They were in the money business only!

****

There will always be that burning question of 'what happened?' This subject has been the topic of conversation for many years and by many people. There have been learned scholars who have weighed in on the matter. This matter has been studied and discussed in great detail by just about every cross-section of scholars, students, laymen, and laborers. The truth is that there was actually no one specific incident or situation that brought about the demise of Modern Continental.

If you look back at the beginning of the company, you notice that the two principals Les Marino and Kenny Anderson were risk-takers by nature. They took chances that others feared to take. They both possessed a raw enthusiasm and the ability to absorb, comprehend, and learn as they moved forward. The two complemented each other in ways that could not possibly be construed when they first met as these traits developed through their lifelong, loyal relationship.

Les Marino was a great philosopher. He provided many memorable astute and profound statements relating to both life and business. Unfortunately, he was better at giving examples and providing eloquent quotes than he was at listening to his own advice.

A perfect example would be 'companies don't go broke from lack of work; they go broke from having too much work'. Another gem would be 'the biggest thing that we have to deal with when you are involved with someone is their ego'.

Les Marino would admit that from the very beginning, as soon as he and Kenny Anderson went into business, he wanted to be the biggest contractor there ever was. He would also admit to having an ego as big as that Northwest-190 backhoe that he bought to perform the excavation work on the Tewksbury

279

sewer project way back in the 1980s. But to achieve what he did accomplish, you needed a big ego!

Wanting to be the biggest contractor and having a big ego probably did factor into the equation when you try to decipher what happened. All in all, though, if you really step back and look at just how two strangers, two guys that came from different backgrounds, heck, different worlds for that matter, and how they wound up accomplishing what they did, you just have to admit, it was nothing short of miraculous!

****

The projects that were on the books for Modern Continental when 'the shit hit the fan' back in 2004 were all completed and finalized. This work was performed and accepted in accordance with all applicable codes, standards, and specifications. No corners were cut and no cheating took place. It needs to be understood that Modern Continental Construction Company did not perform all of the work that they were involved with, there were numerous subcontractors that worked on each project that helped complete the jobs according to how they were originally specified. And all work that was performed was closely inspected and accepted by the owners of the projects.

It took a couple of years to finally complete the work that was uncompleted when the bonding company became involved and Jay Cashman, Inc. took over as the construction manager and the contractor of record.

Were there some 'ugly' accusations made about Modern Continental at the end of their tenure? Yes, and most were untrue or never substantiated. The 'kick the man when he's down' syndrome surely existed in the media near the end.

Officially on 23 June 2008, in federal court in Boston, Massachusetts Chapter #11 bankruptcy was filed by Modern Continental Construction Company.

To quote Kenny Anderson, *it was a hell of a good run*!

THE END

Epilogue by Bill Shields

The rest of the story

It has been an honor and a privilege to collaborate with Kenny Anderson to tell the story of Modern Continental Construction Company. No doubt, this is a story that needed to be told. How this came about, the reason that Kenny Anderson and I decided to actually sit down and finally tell the story of how Modern Continental Construction Company was created, was that every time we got together, we talked about this subject, and it was always exciting and interesting.

Let me first go into just a little more detail about how I was hired by Les Marino back in the summer of 1977. I briefly touched upon the subject in Chapter Ten. I was coming off a very serious injury as I had fallen and broken both of my arms in July 1974. I was down and out and very discouraged as I had tried many times since my accident to get hired, but no one would take a chance with me.

In August 1977, Modern Continental Construction Company had a boatload of safety troubles and their insurance company told them that they needed to have a dedicated safety person to handle the company's safety matters. I interviewed for the job, but truth be told, as much as I desperately needed the job, I was not really qualified. But this is where the magic comes in. The truth about this matter is that Les Marino saw something in me a substance, an unspecified strength, a desire, that told him to take a chance with this guy, he will work out and will be a benefit to the company. It did work out and I was a benefit to the company. I mention this because I was just one of many, many people that Les Marino took a chance with!

Another reason that this story is being told is that back in 2019, the start of the pandemic to be exact, I was browsing my computer looking at different articles, and I came across a Modern Continental article dated '28 June 2008' 'WICKED LOCAL.com' carried this article that was written by Jon Chesto.

This article had a headline that read 'Modern Continental Forever Linked to Failures'. I read the story, and then I said to myself, "If this guy only knew the real story, if he really knew how Kenny Anderson and Les Marino could never be associated with failure, he would retract this article and tell the truth about them." This book, this story about what 'Modern Continental', the company, and specifically Les Marino and Kenny Anderson what they were really all about, that is why this story is being told, and why this book was written.

After I left the employment of Modern Continental in 1987, I remained friendly with both Les Marino and Kenny Anderson. A relationship had been formed with these men that went way beyond employer and employee. As it was mentioned numerous times in this book, both Les and Kenny had a truth to them, an honesty that brought out the best in whoever they were involved with. I'm positive that there are hundreds of people who will attest to this fact. These guys may have been hard, no-nonsense, right to the point, shoot from the hip, rough, and perhaps a bit gruff, but no one cared more about your well-being than they did. And no one would be more of a loyal friend than the two of them.

There was a loyalty factor that needs to be considered when you look at the story of how Modern Continental achieved what it did. The primary component that has always been something that the competitors of Modern Continental could never figure out was the undying loyalty that was instilled in the people who worked for Modern Continental.

If I were to tell you that two hundred former Modern Continental Construction Company employees after spending time working at the company went off to start their own successful business, it would be an understatement. I was one of those employees who went off and started my own business and had a very successful career. Off the top of my head, I could name twenty others, but the truth be told, there are so many out there who owe their success to Les Marino and Kenny Anderson.

The simple idea of two men starting a construction company and then growing it into what it turned out to be, if you take a moment to consider just how much they contributed to the wealth, success, and well-being of thousands of individuals, it becomes mind-boggling.

How many automobiles were bought, how homes were purchased or built, how many children were put through college, how many retirement accounts were established, how many weddings were paid for? If you look at what

Modern Continental did for the economy, the taxes that were paid, both, state and federal, the tolls that were paid, and the groceries that were purchased with Modern Continental dollars? It becomes a staggering amount.

Please understand that the majority of sewer projects, water treatment plants, roads, bridges, tunnels, and buildings built in New England between 1967 and 2008 Modern Continental was probably involved with them.

However, when it comes right down to the success of Modern Continental, you need only to mention two names, Les Marino and Kenny Anderson.

As previously mentioned, it has been a true honor to tell this story. It has been an enjoyable project. Once we decided to go ahead with this endeavor, we first touched base with the Marino family, to let them know that we were going to tell the story of Modern Continental and Les Marino. Kenny Anderson and I would meet weekly and discuss a particular time frame, Kenny would tell the story and I would vigorously take copious amounts of notes. Thank you to the Dunkin Donuts on Ballardvale Road in Wilmington, Massachusetts. Kenny and I would visit this Dunkin Donuts and sip our coffee as we talked about what transpired through the years with the company.

The title of the book comes from what was preached by Kenny Anderson and Les Marino, over the years, to the people who worked for them, something that was their philosophy and what they both truly believed in—*Never Take No for an Answer*!

So now, after reading this story and understanding just what took place and how things were accomplished with the Modern Continental Construction Company, can you really say that they will forever be associated with failure? No, I don't think so!